Pioneering New Frontiers in North America

Pioneering New Frontiers in North America

A Historical Overview of the Board of Church Extension and Home Missions of the Church of God, 1921-1991

By
Louis Paul Meyer

The Board of Church Extension
and Home Missions of the
Church of God
and
Warner Press, Inc.
Anderson, Indiana

All scripture passages, unless otherwise indicated, are from the King James Version or the Revised Standard Version, © copyright, 1972, Thomas Nelson.

ISBN# 0-87162-624-1

Printed in the United States of America
Warner Press, Inc.

Arlo F. Newell, Editor in Chief
Dan Harman, Book Editor
Cover by David Liverett

Contents

Foreword

Louis P. Meyer is the most knowledgeable person in the church with regard to the ministry of the Board of Church Extension and Home Missions. Dr. Meyer joined the staff as director of town and country work in June, 1956. A year later he was appointed by the general board as secretary of the Department of Evangelism. During the 1960s he designed plans to focus the church's attention on urban America, rights of minorities and program development for the board. In 1974 he was elected vice president and served on the management team. Dr. Meyer served as interim president 1986-1987 before officially retiring in June, 1988.

Throughout his forty-three years of ministry in the Church of God as student pastor, pastor, and national staff member, Dr. Meyer was always deeply involved in interchurch work. As a pastor in Ohio, he assisted the Ohio Council of Churches with special town and country research. While a member of the staff of the Board of Church Extension and Home Missions, he served as an officer of the ecumenical Urban Training Center for Christian Mission (1962-1972). This organization trained urban pastors from twenty denominations. In the decades of the 1970s and 1980s, he served as a member and officer of the national interchurch organization—Joint Strategy and Action Committee (JSAC). In 1980 he co-founded the Religious Futurists Network.

Throughout his life, he has recognized the importance of history to inform and remind us of the lessons of the past. At the same time, a review of his forty-three years of ministry reveals a persistent, positive focus on the future. Louis Meyer's personal faith and beliefs are grounded in God as not only the God of the past and present, but also the God of the future. This focus on the future has led him to a personal interest and involvement in matters of ecology, environmental issues, and sustainability as a life goal for all people. He desires that the Church of God become far more global in its views and planning, and provide key leadership on the ever-enlarging multicultural frontier of our nation and world.

In 1989 I requested that Louis Meyer, who had served the board as a staff member for thirty-two years, consider writing the seventy-year history of the Board of Church Extension and Home Missions. In preparing for the assignment, the author gave himself to two years of research and study. During this time, he researched all the minutes and annual reports of the board from 1921-1991, and he read the minutes of the General Assembly and Missionary Board of the Church of God from 1914 through 1924.

Dr. Meyer holds an undergraduate degree from Anderson University. He next attended Oberlin Graduate School of Theology in Oberlin, Ohio where he received his master of divinity degree. Later he attended a post graduate seminar on unban planning at Wayne State University in Detroit, Michigan. In 1987, he received the honorary doctor of divinity degree from Anderson University.

Louis ("Pete") Meyer is the father of a son and a daughter and has three granddaughters. His gifted wife, Marie, has been his companion for almost fifty years. She, too, has been involved locally, nationally, and internationally in the work of the church.

I was pleased when Dr. Meyer agreed to serve as the commissioned author of this history of the board. Our primary aim in this book is to make people aware of the pioneering and diverse ministry of the Board of Church Extension and Home Missions. The board has made a major contribution to the life and work of the movement. As its history reveals, since 1921 this agency has always been on the cutting edge with innovative service programs that have helped to give direction and focus to the Church of God.

The author has striven to maintain objectivity appropriate to this serious study. His work is presented with the hope that it will stimulate persons of all backgrounds to know and recognize the rich ministry of this board. During the time that I had the privilege to work with Louis Meyer, I found him to be a man of integrity, compassion, and focus. As you read the book, I trust you will appreciate the work of a scholar and be reminded of the tremendous contribution the Board of Church Extension and Home Missions has made to the church.

J. Perry Grubbs, President
Board of Church Extension and Home Missions

Introduction

Over the past seventy years thousands of Church of God people have helped to make the ministry of the Board of Church Extension and Home Missions possible. Persons have invested their savings and life earnings with the board to help make the church building loan services possible. Uncounted individuals and congregations have given consistently of their means to enable home mission ministries to be established and maintained. Others, with a passion for starting and developing new congregations, have assisted the board through their prayers, financial donations, and participation in the exciting work of church extension and evangelism.

This book was commissioned to relate the story of the origin, purpose, and program services of the Board of Church Extension and Home Missions on the occasion of its seventieth anniversary. As the research and writing took place, I had as my imaginary audience all the past and present friends and supporters of this board, without whose prayers, backing, and support the history of this agency would never have happened.

In preparation, many volumes of minutes were consulted: those of the General Ministerial Assembly (1915-1925), the Missionary Board (1917-1922), and necessarily, all minutes of the Board of Church Extension and Home Missions (1920-1990). Historical data was abundant from the report books written for each annual board meeting, and from the annual reports of the board's presidents to the General Assembly of the Church of God. In addition, there were hundreds of program files and personal letters, and recorded interviews with former employees, including an interview with Elver F. Adcock, the board's first employee.

I further prepared for this writing by reading books by

Church of God authors: *The Quest for Holiness and Unity,* by Dr. John W. V. Smith; *Miracle of Survival,* by Dr. Harold L. Phillips; *Passport for a Reformation,* by Dr. Lester A. Crose. Several general historical accounts of life in North America from 1910 through 1990 were consulted.

This writing also reflects forty years of my personal involvement with the Board of Church Extension and Home Missions. During six of those years, I served on the board's national Town and Country Committee while a pastor in Ohio, and then thirty-two years as a full-time member of the staff. On staff I served as: director of town and country work, secretary of the Department of Evangelism, director of the Office of Program Research and Planning, vice president, and interim president. Since my retirement in 1988, I have continued to serve as an advisor to the president.

I am aware of the limitations imposed on me as a former staff person in trying to write an objective account of the life and work of this vital organization. I have therefore tried to refrain from too many personal judgments and comments, and have sought to report only what the records reveal. On some occasions, however, I have ventured an opinion based on things that were implied in the minutes and historical files I have used.

This writing is an attempt to give to the church and to friends of the board a broad historical overview, and to share some highlights of the origin, development, and ministry of this Church of God agency—the fourth national agency created by the church. Time and space do not permit a detailed, chronological history of this board. That task will be left to others, but the data revealed on these pages will give a historical perspective of when, why, and how the board and its major program ministries developed.

In this work the full name, Board of Church Extension and Home Missions, is used (BCEHM) even though before 1923 the agency was known simply as Board of Church Extension.

The chief executive officers of the board for its first seventy years were: Dr. Russell R. Byrum, 1921-1927; Dr. Elver F. Adcock, 1927-1953; Dr. W. E. Reed, 1953-1970; Dr. Marvin J. Hartman, 1970-1986; Louis P. Meyer, (interim president 1986-1987); and J. Perry Grubbs, the incumbent, elected in 1987.

The format I have chosen for this historical overview is to cover a decade of history per chapter. At the beginning of each chapter is a brief summary of world historical highlights of the decade as a point of reference. I have also included citations documenting the sources of the stories or events recorded.

Ethnic designations have changed over the period covered. Colored, Negro, black, and African-American have been in common usage. Except in direct quotes, the term African-American will be used in this text. Similarly, Hispanic will be used to designate Spanish-ancestry groups and Anglo will identify Caucasian or white groups.

I have not named in the text all the persons who have served as members of the Board of Church Extension and Home Missions. However, every person who has ever been elected to serve as a member of the board is listed in Appendix A.

Persons who have served in some capacity in the home missions ministries of the board are listed in Appendix B.

Full-time staff persons who served a year or longer during the seventy years of the board's ministry are listed in Appendix C. Personnel records were not complete for the first thirty years or more of the board's history.

For identification of the pictorial sections of the book see Appendix D.

I am grateful to Faith Phile, Mary Lee Huff, Paula Snyder, Vickie Rice, and Lisa Fowler of the board staff for their help with the research and for pulling together the names listed in the three appendixes.

I am most appreciative of my wife, Marie L. Meyer, who spent many hours editing three drafts of the manuscript. In addition she has been encouraging, understanding, supportive, and patient during the twenty months it took to research and write this document.

Louis Paul Meyer
Anderson, Indiana
June 1991

Chapter 1
Beginnings
(1915-1920)

The Civil War of the United States of America had been over only about fifteen years when the Church of God reformation movement came into being, in 1880-81. This war had helped to catapult the nation into the industrial age, an age which in itself was to force major changes in lifestyles, viewpoints, and traditional values across the nation.

As with all wars, the Civil War dreadfully divided families, institutions, and particularly the churches. The mainline denominations of the time were badly split over slavery and other controversial issues. This split manifested itself as the Methodists, Baptists, Presbyterians and others divided, each one with its northern group and its southern group. Such division brought about a struggle for funds, members, church property and leadership. Competition was fierce. Some denominations, with attention focused on their internal struggles, were not addressing the key issues of the frontier and westward movements. Failure to attract new members resulted, and stagnation became a reality.

Into this setting came Daniel Sidney Warner and other pioneers of the Church of God movement with the message that one's personal commitment to Christ as Lord and Savior makes one a member of the family of God, that all believers are united in Christ, and that God's Holy Spirit can empower each believer to live life to the full. This powerful and appealing message attracted many followers.

The early leaders strongly felt that this message of holiness and the unity of all God's people needed to be spread anywhere and everywhere that an opportunity presented itself. These pioneers had a burning passion: the message must get out. Two primary methods were used to spread this good news. One was the written word. The *Gospel Trumpet* was printed each month as a herald of the message. The other method was through traveling evangelistic teams with their singers and testifiers. These small bands went from rural areas to villages and small towns, proclaiming the message in sermon and song. For the first thirty years or more this was the primary method of "extending the truth."

It is interesting to note that in the beginning of the movement there seemed to be little or no discrimination against minority and ethnic groups. According to the former church historian John W. V. Smith:

> The reformation proclaimed a message for all people, and so it is not unexpected that the early pioneers of the movement would extend their evangelistic endeavors to reach those of various ethnic cultures. Significant efforts to reach at least five of these groups—the Blacks, Germans, Slovaks, Scandinavians, and Greeks—took place early in the movement's history, and major segments of the work of the Church of God developed among the Blacks and these European ethnics in the United States and Canada (Smith 1980, 161-62).

This helped motivate the early leaders to see that the message was taken wherever doors were opened—in foreign lands or here at home. It was this conviction which later led to reaching out in an organized manner to a wide variety of ethnic groups in the homeland.

Within the first fifteen years of the Church of God, evangelistic efforts were made in a number of countries, including: Mexico (Baja), India, England, and Germany. By

1909 a missionary board was formed by action of the ministers. Later, in 1912, a Home and Foreign Missionary Fund was established.

1915-1920—Disruptions on a World Scale

In order to understand the setting from which the Board of Church Extension and Home Missions came, a brief look needs to be taken at the world as well as the nation in the years between 1915 and 1920.

One of the profound changes in Europe at that time was the population explosion. European population at the beginning of the nineteenth century was roughly fifty million; by 1820 it was one hundred million; by 1870 two hundred million; and by 1914 the population of that region was three hundred million. Of this period of time, author James L. Stokesbury says:

> A series of profound social changes had led to dangerous imbalances in politics, and these in turn led to one crisis after another. It was in that memorable summer of 1914 that the states of Europe finally used up their maneuvering room, and the resulting explosion brought their complacent society tumbling down around them. . . . The greatest of all the new "isms" of the time was nationalism. . . . "This is my own, my native land," was the cry of millions; all good stemmed from the Nation. . . . These nations had all become intensely egocentric—so intense was nationalism that the states or powers were inevitably spoken of as if they were individual persons—because a sense of national self-satisfaction was achieved only at the expense of another nation. . . . Another son of nationalism was therefore born, called militarism. . . . Therefore, technology and a growing interlocking system of alliance helped set the stage for an inevitable clash of nations (Stokesbury 1981, 11-14).

By 1915 World War I was in full swing. The Allies were in great need of guns, machines, ammunition and troops. Financial conditions in the United States were difficult. The mood of the country was one of isolation and neutrality.

However, in the spring of 1917 German submarines sank four unarmed and clearly marked American merchant ships. Thirty-six lives were lost. A reluctant President Woodrow Wilson could wait no longer. He went to Congress on April 2 to ask that war be declared against Germany, stating, "The world must be made safe for democracy." On the afternoon of April 6, 1917, the United States, after an overwhelming vote of Congress, was at war with the German empire. By the spring of 1918 325,000 American troops were in France, and more were on the way.

In this tragic world conflict from 1914 to 1918, sixty-five million human beings were mobilized. Of this number, 5.5 million were killed and twenty-one million others were wounded.

These war years changed the way America saw itself and the world. There was a gradual shift from isolationism to a broader view of the world and the need for alliances. The United States emerged from the war to become the strongest industrial and financial power in the world.

The war effort caused shifts in the United States population from the rural areas to the city. This was disruptive to rural and small town churches and public schools. Materials for building homes and churches were scarce. This created a great need for new buildings and repairs in 1919 and 1920.

The Beginning of a Church of God National Consciousness

For its first thirty years or so, the Church of God approached its mission from an individualistic focus. Most evangelistic and missionary work was carried on by individuals who felt a particular call, or carried a burden for some specific work or mission. Warner and other early leaders believed the end of time might occur in their lifetime. This conviction added an urgency to their message and caused them to focus more on "getting the message out" than on conserving the results of their evangelistic efforts through the establishment and nurturing of congregations.

A March 10, 1892, *Gospel Trumpet* editorial admonished local groups not to entice preachers by offering to build a home for them. D. S. Warner said:

> Beware, how you, through selfish motives of having frequent preaching, lay a snare to entangle God's flying messengers. . . . This is the time of the end, and God's messengers must run to and fro.

Addressing the need for some form of organization, Lester Crose noted:

> To bring together and coordinate the missionary outreach of the Church of God reformation movement, the need for some plan became evident by 1909. Twenty years of voluntary and independent expressions of missionary endeavor were now culminating in the formation of a Missionary Board (Crose 1981, 35).

By 1910 there was growing evidence of the need for a more cooperative approach to the way missionary work was done and the way regions of the country were evangelized. Around 1915 a national consciousness within the movement was beginning to develop. A growing number of ministers recognized needs which the entire church ought to be addressing, rather than being left to a congregation or a popular leader. One of these needs was better training for the leadership of the church. In 1917, under the sponsorship of the Gospel Trumpet Company, the Anderson Bible Training School was started. In June of 1917 the General Ministerial Assembly of the Church of God was established to develop a listing of the ministers who qualified for clergy rates on the railroads, and to more formally tie the publishing work and the missionary outreach to the whole church. John W. V. Smith writes:

> The years from 1916 through 1928 proved to be a time of very dramatic change in the whole structural pattern of the Church of God reformation movement. The organization of the General Ministerial Assembly with a written constitution and bylaws, major corporate changes in the Gospel Trumpet Company, the establishment of Anderson Bible-Training School, the printing of the Yearbook of the Church of God, the formation of various boards for foreign missions, church extension, and religious education, and the beginnings of Associated Budgets highlight the major changes of this twelve-year period (Smith 1980, 205).

Critical Need: Funds for Expansion

Every expansion of ministry eventually requires additional financial commitments. In addition to the creation of the new agencies and the yearbook publication mentioned above, there was a vote by the General Ministerial Assembly to build a permanent tabernacle. The June 21, 1917, minutes of the assembly record that F. G. Smith addressed the assembly on the question of a permanent tabernacle capable of seating seven thousand, which was recommended by the Campground Committee. The motion to accept the plan lost, but a new motion to erect a tabernacle capable of seating ten thousand carried.

Special appeals for funds were made, and the tabernacle was built in 1918 and 1919. It is interesting to note that in this same business session, June 21, 1917, action was taken to set up a ministerial relief fund, which also required additional funding. The Gospel Trumpet Company also faced some severe financial problems at this time:

> When J. T. Wilson reported to the Company on June 24, 1918, he had startling and disturbing news for them. On October 27 of the previous year the company indebtedness had leaped to an all-time high of $88,434.29 and had increased by $16,000 in one single month that fall. Drastic measures were required to meet this crisis (Phillips 1979, 154).

Travel was restricted at this time because of World War I, but in spite of the war Church of God missionaries were finding many opportunities to expand the church's witness on foreign soil. These opportunities far exceeded the church's leadership supply and financial support.

The minutes of the Missionary Board of the Church of God give insight into the increasing problem of finding adequate finance to carry out its work. The June 7, 1915, minutes state:

> Fewer missionaries have gone this past year to foreign fields because: we have as many missionaries as we are able to support, and due to the great European war. . . . The paramount needs are the same as those pointed out last year—capable men and more money.

In its annual business meeting on June 5, 1916, it was reported again that attaining adequate funds was a real challenge for the Missionary Board.

> The collection of missionary funds this year has been attended with considerable difficulty, and we have, because of the lack of funds, felt at times considerable anxiety for the welfare of the work. . . . Our collection through our special Missionary Boxes was down again this year.

During 1916 F. G. Smith, editor of the *Gospel Trumpet,* was elected to serve also as president of the Missionary Board and E. E. Byrum was elected its vice president.

Missions: Home and Foreign

It should be noted that the Missionary Committee (later changed to Board) was created by the ministers assembled at the 1909 Anderson camp meeting. In 1912, when some of the brethren raised questions concerning excessive organization, a rationale was presented by H. M. Riggle. One of the functions of the committee was to collect and distribute the Home and Foreign Missionary Fund (Smith 1980, 210-11). John W. V. Smith wrote:

> When the Missionary Board was reorganized under the General Ministerial Assembly in 1917 it was assigned both home and foreign missionary work and was called the Board of Home and Foreign Missions of the Church of God (Smith 1980, 218).

With the growing financial crisis, some members of the Missionary Board began to question the wisdom of one board's being responsible for both fields of mission service. The Missionary Board minutes of June 10, 1918, record the following issues:

> Brother E. A. Reardon raised for discussion the question of supporting the Kansas City and the New York City mission homes. The Secretary explained the reason why these homes had been supported and the use that has been made of the money. Brother Reardon said he had no objection to the schools run in these two places. . . . Brother F. G. Smith said the main question is whether or not the Board shall confine its efforts to foreign missions or divide its efforts between the foreign field and work in this country. . . . After some discussion, D. O. Teasley moved, That our president (F. G. Smith) be hereby requested to ask the advice of the General Ministerial Assembly concerning whether money from the General Missionary Fund

should be spent in the home work and what responsibility this Board is expected to bear in such work. Motion carried.

In the General Ministerial Assembly meeting of June 20, 1918, F. G. Smith, president of the Missionary Board, made the report to the assembly on missionary interests. He again raised the question of the wisdom of one board's being responsible for both home and foreign missions in that the two functions were different in nature, and the question of inadequate funding for the growing foreign mission outreach again was raised.

The assembly set up a committee of five ministers (D. O. Teasley, J. W. Phelps, R. L. Berry, A. F. Gray, and R. H. Owens) to "investigate this matter and report back to the Assembly." The next day the committee's report resulted in the following resolution:

> Resolved, that we, the General Ministerial Assembly of the Church of God, hereby advise our Missionary Board to use all moneys contributed to the general missionary fund in the prosecution of foreign missionary work, leaving all home missionary work to be supported by local congregations in the several States in such manner as the congregations see fit. Upon a motion and second the resolution was adopted as read (GMA 21 June 1918).

This action meant there was now no plan for sustained mission work here at home. Many leaders were troubled by this. At the next year's meeting of the Missionary Board, on June 9, 1919, ways of setting up a special fund campaign for foreign mission work were considered. The following discussion took place:

> Brother Teasley then got the floor and said that if we are to make a successful campaign for foreign

missions, we must also do something for home missions. He believed that we should make a drive to supply a truth extension fund. It was agreed that we should by all means have a home missions fund and also a foreign missions fund, but the real difficulties that face the Board were finding a method of getting the money and of distributing it. . . . A number of the brethren thought they saw many insurmountable difficulties in the way of equitable and satisfactory distribution of such a fund. Moved by Brother Teasley that the chair appoint someone to present the budget plan supporting foreign missions to the General Ministerial Assembly for their approval, and that he appoint someone to write a paper to be read before the Assembly, discussing the advisability of creating a Home Missions or Church Extension Fund. Thus committing the problem to the ministers for their consideration during the year, so that some definite plan be formed at the next meeting if advisable. . . . This motion was amended to name F. G. Smith to write the paper and make the proposal to the Assembly, and thus voted (MB 9 June 1919).

Conditions Calling for United Action

Following is a brief summary of the conditions and circumstances of the church and society which resulted in the creation of a new national agency. World War I was over. Many citizens had migrated from rural areas and small towns to the cities of America. This caused many of the small congregations and preaching points of the Church of God to decline. There was also a growing concern that the starting and developing of new congregations had slacked off, due in part to war and in part to the methods being used. Several leaders charged this decline to the early practice of itinerant evangelists preaching in one place for a few weeks, and then, after a few converts, moving on to the next preaching point. This left no one to shepherd the newly converted. The method which had worked effectively for the early years of the movement was now being questioned.

Some years later, H. M. Riggle wrote an article, "Pioneer Evangelism," in the *Gospel Trumpet* (1924). Here he said:

> One of the greatest mistakes of my early ministry was to open up new fields and then rush off and leave them. Had I remained and taken care of the tender flocks until capable pastors were raised up, there would, today, be a mighty work to show the fruits of our labors. Instead of doing this, being one of the "flying ministry," I felt it my duty to hurry off to other new fields.

As the 1920s approached, some leaders began to point out that there were many entire states and large cities with not a single Church of God congregation. There was no organized plan designed to reach out to the ethnic groups of the nation—native Americans, African-Americans, Hispanics, Appalachian Mountain folks, and others.

There were approximately 743 congregations of the Church of God in 1920. Of these, over three hundred did not have buildings of their own for worship and church school. They met in homes, rented facilities, storefronts, and schoolhouses. Local church finances left room for great improvement. Most banks were reluctant to make loans to these congregations because they had little or no equity or collateral.

After the war there was still a keen mission zeal in the Church of God. It was widely felt that the church had responsibility for getting the message of salvation, unity, and holiness to foreign lands and throughout North America. Several key leaders who were strongly committed to the cause of foreign missions recognized that in order to have strong overseas missions and evangelistic outreach, there must be a strong church in America. Missions at home and missions in other lands were seen as being equally necessary and important.

A New Agency to Meet Specific Needs

In 1920 all of these needs and concerns converged and the General Ministerial Assembly decided to take decisive action. A study committee of nine ministers, called the Committee of Schools and Church Extension, had been appointed to draft an educational policy for the assembly. This committee was also assigned the task of studying the issue of church extension. In the June 25, 1920, meeting of the General Ministerial Assembly, J. A. Morrison presented the report of the Committee on Schools and Church Extension. The minutes record the following two actions:

> Moved and seconded that we recommend to the General Ministerial Assembly that they nominate a Committee of twenty-five men to select a Church Extension Board of nine men and that these nine men be elected by the General Assembly. Motion Carried. . . . Moved and seconded, that we recommend that the duty of this Board of nine men shall be: first, to establish work at strategic points where there are no local agencies sufficient to establish a work, and second, to assist struggling congregations by lending them money for the erection of necessary church buildings. Motion Carried.

The assembly nominated these twenty-five persons to select a church extension board: B. E. Warren, R. H. Owens, W. H. Oldham, A. Q. Bridwell, W. A. Sutherland, E. E. Byrum, R. L. Berry, J. T. Wilson, J. D. Smoot, O. E. Line, Russell Byrum, W. D. McCraw, S. L. Wingert, F. G. Smith, J. W. Byers, A. F. Gray, Earl Martin, A. C. Harrison, J. C. Blewitt, C. J. Forsberg, W. E. Monk, Charles Brown, I. S.

McCoy, Merton Mercia, and C. H. Tubbs.

The next day, the minutes record that the Committee on Church Extension presented the following names in nomination for the Board of Church Extension: A. T. Rowe, J. T. Wilson, W. D. McCraw, A. F. Gray, L. W. Guilford, R. R. Byrum, Earl Martin, C. E. Brown, and A. C. Harrison. These persons were all elected by the assembly to compose the Board of Church Extension (GMA 16 June 1920).

The nine spent the next twelve months studying the needs of the church, ways to organize, how to focus the charter, and what to include in the bylaws. J. T. Wilson served as chair of the group. Appearing in the 1921 yearbook for the year 1920 is a report written by Wilson which gives some rationale for the need and the purpose of this new agency about to be born, as follows:

> As the work of the church increases, it is constantly becoming more evident that no man or set of men can look after all the general phases of the Lord's work. This fact makes it necessary that certain agencies be made responsible for certain phases of church work, otherwise much important work will be neglected. It is a well known fact that there are several states in which there is not an established congregation of people enjoying these truths of this last reformation, and for many years very little has been done toward planting churches in these states. It is the purpose of the Home Missionary and Church Extension Board to undertake the planting of new churches in new places. There is also another phase of work which this Board is undertaking, namely, to assist worthy congregations that are not able to carry on their work alone. These congregations are aided by helping them to establish a financial system and by loaning them money when it is deemed advisable to do so.
>
> In one sense this is work of a purely missionary character, and the church in general must help bear the

financial burden if new fields are to be opened up and struggling congregations established.

The articles of incorporation of the Board of Church Extension and Home Missions were adopted by the General Ministerial Assembly on June 15, 1921. Ballots for the new board were presented the next day, June 16. There were thirty names on the ballot: ten names paired for five one-year positions; ten names paired for five two-year positions; and ten names paired for five three-year positions.

On June 17, 1921, the following fifteen men were elected as members of the first Board of Church Extension and Home Missions: for one-year terms: A. T. Rowe, J. D. Smoot, S. P. Dunn, J. T. Wilson, W. A. Sutherland; for two-year terms: R. R. Byrum, H. A. Sherwood, C. H. Tubbs, C. E. Byers, C. S. Sisler; for three-year terms: L. H. Morgan, C. C. Mansfield, W. T. Seaton, J. L. Williams, and W. P. Long.

It is interesting to note that of these original fifteen board members, two were African-American—S. P. Dunn and J. D. Smoot. The latter received the highest number of votes of all thirty persons on the ballot.

The Articles of Incorporation

Article III

A. The object and purpose of this Corporation are hereby declared to be benevolent and religious, to obtain and diffuse information on the subject of home missions, and missions in general, to promote education and the knowledge and acceptance of the Gospel of Jesus Christ among the heathen and benighted people within the territorial limits of the United States of America and Canada and in foreign countries, and to that end may do home missionary work among immigrants, Indians, Mexicans, mountaineers, in the city slums, and other unevangelical regions, and it may also seek to establish churches in large cities and strategic centers or other places where work has not been opened, especially in those states or provinces where the church is not well represented. It also may assist in the work of the church by supporting evangelists in the new fields; by assisting struggling churches in support of a pastor; by loaning money for the erection of church buildings, parsonages, etc.; by holding church property; by acting as Trustee of designated trust funds when required; and by doing and transacting any other business of and for the above named objects. June 15, 1921.

The objectives of these articles summarize the many concerns that had been developing for more than eight years. They outline a broad area of assignment and represent a timeless charter. The ministerial assembly gave this agency an assignment which is needed as much in the 1990s and beyond as it was in the 1920s. There is always a need to help the church in evangelism, church planting and growth, ministry to minorities and the forgotten of the land, and in church building and loan services.

Chapter 2

Getting Ready For Mission

(1921-1929)

God always has a need for pioneers, for people who will forsake the socially comfortable, settled places and set out on new paths that involve creativity, hard work, and the spirit of adventure. The Church of God itself is a product of the pioneering spirit of people like Daniel S. Warner and others. In 1921 fifteen of the best-known leaders of the decade of the twenties were elected to organize a new, pioneering national agency of the Church of God—the Board of Church Extension and Home Missions.

Executive Committee Named

On the morning of June 17, 1921, the fifteen member BCEHM was elected. At 1:00 p.m. of the same day, they met to organize and set priorities. J. T. Wilson presided. This included the adoption of articles of incorporation and bylaws to govern the new board. H. A. Sherwood was elected president, J. T. Wilson was selected vice president, and Russell R. Byrum secretary-treasurer. An executive committee was named to do the immediate work of organizing, planning, program development, and handling of week-to-week operations. Its three members were officers Sherwood and Wilson, plus A. T. Rowe from the general board. (The term general board refers to the total Board membership, which met annually.) The minutes of this first organizational meeting report an interesting action which would serve as a sound policy for the years ahead. "Motion and passed, That the Executive Committee spend no more money during the coming year than they receive."

In this first board meeting a lengthy discussion took place as to where and how to begin their assignment. The real challenge, however, was to discover where to get the funds to carry on their assigned ministry. The action by the General Ministerial Assembly authorizing this new agency had made no mention of funds to support its work. After many ideas were suggested, it was decided that for the first year, "$25,000 was a reasonable amount to request from the Church for Extension Work (GB 17 June 1921)."

Possible areas for church extension work were discussed and the rationale given as to why each was important and strategic. The minutes record: "We recommend to the Executive Committee as fields for work this coming year: Western Canada, Omaha, Boston, and New Orleans. Voted." It would be the task of the executive committee in the next twelve months to study and explore which of these options would be feasible and most appropriate. Then another action was taken to establish a board policy: "Moved and Passed. No minister be sent to any field until all members of the board are consulted."

The primary task of shaping the legal structure of this new organization was placed on the shoulders of Russell Byrum, its first executive. Since he had been involved with the process as a member of the original committee of nine in 1920, he had given thought to these organizational needs. He had a rough draft of what he felt should be included in the bylaws. These he took to Judge William Diven, a well-known attorney in Anderson. According to Elver Adcock:

> Attorney Diven advised that the agency be incorpo-

rated under Indiana statutes to give full authority and legal sanction to a corporate body. Mr. Diven prepared the Articles of Incorporation under an act of the Indiana legislature which formed a proper setting for a religious body of this kind and helped in the final shaping of the governing rules and by-laws (Adcock 1986, 6).

Some of the reasons the board asked Russell Byrum to be its new executive as secretary-treasurer were his: keen insights; organizational skills; ability to see the larger picture; and effectiveness at getting things done. From 1920 when the committee of nine was set up to develop a broad draft of the task of the newly proposed board, Russell Byrum began searching for sources of help and information. He wrote letters and made visits to other church groups which had been operating church extension and home missions programs for years.

The Methodists and Disciples of Christ were contacted for information on how to operate a lending program for congregations needing church buildings. How and where did they get the funds to make building loans? He contacted the Baptist and Presbyterian boards, as well as home missions departments of other church groups, regarding their methods and materials on evangelism and home missions operations. From these contacts he gathered a valuable supply of resources, forms, methods, and helpful insights which served him and the board well for its first six years of organization and operation.

In order to help the church at large to see its role in the work of church extension, Russell Byrum wrote these words in the report section of the *1922 Yearbook of the Church of God*:

> A glance at a map indicating the location of congregations of the church of God shows that our work is not very evenly distributed over the country. While in

> some states there are large numbers of congregations, in other states there are almost none. The evangelization of these larger districts is the responsibility, not of a particular individual minister nor of state evangelistic boards, but of the whole church throughout the country. A general board is needed as a medium for the evangelization of these districts in the same sense as a foreign board serves as a medium for the evangelization of foreign countries.

The executive committee agreed to meet on a monthly basis, but the pressure of organizing policies, programs, rules of procedure, and priorities often required them to meet weekly and sometimes more often—a heavy commitment of time from each member. Each had full employment with other assignments. In fact, the board did not have a full-time staff person for the first two years of operation.

Before 1921 was over they had made some crucial decisions. On August 26, 1921, executive committee members discussed the prospects of beginning a new work in Boston, Massachusetts. They felt that the need there was great, and this ought to be the first place to begin church extension efforts. It was "Voted, to ask Earl Martin to go to Boston from Houston to start the Church of God in the Northeast. Weekly allowance at first to be $35. He will be asked to develop a budget of expenses after arriving, for the board's consideration. . . . And the board is to pay for moving for the Martins from Houston to Boston." Earl Martin and family made the move from a pastorate in Houston, Texas, to pioneer a new start in Boston in the fall of 1921.

By year's end, the executive committee had set priorities for starting additional new works: first, Omaha, Nebraska; then New Orleans, Louisiana; and western Canada. Experienced leadership for new congregations was scarce. It took a while to get leaders for each targeted area.

New Orleans was chosen because of the large concentration of African-Americans there. The executive committee decided to write leading African-American ministers, especially board members S. P. Dunn and J. D. Smoot, concerning the method of approach, possible leadership, and the strategy in raising necessary funds.

First Annual Report to the Assembly

In the June, 1922 meeting of the general board, it was reported that a good start had been made toward shaping the board's policies, program, and organization. Considerable progress had been made in just twelve months. The progress was outlined in President H. A. Sherwood's written report to the General Ministerial Assembly. This report gave some insight into the scope and methods of the new board's work.

He began by restating the purpose of the BCEHM as set forth in the articles of incorporation. Then his report continued:

> The plans of the Board of Church Extension were announced through the *Gospel Trumpet*, and by form letters to the ministers. . . .
>
> Brother Earl Martin became pastor of a congregation in Boston last September. He made a trip throughout New England to visit the isolated saints in that section. He held a short series of meetings on Cape Cod and preached at different places on this trip. Some conversions were the immediate results of these meetings. He is planning also to hold a series of meetings in the state of Maine where there are a few saints. Brother Martin is laying a solid foundation for a good work by preaching and by securing cooperation among the saints. The field of his labor is one of the most populous regions which has not yet been evangelized by ministers of this reformation. It is a well-known fact of history that the people of this section are very conservative in their dispositions and tendencies and hence it

requires more patient effort to establish a work there than in some sections, but once established, the work is almost certain to be reliable and enduring.

The work in Rochester, New York, was opened by Brother Fay C. Martin in February, 1922. This work has received assistance from the Board of Church Extension since the beginning of April. Rochester is one of the populous cities in the state. The first service was held in a large auditorium in the heart of the city. A number have taken their stand for the truth and are very enthusiastic in the work. . . . Arrangements are being made to carry on a tent meeting through the months of August and September.

The work in New Orleans was begun late in April, 1922 by Brother J. D. Smoot. The population of this city is 400,000, of which number about 112,000 are colored. . . . The outlook is good for future success. He emphasizes the great need for a strong church among the colored people in that city and feels sure that the best way to accomplish this result is through the assistance of the Board of Church Extension.

The work in Omaha, Nebraska has not yet been opened up for the reason that the Church Extension Board has thus far been unable to secure a minister for this field. The prospects seem brighter just now, however, and we hope to have the work started there before very long.

Western Canada had also been mentioned as a field that should be encouraged by the Board of Church Extension, but financial aid is not so much their special need for the present as that of good ministerial help.

President Sherwood concludes his first report to the ministerial assembly with a reminder of the need for funds:

Had it been possible to have secured sufficient ministerial help to open up the work in the various fields according to the original plans of the Church Extension Board, the contributions received for this purpose would have been scarcely one-sixth of the amount required to meet the expense. If the work is to be opened up in Omaha and other places that have been suggested, the average contributions for this work must be greatly increased. Liberal offerings from the church at large for the worthy cause of Church Extension will not only plant the glorious truths of the Reformation in important but neglected fields in the homeland, but will marvelously quicken every other phase of our work both at home and in foreign fields (GMA 20 June 1922).

Getting Operational Funds

By 1921 there were four national agencies: the Gospel Trumpet Company, the Missionary Board, Anderson Bible Training School, and the Board of Church Extension and Home Missions. In 1923 the fifth agency, the Board of Sunday Schools and Religious Education, was voted into being by the General Ministerial Assembly. Each agency required funds for operation, but there was no agreed-upon procedure for raising and allocating funds. This was a particular hardship on the newest agencies. Their purpose and ministry were not as well known. How were operational funds to be secured?

An insight is given by Elver Adcock. Adcock had come to Anderson, Indiana, from Iowa in the fall of 1919 to attend the Anderson Bible Training School. As a student he obtained employment at the Gospel Trumpet Company, working in the Editorial Department. Upon his graduation in 1921 he began full-time work as an editor and writer under Russell Byrum, managing editor of the Gospel Trumpet Company.

Russell Byrum, at the age of thirty-two, was asked to be the executive secretary-treasurer of the newly formed

Board of Church Extension and Home Missions. In addition to his work at the Gospel Trumpet Company, he was teaching at the Anderson Bible Training School and was writing a large volume which was published in 1925 under the title *Christian Theology*. With such heavy commitments, Byrum soon saw he needed help with getting this new agency in to operation. "I needed an assistant to do the routine work of the board," he said, "I chose a young man in the Editorial Department of the publishing plant to do this work. He had just graduated from our new school and was a good writer. His name was Elver F. Adcock (Byrum 1976)." Adcock recalls Byrum's invitation this way:

> I was willing to do whatever Russell Byrum felt was needed. With my consent to help, I was stepping lightly through the opening of a whole new mission enterprise. That was the beginning of my connection with a vital new cause which would for over forty years, become an all-absorbing, challenging-in-new-ways-every-day ministry. I was to be part of a working fellowship with the top leaders of the Church of God. It was a lifetime of learning from the best the church had to offer. It was to be a term of service on the new frontiers to which this new agency was commissioned.
>
> So I began to get acquainted with the new agency I would serve. I found out that a hustling, fast-working teacher, managing editor and writer, Russell Byrum, was the only employee. I found out that the new Board did not own a desk, nor a typewriter, not even a pencil or pen. What stenographic and bookkeeping help was needed was provided by arrangements with the Gospel Trumpet Company in whose building we were situated. Russell gave me a few checks and some currency that had come in the mail as contributions to the new cause. It would be my job, he said, to send thank-you letters to each contributor, report all contributions, deposit them in a checking account at Ander-

son Banking Company, and be sure a record of receipts was given to Wayne Moore, a Gospel Trumpet bookkeeper who would handle the accounts for the Board. An acknowledgement letter was to go to each contributor, with name and address kept for the office file. The first month I was to have less than ten names for the file.

> Russell wanted me to prepare what he called an ad each month for the *Gospel Trumpet* magazine, which was to be our way of reporting the work of Church Extension and Home Missions and of asking for contributions to support the program (1986, 2).

Direct appeals for funds through ads in the church's one publication, the *Gospel Trumpet*, was a primary method of getting the program dollars necessary to carry out each agency's mission. The church slowly developed a national consciousness. It began to realize that national agencies were necessary to help with its ministry in evangelism and missions. Then came the realization that a cooperative plan for funding such ministries must be developed.

Soon after the new board started telling its story of needs here in the homeland, some of the church people began to respond, slowly, with financial support. Adcock relates:

> At first it was only a dollar or two, just to try us out. Occasionally it was five dollars. Then we got a pleasant surprise when we received our first one-hundred-dollar check as a contribution to the new work! Actually, the people were pleased that something was being done to carry the message of the Church of God to the needy places. And it was a response to many of the pleas which came to the publishing company for ministers and literature to help present the Gospel in new and neglected areas (1986, 15).

First Year—Bottom Line

Research of the board's finances for its first year of operations, June 1, 1921, to May 31, 1922, reveals a most meager beginning. A balance sheet reconstructed from financial statements shows income for the year as $4,402.39! Expenses for the twelve months totaled $2,544.21. This left a general fund balance of $1,858.18. This was proof that the executive committee lived within the board policy of "not spending more money than they received"! By May 31, 1924, after three years of operations, the general fund balance was $6,093.53, and the board's net worth was $22,656.08.

In its June 2, 1922 session, the General Ministerial Assembly approved what was called a "Benevolent Budget." The budget included $144,000 for the Missionary Board, $95,000 for a general Benevolent Budget, $50,000 for the newly established Board of Church Extension and Home Missions, $35,000 for the publishing work (Gospel Trumpet Company), and $10,000 for Anderson Bible Training School. This was more of an approved targeted amount than an actual budget. It was expected that each agency would bear the responsibility for soliciting its own funds by whatever methods and ways it could.

A Vast and Exciting Assignment On the Advance Front

Adcock wrote concerning the large assignment given the board and the fact that there were no start-up funds:

> It could be described in a comparative way as a David-and-Goliath situation. It was like Peter and John outside the gate when the crippled person was crying out for alms. Peter responded, "Silver and gold have I none." There was so much the Board of Church Extension and Home Missions could have said they did not have. They did not have experience in the field to

> which they were assigned. They had absolutely no funds with which to begin. They had little acquaintance of the church they would represent, and no surveys or preparation of programs for approach to the work in hand. They did have an appointment by the church, a charter from the state of Indiana, and a rather long name (1986, 16)!

Under such adverse circumstances, it is interesting to discover just how the board survived. Although the actual funds were not available the first year or two of operations, there were some powerful dynamics at work. The church and the new agency felt that the message of the Church of God could and would make a difference in society at home and abroad. They had been entrusted with a powerful bit of good news! Somehow, if God had called them and entrusted them with this welcomed message, ways would be found to carry it out. There was also the dynamic of the conviction that in order to get the truth out to the entire world, there needed to be strong congregations. This new agency was brought into existence for the very purpose of helping to start, develop, and nurture strong congregations. There was also the dynamic of a thrilling and exciting assignment given to the board and staff.

Adcock gives some insight into the feelings and excitement of those first years:

> The assignment was new, all right. And it was a new concept to the church. To Church of God folks, India, with all of its "benighted millions"; or Africa, the dark continent; or Japan, or China—this was missions. But America? It is hard to think of your own country as a mission field.
>
> But when the Church of God looked, really looked at North America, the picture was plain. It was a vast mission field. But its physical size, its mixture of cultures and diversity of peoples in its strategic world

situation, was a bit awesome to the small church body and its new agency to which the assignment was made. The assignment was the whole continent from the Atlantic to the Pacific, from pole to palm tree.

How do you see it all: the mountains, the rivers, the diverse climate, the grain and vast farm lands, teeming cities, the people of every color, the rich and the poor, the illiterate and the educated? How do you get to it? How do you deal with a continent? To the peoples in this vast area—what do you have to say? How strong is your mission? How many days are you willing to be on the road to reach the spots where you hope your service will be full of meaning?

Yes, in any way you look at it and size it up, it is an astounding mission field! . . . In a very special sense, there was a keen realization on the part of those of us in the beginning years that the Board was called upon to carry on a prophetic ministry, as a pioneer reaching out to new fields and to new people. Born to the role of pioneer, the Board would ever remain on the advance front (1986, 15-19)!

Discovering Areas of Need

From the beginning of this board there was a constant desire to work closely with the church. Each decade of board ministry was highlighted by various attempts and methods to keep discovering the needs and desires of the congregations and church leaders. This desire to keep in touch manifested itself, in 1925-29, in the form of automobile tours. The first such tour was made by five men—E. F. Adcock, A. T. Rowe of Atlanta; F. M. Dodge of Cleveland; W. T. Wallace of Louisville; and Fred Higgins of Anderson, the driver and owner of the 1926 Buick. The primary purpose of the trip was to get acquainted with pastors in the southwest and learn of their needs and fields of service. The group of five leaders also wanted to have a look in San

Antonio at the work of M. F. Tafolla among Hispanics. The BCEHM had been supporting this Spanish-speaking pastor with a modest monthly check, and now the leaders wanted to get an on-site look at this effective leader and his field of labor.

This first tour took the five men through Missouri and Oklahoma, into Texas, and across the border to Monterey, Mexico. While in San Antonio they discovered that the Hispanic, Anglo, and African-American congregations were all worshiping in woefully inadequate facilities to effectively represent the Church of God to this fine city. This was discovered in many cities where there was a Church of God congregation.

The next field discovery automobile tour took seven weeks and clocked a total of over 11,000 miles. After leaving Anderson, the first stop was Milwaukee. Then the team drove on to St. Paul, Minnesota, a tent meeting in North Dakota, and Winnipeg and Edmonton in Canada. They came down to Montana and the Inland Empire, to camp meetings in Oregon, and south to California—San Francisco, Fresno, Los Angeles, and San Diego. They returned home with stops in Utah, Colorado, Iowa, and Illinois.

Such exposure to the front lines of church extension and missions enlarged the vision of the five who made the tour. Adcock wrote:

> Out of the tours like these two came an appreciation of the bigness, and in many cases the emptiness, of our country so far as our church development was concerned. The tours also gave us an appreciation for the brothers and sisters who were working in more or less pioneer situations. After these trips we had an awareness of a vastly greater field than we had formerly. . . . such discoveries brought us nearer to working arrangements that would result in greater developments in the work of the new Board. We were able literally to

see that the field was large, the laborers few, and the great necessity for an agency like Church Extension and Home Missions to be busy at the task (1986, 23).

In addition to tours of the territory by the chief executive officer and staff, there was an attempt to keep informed by frequently having pastors who were doing effective work or who had ideas on church extension or missions to share their insights and suggestions with the board in its annual meetings. Such teamship enhanced the effectiveness of the board.

Early Patterns of Program Development

Evangelism and Church Extension. A major assignment of this new board was evangelism. The focus from its first year was to help the church become more effective in winning the lost to Christ. The board's strategy for evangelizing North America was through starting and developing congregations.

Until the 1920s, most all Church of God congregations had been started independently by individual pastors or evangelists. The board decided to try to find a more cooperative approach for new church development. It felt that the church at large should become more directly involved in the process of church extension. Board members hoped that the moral and financial backing of the entire church through the BCEHM would result in the establishment of stronger congregations. It was the beginning of a pioneering cooperative strategy.

Within its first three years, 1921 to 1924, the board helped start new works in Boston, Rochester, New Orleans (African-American), Omaha, Atlanta, San Antonio (Hispanic), Dallas, and Edmonton, Alberta, Canada. Monthly financial support for each project varied according to need, and was modest but adequate in light of the meager funds available.

The conviction that church extension must be a primary goal of the board was indelibly established in its first decade of operations. It has been a centerpiece of the board's program for seventy years.

Russell Byrum, in his report in the 1923 *Yearbook of the Church of God,* gives insight to the high priority for establishing new congregations:

> The purpose of this Board is the evangelization of the larger unevangelized portions of North America. It will seek to establish churches in such regions as strategic points, so that they serve as centers from which the work may spread to surrounding territory. Its purpose is also to assist evangelists in new places by furnishing them support as needed, and to assist struggling churches in the support of pastors.

To impress his readers with the scope and urgency of evangelism through church extension, Byrum continued:

> Of the 105,000,000 people in this country, only 27,500,000 are members of evangelical churches. . . . The 78,000,000 non-evangelical people of the United States are more than the entire population of the whole continent of South America, or the continent of Australia with the thousands of South Sea Islands added, or all of the British Isles, or Germany, France and Italy, or Japan. The non-evangelical people of the United States are nearly as many as the combined population of all the countries of South America, Mexico, and Canada.

Church Building. A second dominant ministry of the board was church building. It was often referred to in the first decade or two as church erection ministry. In the 1921 yearbook there were listed 720 congregations of the Church of God. Of this number more than 312 did not have their own places of worship. These congregations met for worship and church school in rented halls, school buildings, private homes, tents, and a variety of other places.

As mentioned earlier, this lack of congregationally-owned property was partly due to the feeling of the early leaders that the end of time would happen in their lifetime. Therefore, little thought was given to the buying of land and the building of buildings for church use.

During World War I, building supplies were either limited or prohibited from being sold. For the few congregations wanting to build this created further delay and discouragement. Also, at this time the majority of Church of God congregations were caught in the transition from conducting church work with volunteer leadership and preaching, plus occasional evangelistic services, to full-time paid leadership. Regular weekly giving and keen stewardship principles had not been adequately developed by the 1920s in many congregations.

Many of the congregations with enough financial strength to build church facilities had done so with improper planning. Often the pattern was to purchase a single lot, hopefully on a corner, and to build a one-room frame building on it. Then they discovered, often after the first year, that the building was not adequate. Scores of congregations of the Church of God in the early 1920s followed this pattern.

In this setting, it is understandable that the desire for adequate facilities for church worship and ministry would become a high priority. The increase in starting new congregations helped to heighten the urgency for better and more adequate facilities.

The records and minutes reveal that, from the beginning, the board worked hard through conferences, writings, sermons, and staff visits to help the congregations keep physical facilities in proper perspective. The refrain down through the years of the board's ministry was that the work of God demands our best, and that the buildings we build should reflect our beliefs and concepts of worship: build the best building you can afford, but always keep in mind that the building is not an end in itself; know what God has called you to do as a congregation, and let your building be a tool to help you fulfill your congregational mission.

Highlighting the need for another service of the new board was a backlog of congregations wanting to build but not able because of the restraints of the war. Also, there was a growing awareness that Christ might *not* come back in the immediate future. The recognition of need for more permanent and better facilities was developing.

In such a setting it is understandable that another primary program service of the new board was church building. As soon as it became known that the board would loan funds to help new and struggling congregations build adequate church facilities, there was an avalanche of requests for such aid. With a growing movement, these demands would prove to be fairly constant over each decade of the board's history. It is interesting to note that, in spite of the limited supply of loan funds, on several occasions the board approved loans for overseas projects through the Missionary Board. In 1928, President Sherwood in his report to the General Ministerial Assembly states:

> The benefits of the loan phase of our work (as a board) is not restricted to this country. Loans have been made in South America, Jamaica, Egypt, Syria and Germany (YB 1928).

Home Missions. The other half of the new board's name and special emphasis was home missions. Early in his ministry with the board, someone asked Adcock what the difference was between evangelism and home missions. His reply was to give a definition of home missions which has held up across the years of the board's program:

> Actually, home missions is a ministry to reach people who by reason of race, economic status or maybe by a prejudiced social attitude, were not included in the mainstream of the church's ministry (Adcock 1986, 25).

To include such groups of people in the life and ministry of the church requires special skills and knowledge of each group. It also requires a greater outlay of budget. The BCEHM was to learn that to start and develop a self-supporting congregation for those of the mainstream may take five or more years. On the other hand, to assist those who have been excluded from the mainstream and deprived of their rights to earn a fair wage would take much longer. In many special situations, a sustained financial backing over decades would be required.

It is highly understandable, then, that in its earliest years the board did not have a major emphasis on home missions. There were no full-time staff members for the first two years. There were no program budget dollars for missions at home. It was soon discovered that the church responded more quickly and generously to the board's call for invested dollars for the making of loans than for gift dollars for missions and evangelism. For example, 1927-28 was the best year for the board since its beginning, in regard to gifts from the church for home missions. Financial records reveal that the sum of $18,641.91 was given that year. Yet, in the same year the sum of $100,000 was invested with the board for the purpose of making church loans.

With the limitations of dollars and staff, the board recognized during its first years of operations that one of the most ready opportunities for mission and evangelism was some form of special ministry to Spanish-speaking Americans located in the southwest United States:

> The first Hispanic Church of God congregation in the United States was started in San Antonio, Texas, in 1921, by the Reverend M. F. Tafolla, a Mexican-Ameri-

can minister who came in touch with the Church of God through reading a *Gospel Trumpet* magazine. . . . Later, Brother Tafolla conducted camp meetings on property along the Medina River, near the town of Somerset ten miles southwest of San Antonio. . . . He was the first home missionary of the Church of God to receive direct support of the Board of Church Extension and Home Missions (Telfer 1981, 10).

There was a gradual build-up of concern for Mexico. As the board developed more contacts with Hispanics and supported new projects for Spanish-speaking people in the United States, this naturally led to a greater concern for the Mexicans below our southern border.

Other areas of home missions concern in the board's first decade were: Alaska; the native Americans; people of the Appalachian Mountains; the African-Americans, largely concentrated in the South; and ethnic groups in the cities. Adcock writes:

> Developing a missionary thrust into these areas and to these peoples was slow at first, but gradually took on the importance of a real mission to our neglected friends within our own borders. For a long time our Church of God folks had thought of missions as being an overseas ministry, and there was a great deal of romantic interest in places outside of our country. Perhaps it is harder to get excited about reaching out to Mexicans in the United States than in sending missionaries to the continent of South America. It would, of course, be more alluring to develop missionary work in Africa among the blacks there, than in taking the Gospel to black folks in Alabama or Mississippi, or anywhere within our borders. But as the need was presented and as workers went out, supported by the Board of Church Extension and Home Missions, a real home missions program gradually developed (Adcock 1986, 27).

Getting the Funds to Loan

If there is a great demand for loan funds by congregations wanting to build or remodel, and if the Church has made no provision for loan funds in its charter, how does a new agency meet the tremendous need? That was the key question faced by Byrum and the executive committee of the board in 1921.

Before the first year of operations was over, the board had a plan to go to individuals of the Church of God to ask them to invest some of their personal savings with the board. The investors would receive interest, and the board in turn would loan these funds to congregations for their building needs. Adcock explains the establishment of the church building loan program:

> The Board had to depend solely on funds which it could obtain as loans from members of the church. Appeals were sent out, largely through the medium of church papers, for those who had savings to deposit them with the Board and let them be used by the church, rather than in a purely secular way.
>
> The Board started out offering the current rates of interest for the time, 5% on a straight promissory note. The first notes were made for one year, and then renewed if continuing use were desired. . . . The Board explained that reserve funds were kept, so that a note presented for payment would receive immediate attention; the investor would not need to wait the period of ninety days named in the note.
>
> In describing this plan, we made three claims. One, safety of principal. Two, availability of principal when needed or desired. Third, satisfaction of Christian use of the investor's savings. . . . The Board operated on the principle that we must prove to be trustworthy borrowers (1986, 37-39).

In addition to the promissory note, the board offered a life-loan note. This plan stated that the investor would receive income on his/her money and have the privilege of withdrawing it at any time. It was also stated that at the investor's death, if the money were still invested, it would be considered a donation to the board for its church building loan program. The board also set up a life annuity contract as another method of getting building loan funds. This offered an annuity for life without provision for withdrawing the principal.

The June 1922 records reveal that just a few hundred dollars were invested with the board for its lending ministry. But by the end of the year the plea of "invest some of your savings with the board" was being heard. Church members began to respond. By year's end, there were enough investments for the board to make these six loans: five hundred dollars to Muskogee, Oklahoma; three hundred dollars to LaPorte, Indiana; one thousand dollars to Louisville, Kentucky; twenty-five hundred dollars to Pomona, California; fourteen hundred dollars to Edmonton, Alberta, Canada, and $320 to Enterprise, Oregon.

Gradually the church began to respond as it realized the partnership possibility with the board in providing church building funds. In 1923, there was a total of twenty investors with the board. By 1925, there were fifty-eight investors. The personal investments ranged from fifty dollars to twenty-five hundred dollars each. The BCEHM had a lending fund of $108,295 by the end of 1925.

Once Church of God people saw the need and realized their own personal savings could be used to help erect buildings for Church of God congregations, many responded with deep commitment. The annual reports and minutes of the organization record many human interest stories of the joy of partnership with the board in providing loan funds. An example of how people responded is told by Adcock:

> One day an elderly couple from Ohio came into the campground office during the Anderson Camp Meeting. The man was clutching a small pamphlet, which we recognized as one that had been sent out several years before, telling about the life-loan note plan. These good folks came in with their statement, "We are ready now." They went on to explain that they had heard W. E. Monk, when he visited their congregation, telling about how money could be used in the Lord's work. They were living on the farm at the time, and all of their funds were tied up in their own farming enterprise. Now, with advancing years, they were retiring from the farm. They had sold it and bought a small place in town, leaving them funds with which they could make an investment with the Board. All these years it had been in the back of their minds that they would want to do something like that if ever they could get the funds with which to do it. They left the office that day with a life-loan note and the real satisfaction that their money was going into the work of helping congregations of the Church of God (1986, 41).

During the first five years of the lending operation, over $250,000 was loaned to congregations. During the 1926-27 fiscal year $86,000 was loaned. In 1926 President Sherwood reported to the General Ministerial Assembly, "All told the Board through its church erection fund has granted loans on nearly one hundred houses of worship (GMA June 1926)."

Although the board was receiving hundreds of thousands of dollars in personal savings investments from the church, it had very little funds of its own. Some plan was needed to make sure the invested dollar was safe and available if the investor needed it. Very early, the policy of keeping twenty-five percent of each invested dollar in a reserve account was established. This would keep adequate funds available in the event an investor had to withdraw funds earlier than the terms of the note. This policy, established at the beginning of the lending program, proved to be of great value to the agency. This would be particularly true in the 1930s.

In spite of the increase in invested funds for making church building loans, the demand far exceeded the supply of money. In 1925, after a year of searching for an answer to this dilemma, the executive committee recommended and the board approved the hiring of W. E. Monk as a field man on a part-time basis, to help find the loan funds so urgently being requested by the church. He was the first field staff person to be employed by the agency. His effectiveness increased with each year of experience. He was one of the most persuasive and effective development persons the board had in its first thirty-five years. He not only helped increase the loan fund of the board, but also was effective in securing gift money for home missions, evangelism, and new church development.

Help for State Organizations

Before its first decade was over, the board saw that if the task of developing new congregations was to be as effective as possible, help must be offered to the newly-forming Church of God state organizations. In 1920 Michigan was the first state to organize its work on a statewide basis. Other states in which there were a dozen or more congregations began to see the advantages of organizing their work on a cooperative basis. In 1928 authorization was given for the executive committee to develop a state aid plan to assist the states in church extension work, particularly with opening up new works in the cities. This was the beginning of a partnership between the state organizations and this national agency which would be enhanced in the decades to come.

By 1929 there was an urgent need for help in erecting houses of worship in New Orleans for both the African-

American and the Anglo congregations, and for both the Anglo and Hispanic congregations in San Antonio. Under Adcock's leadership an Every Member Extension Campaign was set up. The goal was to raise forty thousand dollars for these four congregations. The money was raised.

Cooperative Funding

In 1923 a fifth national agency was formed: the Board of Sunday Schools and Religious Education. With this new arrival, the issue of equitable and adequate funding became more critical. That same year, R. L. Berry, a pastor from Missouri, had proposed that the representatives of all the agencies meet and discuss their benevolence askings and that such askings be combined into "one general budget (Phillips 1979, 191)." However, it was not until 1927 that official action was taken. This was the beginning of a process which produced the Associated Budgets. Adcock was a participant in this process. Years later he recalled:

> It is an interesting fact that the agencies always got along well together. That is not to say they were always in agreement, but always in fellowship and unity. There was unity in spite of the fact there was no corporate structure to bind them together. Each agency did well its assigned task, but still problems arose. One key problem was in regard to the gathering and distributing of the general budget funds of the Church of God.
>
> It was easy for the little new agency, Board of Church Extension and Home Missions, to feel a bit crowded and a bit left out. At times it felt it had to cry a little louder and scramble a bit harder for the attention of the Church for funds.
>
> By the time the Board of Christian Education was added to the family of agencies and began asking for its share of attention and subsistence from the church,

some sharper tensions began to develop. There was some murmuring from investors and donors across the church regarding the frequency of appeals from the five national agencies. There were some informal discussions by agency people in Anderson about the problem and suggestions of what might be done about it.

A family conclave was called. Each agency was asked to send to this meeting its executives and any others they desired to be in the consideration of the issue. In the discussion it was soon evident that agency people were of two very different opinions. One group held to the old way of direct, individual relationship of each Board with the Church as an essential and almost sacred manner of operating. The other viewpoint held that some form of united appeal and sharing of funds was the way, required by the changing conditions and strong urging from the field. These two positions were strongly debated.

There were twenty to thirty persons present in this discussion. A committee of three was appointed to prepare a plan and bring it back to the conference the next day. Two members insisted on going about the task as it was being done, and suggested no change. They put their recommendation in the form of a report for the next day. However, one committee member brought in a minority report advocating a real united budget.

After hearing and discussing both reports, it became evident there was strong support for a change of some kind of plan for united promotion and fund distribution. Finally, a compromise was worked out and a new modified plan, termed the Associated Budgets was agreed upon. This plan allowed for a great deal of freedom of field promotion, and opportunity for donors to designate who should be the recipients of their general church giving. The final agreement was reached amicably. A fine family spirit was maintained and the desire of the field was satisfied. Although the plan was a compromise, it was a move toward unification (1986, 72-75).

An Associated Budgets part-time office was set up. Elver Adcock, who by this time was secretary-treasurer of the BCEHM, was asked to assume the oversight of this cooperative budget plan. Later, R. L. Berry was invited to become the first full-time secretary of Associated Budgets.

Changes of Leadership

From the beginning of his leadership as chief executive officer of the board, Russell Byrum knew he could never give it his full-time attention. He had been training Elver Adcock to handle much of the day-to-day operation of the new agency. He had suggested that Adcock be nominated as a board member. In 1924, the General Ministerial Assembly elected him to the board. Then in 1925 Adcock was unanimously elected by the board as assistant secretary-treasurer and asked to serve on the executive committee.

In 1927, Byrum notified the board that he was going to resign as secretary-treasurer. He urged the appointment of Elver Adcock as his successor. The board approved and submitted Adcock's name to the General Ministerial Assembly. He was elected as the first full-time chief executive officer of the agency, at the age of twenty-nine.

The same year, H. A. Sherwood felt he could no longer continue to serve as president of the board. His resignation, in the board's annual meeting on June 14, 1927, was accepted with regret. The board then voted to elect Earl Martin as the new president of the board (GB 14 June 1927).

The responsibilities and risks of operating this expanding agency were increasing with each new year: greater investments, larger church loans, an increase in new church development, and a broadening of home missions ministries. Under such conditions, the board felt that a wider representation was needed on its executive committee. They voted to increase the membership from three to five members.

Patterns and Principles of Operation

By the end of the board's first decade, certain patterns and principles had been established. Many of these would continue throughout the following decades.

One point was clear to the members: the BCEHM was brought into being as a service agency through the vote and empowerment of the General Ministerial Assembly. It understood that it was not a law unto itself, and that it must carry out its assigned tasks from the stance of cooperative ministry, as opposed to independent work.

The vastness of the North American continent as its mission field and the crucial ministry assigned this agency caused the leaders in this first decade to stay close to the church. The two staff tours taken in 1928 and 1929 were symbolic of the board's desire to see the needs firsthand and hear directly from those serving in front line ministries. This helped to establish the principle that in order to carry out its assigned task the board must be constantly exposed to the daily work of the church. The desire to keep informed of the needs of society and the church was strongly established in the formative years.

The early experiment of starting new congregations on a planned, cooperative basis proved successful. Mistakes were made, and there were some failures, but the principle of church extension through cooperation became the primary means whereby new congregations were established. Battles were fought over this new concept in the 1920s and more would be fought in the 1940s, but cooperative church extension as a sound method of work would win out in the end.

With no full-time staff for the first two years, and with very limited funds for operations, the board established the practice of utilizing volunteers in carrying out its assigned tasks. Its elected members were expected to serve the needs of the board in their respective states and regions. Certain pastors and leaders were co-opted for special tasks and assignments. This helped to establish the pattern that volunteers would play a key role in the agency's life and ministry.

The only funds the board had for church building loans were in essence borrowed funds. Hundreds of individuals deposited savings with the agency. They viewed this as a partnership with the board in helping the Church of God get proper church buildings. Therefore, because the church building loan funds did not belong to the board, it took a very cautious and conservative stance regarding these funds. The mandatory twenty-five percent reserve fund was set up in this first decade. Later, other controls and actions were established to give every protection possible to those who entrusted their funds to the agency. The trust of the investor must never be violated was a principle established early in the board's history.

By 1928 it became clear to the leaders of the Board of Church Extension and Home Missions that there was a natural affinity between cooperative church extension, evangelism, home missions, and the newly developing state organizations.

Chapter 3

Struggle and Survival

(1930-1939)

The young board was only in its ninth year of operations when it met the most severe test of its existence.

The Great Depression started with the Wall Street crash on October 24, 1929. This event wiped out millions of dollars of investments at a single stroke. Just eighteen months prior to that date, a bull market was at full steam and appeared to be unstoppable. Some major industrial stocks had more than doubled in value, and speculators were rushing to the market in ever-increasing numbers to make quick profits.

European funds were flooding into the United States. Banks had lent some eight billion dollars to brokers trading on the New York Stock Exchange. Herbert Hoover had just been elected president. He tried to control the market by refusing to lend money to banks that financed speculation. An all-time stock market high was reached on September 3, 1929. Over eight million shares were traded.

Four weeks later, the bottom dropped out. More than twelve million stock transactions were recorded that day. Five days later, the value of some of the leading stocks had been slashed by sixty-six percent. Thousands of Americans saw their life savings wiped out in less than a week.

Across the World

The 1930s witnessed massive depression and unemployment throughout the entire western world, and the road back to economic health proved steep and costly.

Unemployment in the United States remained at about eight million in spite of all the reconstruction programs of President Roosevelt and the New Deal. In Germany the cost of recovery was higher still, and by 1934 could be borne no longer. This created a ripe setting for the rapid rise of Adolph Hitler and the Nazi party. All civil powers were suspended and absolute, dictatorial power was given to Hitler to run the country.

There was civil war in Spain. Joseph Stalin used the turmoil to strengthen his grip on the U.S.S.R. with a ruthlessness equal to that of Hitler. There were massive hunger marches in Britain. Unemployment was unprecedented in Germany, Britain, and the United States.

The situation was made even worse by a long and costly drought in Midwest America. In 1935 more than seventy thousand farm refugees and their families fled the dust bowl states. That year the federal government created the Works Progress Administration (WPA). Its purpose was to create jobs for some of the ten million unemployed Americans. Such jobs included the building of roads and facilities for community health services. By 1937, in spite of all the government was trying to do, millions of people were still jobless.

In the United States by 1932, five thousand banks had failed and eighty-six thousand businesses had closed their doors. This particular year was referred to by some as the cruelest of the entire depression. In this year alone more than 275,000 families were evicted from their homes because they could not make the mortgage payments. Some men took their own lives rather than go on relief. During this year corn sold, if it sold at all, for seven cents a bushel, oats brought ten cents a bushel—if buyers could be found—

and sugar was down to three cents a pound. It is no wonder that this period of the 1930s is referred to as the Great Depression.

By 1939 Germany had marched in and taken Austria, Czechoslovakia, Bohemia, Poland, and Moravia along with other parts of nations. France and Britain declared war on Germany on September 1, 1939.

Adapting to the Situation

Before the economic crash, the young Board of Church Extension and Home Missions was just gaining the experience and economic strength it needed to carry out its assigned tasks. It had been successful in helping the church to focus on evangelism and the starting of new congregations. Requests for its church erection service far exceeded everyone's expectations. This was due in part to the broad recognition across the church of the importance of adequate church buildings. This made it easier for the board to appeal for and to get favorable responses from church members, who invested their savings with the BCEHM for church building loans. By the end of the board's first ten years, it had loaned one million dollars to Church of God congregations for building purposes. None of this ministry would have been possible without the hundreds of investors across the church who saw the need, believed in the board, and entrusted their financial savings to it.

Impact on the Church

The arrival of the decade of the 1930s ushered the church and the board into totally new and undreamed-of situations. In light of the reality of worldwide economic turmoil, all of the church's agencies were forced to an examination of their organizational structure and programs.

From 1921 to 1932, hundreds of congregations of the Church of God had borrowed funds from the board for erecting or remodeling church building facilities. In addition, scores of congregations had borrowed their building funds from local banks or insurance companies. This was a rapid growth era for the Church of God.

Then came this overpowering economic crash. Congregations, families, and individuals alike were impacted and changed by its devastating force. The board's files of letters and committee minutes reveal a wide variety of situations and reactions on the part of pastors and congregations.

The loss of jobs affected every congregation of the Church of God. In many congregations the majority of members were without employment of any kind. In some congregations not a single family had employment. This was a severe test of commitment for each member and for the pastoral leadership. Some insight is gained by the description of a visit Elver Adcock made to the Mt. Carmel, Illinois, congregation in 1932. He wrote:

> I visited Mt. Carmel during the worst of the depression and stayed with the pastor overnight. He told me not to be surprised if I heard considerable commotion under my upstairs bedroom window. Some of the church people would be out there early making their daily volume of homemade soup to be distributed to the community. I did wake up about 4:00 in the morning and saw there was a light in the back yard and heard voices and the banging of pots and pans. The fire had been built under a large iron kettle and about a dozen people were working diligently. I had to see what was going on, and when I joined the group, I learned that the church had found regular customers in their community who would buy a quantity of homemade soup when it was delivered to them early in the morning several times a week. This church did not have a single man holding a job. Besides their Church Extension loan, they owed a sum at the local bank, and I went with the pastor later that morning to

talk to the banker about the loan situation. The banker told me the church had kept up regular payments to the bank, though he did not understand how in the world they could do it. He highly praised their attitude and effort and said it must be that the Lord was with them (Adcock 1986, 61-62).

Records reveal that other congregations made and sold baked goods in order to raise funds to pay on their loans. One would hear about "Church of God" donuts, pies, pastries, or bread being made and sold. Stories were also told of how local groups of the National Woman's Home and Foreign Missionary Society were involved in helping to raise funds for local congregational needs, including pastoral support and building needs.

Conditions Worsen

The depression lingered several years. In spite of the resourcefulness of the congregations, conditions worsened. Each month that the depression continued, the situation grew more desperate. Loan payments to the board became delinquent in increasing numbers. Delinquent interest on the church building loans also climbed.

Before 1930 quite a few Church of God congregations had built up enough equity and financial reputation to be able to borrow funds for building from their local banks. Others had first mortgage loans through insurance companies. When the depression came, these congregations were very vulnerable. Most of the banks and insurance companies were understanding, but the continued period of joblessness and dwindling loan payments forced many financial institutions to demand that congregations make full monthly payments on their church loans or face the reality of foreclosure.

Congregations began to write or call the board to plead for help. Could the BCEHM refinance their loan? Was there any way or place to find help or relief?

The BCEHM itself was very vulnerable at this time. When the Great Depression hit, the board had out over $500,000 in church loans. These were funds made possible by individual investors. The board was making monthly, quarterly, or annual payments of interest to each investor. As the congregations were having difficulty making their loan payments, a problem was created for the board in generating enough cash to pay that interest. It was a time when the investors could have become fearful and decided to withdraw their funds. But fortunately they were understanding of the situation and stood firm and faithful. They knew that thousands of banks and financial instituations had become insolvent. Letters came from investors giving the board a vote of confidence and thanking it for the regular payments of interest. Some said that if there were any doubts, they would rather trust their money in the work of the Lord than in a secular institution.

Saving Church Property

The continuation of the depression increased the congregations' inability to make full loan payments. By 1934-1935 over one hundred and twenty congregations were behind with their mortgage payments to the board and to local financial institutions.

This forced the board to come up with a plan of help for these troubled congregations. There were many prayers on the part of the board members and staff. A variety of approaches and methods were tried. Each local situation presented its own unique challenge.

In some situations where a congregation was falling behind in its monthly loan payment, a letter was sent or a call by a staff member was made. Inquiry was made as to the specifics of each situation. Many staff trips were made to sit with a pastor and local leaders to hear their story and decide on alternatives. Often the situation was eased by allowing the congregation to make partial or interest-only monthly payments for a few months.

The demand by the church for financial counsel and advice grew. The board decided this should be one of its major priorities in the mid-1930s. At the time, Steele C. Smith was pastoring in Boston. He had some training and experience in banking and business. He accepted an invitation to join the staff in 1935 to work as a special consultant and counselor with congregations facing foreclosure by local financial institutions, and those who were delinquent in their loan payments to the BCEHM. The year Smith came to the staff, congregations owed over fifty-eight thousand dollars to the board in delinquent interest alone.

In situation after situation, Steele Smith went with pastors and lay leaders to local banks or financial institutions. They discussed the options. Time and again he was successful in pointing out to the local lender that partial payment was better than foreclosure. In a particular situation, Smith and Adcock went to meet with a local lender. The man was very rigid and unsympathetic at first. Then it was learned that in that small town the financial institution had already foreclosed on two other church groups, and the buildings were vacant. Smith and Adcock were able to convince him that six months of interest-only payments by the congregation was better than having a third vacant church building on his hands. An agreement was reached. By the end of the year the congregation was able to resume making full loan payments.

Each congregation was treated with compassion and understanding. Some congregations had been discouraged for so long that it was hard for them to believe they could ever pay their debts. Part of the board's job was to offer encouragement, and help them find alternatives.

One congregation found itself unable to make full loan payments as well as payments on its delinquent interest. The pastor and chairman of the board wrote that they felt sure they could make the loan payment, but due to local unemployment did not see how it would be possible to pay anything on the delinquent interest account. A letter from the office went back, expressing thanks for their efforts and for the full loan payments. The letter stated that every additional dollar the congregation could pay on the delinquent interest would be matched with a dollar by the board over the next six months; this achieved the desired result for the congregation and the board. Within a year the group was back on track with full loan and delinquent interest payments.

Another approach to helping the congregations in loan payment trouble is told by Elver Adcock:

> Believe me, the money situation was tight! It was during this time that many building and loan associations were in difficulty. The stock from some of them, particularly in Indiana and Ohio, was selling for less than one-third of its face value. Some of these institutions encouraged their loan customers to buy the stock at these low prices and turn them in for full value on indebtedness. In some cases, like in Canton and Dayton, Ohio and Indianapolis, Indiana, loan balances were more than cut in half when the Board was able to come up with enough money with which to purchase the stock. In no case did the Board ever ask a lending institution to cut its loan, but only acted upon the suggestion and readiness of the loan association to deal in this way (1986, 63).

In just two years' time, primarily through the efforts of Steele Smith, the delinquent interest balance at the board had been reduced from fifty-eight thousand dollars to only ten thousand dollars. He left the employment of the board in 1935 to work for the Gospel Trumpet Company, and became its general manager in 1949.

Perhaps one of the most unique accomplishments of the BCEHM in this decade was its help in keeping the church financially solvent. Over a hundred congregations were able to escape foreclosure because of the ministry of the board. Many members of the church lost money they had invested in banks. However, every single investor with the board received one hundred cents on the dollar of both principal and interest. This fact alone helped church people to increase their trust in the board and view it as an institution of integrity with sound business principles.

Cash Flow Needs of Agencies

The policy of keeping twenty-five percent of invested funds in a reserve account proved prudent and helpful. If an individual investor needed to withdraw his or her investment early, the reserve funds allowed this to be done without interupting the church loan program. Just as congregations were hard hit by the depression, so were the national agencies of the church. The minutes of the executive committee of the BCEHM periodically reveal that through the years Anderson College, the Missionary Board, the Gospel Trumpet Company and others came to the board for a ninety-day loan. It was always related to a cash flow problem and the need for money until income resources were built back up. Often it was for the purpose of meeting payroll of staff or of missionaries, or to purchase equipment. At the end of the ninety days, the loans were repaid with interest. These quick rollover loans came from the twenty-five percent reserve account of the board.

Commission on Reorganization

The minutes of the 1930 General Ministerial Assembly note that authorization was given to appoint a Commission on Reorganization. Concerns had been expressed regarding the organizations of the church in the 1930s as compared to the early teachings of the church on the matter. Does the church have enough organization? Too much? There was also concern for more lay leadership and involvement in the church. A proposal was presented that, in essence, would change the annual meeting from a voluntary association to a delegated body. This was defeated.

In 1931 a resolution was sent to both the Missionary Board and the BCEHM. The source of the resolution is not clear. The June 15, 1931 minutes of the board record a Resolution of Dissolution (Merging of Home and Foreign Missions). It called for both existing boards to be dissolved and merged into a new board, to be known as the "Board of Home and Foreign Missions of the Church of God." Some saw this as a proposal to save money during the depression. It was a call to return to the missionary agency structure of 1917. The secretary-treasurer reported that the Missionary Board had tabled the resolution of dissolution, and moved that the BCEHM do the same. The motion carried.

No mention of this proposal was ever made again in the General Ministerial Assembly minutes nor in the minutes of either of the missions boards.

Golden Jubilee

One of the bright spots of this difficult decade was the Church of God Golden Jubilee. 1931 was the designated year for the Church of God to have its first all-church celebration in honor of its fifty years of history. The Gospel Trumpet Company was the prime mover of this event. It had developed the basic concept and widely promoted the celebration. One primary event was the publication of a commemorative golden jubilee book with pictures of all pastors, evangelists, and ministers. The book also featured a history of the Church of God.

An examination of the Church of God yearbooks for 1926 and 1935 reveals rapid growth in the number of congregations. The total number of congregations in the United States and Canada increased from 635 in 1926 to

1,352 in 1935. This was an average of a new church start every five days. The BCEHM often used this figure to inspire and encourage states and districts to keep involved in the work of church extension. This growth rate was also a cause for celebration during the golden jubilee:

> Even though the major impetus for the 1931 Golden Jubilee celebration came from the Gospel Trumpet Company, all of the other church agencies became involved and contributed toward the accomplishment of the objectives which had been set forth. It must be noted also that not all the special emphasis action was confined to this one year. Many things initiated at that time continued. A look at some sample events and activity during these years will help to round out the picture.
>
> The Board of Church Extension and Home Missions, for instance, contributed greatly to the already noted tremendous thrust in church growth during the Golden Jubilee years, when the movement experienced its highest rate of growth ever. The Board was very active in planting new congregations and strengthening churches in need of assistance. There was also a home missions thrust to reach Native Americans, the Spanish-speaking people of the Southwest, migrant workers, Orientals in the U.S., southern mountain folk, immigrants, and others in need of the gospel in America. . . . In many ways this Board helped to implement a great organized thrust for expansion (Smith 1980, 265-69).

Another event took place in 1931 and 1932 which was to have positive and lasting results for the Board of Church Extension and Home Missions. Through the efforts of Nora Hunter and others, the National Woman's Home and Foreign Missionary Society was organized. Its first objective was "to cooperate intelligently with the Missionary Boards of the Church of God in helping promote missionary work in various fields at home and abroad." This organization, today known as WOMEN OF THE CHURCH OF GOD, has been a loyal and dependable partner with the BCEHM in a wide variety of home missions endeavors. Early in its history the organization began providing annual budget support for home missions projects. Many special ministries among minority groups and in urban settings have been made possible because of the financial and moral support of this creative organization.

Missions in Difficult Times

The records in 1928 reveal that the Associated Budgets total for the year was $275,000. Seven years later, in 1935, that total had shrunk to $150,000—a thirty-seven percent reduction.

Mission and evangelism programs of the BCEHM were made possible by donated dollars. When donated giving was down or ran short in any particular year, this immediately affected the mission outreach program. Borrowed funds were used only for making loans for church facilities, never for program ministries.

As one would expect, the depression greatly reduced the board's receipts of gift income. In 1931 donated income was only ten thousand dollars. This was eight thousand dollars less than had been received in 1930. In the annual reports of the president of the board, printed in the yearbooks for 1931 through 1934, such statements as these give some insight into the harsh realities of that era: "Donated income continues to decline." "No new projects have been undertaken because of the decline of gift income." "This year (1933) the treasurer's report shows a deficit, due to decreased income in donations." "Decreased donations have made further retrenchments than those reported a year ago."

Under such circumstances there was the temptation to

give in to the harsh realities of the times. But the church and its homeland ministries board felt they had a message that could make the difference in the lives of Americans. They also saw and were deeply moved by the vast unmet needs of the unchurched and the minorities of the nation. In spite of the odds, the conviction grew stronger that ways must be found to minister. Before the decade was over, new ways would be found to continue planting new congregations and opening new mission fields, despite the cruel budget realities.

In the 1935 yearbook, reporting for the program year of 1934, Earl Martin wrote in his president's report to the church:

> We are glad to report that some advance has been made in new evangelistic enterprises such as the tent campaign of last year. At least fifteen more tents have been put to work in the field in a way that will mean the building up of new churches. Already several new congregations have been raised up through one summer's campaign and we are arranging now for several tents to be put into use in the South during the winter months, and in the North as soon as the tent season opens up again. . . . We are attempting to place the tents where they will have a State Board to back up the work that is done in any tent campaign and to follow it on to a successful established church. . . . In Home Missionary work there is a particularly fine opportunity for a good work among the Spanish-speaking people of Los Angeles, and of course, the Board is continuing to help M. F. Tafolla in San Antonio. . . . Then, too, an opening has come in Alaska in a wonderful way (YB 1935, 27-28).

Following is a brief synopsis of some of the key events, mission and evangelism ministries, and other assignments carried out by the board in these difficult days.

1930-1935:

W. E. Monk was invited to join the staff on a full time basis as field secretary. His assignment was to assist in getting investments deposited with the board for loans. Getting gift funds for missions and evangelism was also included in his assignment.

A decision was made in 1931 to explore radio broadcasting as a means of evangelism and church development. The next year a pilot radio project was set up. A monthly broadcast was made from Fort Wayne, Indiana over station WOWO. A. F. Gray was the speaker, and an Anderson College quartet helped with the music. The records do not reveal how long this experiment lasted. From that year on, the board's interest in radio as an evangelistic tool continued.

The June 13, 1934, general board minutes record the decision that in spite of the depression, further exploration ought to be done on how the Church of God could get more involved in radio outreach. Several of the board members were from larger cities and had their own radio broadcasts. In this annual meeting, member S. P. Dunn suggested that the board ought to investigate buying a radio station, to be owned and controlled by the church through the BCEHM. Several trips were made to research this idea, but budget shortages dictated other priorities at that time. This interest in radio continued, however, until 1946, when it resulted in the development of a weekly national Church of God radio broadcast, called The Christian Brotherhood Hour.

In 1933 Adcock was asked by the assembly to serve as registrar of the yearbook of the Church of God. He assumed this assignment in addition to his BCEHM responsibilities.

In 1925 J. T. Wilson and others felt there was a need for a Christian college in the southwest. He had been instrumental in the starting of Anderson Bible Training School in

1917. Wilson got the approval of the ministers of Texas, Oklahoma and Louisiana to begin the school. It was named Warner Memorial University and was located in Eastland, Texas. Wilson served as its president. He also continued to serve as a member of the Board of Church Extension and Home Missions.

A down payment was made on sixty acres of land on the edge of Eastland. By 1930 two buildings had been erected on the property. There was great controversy surrounding this project from the beginning. The economic crash in 1929 increased the tensions and, in reality, doomed the project. Wilson was putting heavy pressure on the BCEHM to take over the school and try to salvage the situation. Many long and often heated debates resulted. The board repeatedly refused to take over the school, stating that higher education was not in its charter nor in the assignment given to it by the church. In reality, the board did not have the financial resources to assume the debts at Eastland. The doors of the infant school closed after only three semesters. It was years, however, before a final solution could be worked out regarding the property and the debts which had built up.

The BCEHM was asked by the General Ministerial Assembly's Committee on Pensions to administer the line item of two thousand dollars in Associated Budgets for ministerial pensions in 1933-34 (GB 14 June 1933).

The executive committee of the board approved a plan on October 18, 1934, to raise $100,000 for a permanent revolving loan fund. This was an act of faith because of the depression.

In the summer of 1935, the need for funds to lend and for operations was getting heavier. A letter was sent to several investors asking if they would voluntarily agree to receive less interest on their investments with the board. Several investors, with a total investment of thirty thousand dollars, agreed to do this. This illustrates the sense of partnership and cooperation manifested by individuals who strongly believed in the Church of God and the work of the BCEHM.

By the mid-thirties, the board members began to see some small signs of economic recovery. They asked Elver Adcock to update the church's call to mission in North America. In 1924, Russell Byrum had given the first broad overview of the home mission field in a small book, *America's Millions for Christ*. In 1934 Adcock wrote a 96-page paperback, *Our American Missions*. In the preface he said:

> Home Missions is more than a program; it is a spiritual undertaking. We are facing a new day of opportunity in Home Missions which calls for a thorough understanding of the field and a new sense of obligation in the task of saving America (Adcock 1934, iii).

The book briefly highlighted all major ethnic groups of North America, and the many opportunities awaiting the church's response. It was a brief but comprehensive call to mission.

There was a growing feeling on the part of board staff that it needed to hear from more key leaders of the church. There was also the feeling that as pastors and ministers discussed and learned of the wider needs in home missions and evangelism, they would become more involved. In 1934 the board took action and appointed what it called "state secretaries" to represent the states (YB 1935, 10). Adcock gives this background:

> The board was very serious about keeping close relationships with the church throughout the field. We worked hard at staying close to the church and hearing what pastors and lay leaders were saying and requesting. We did not depend solely on the feedback the Board members gave. In 1934, the Board appointed thirty-five state representatives. We sought leaders . . . usually pastors who were active in cooperative minis-

tries and who could help the Board's program in their state. Also we wanted leaders who could give constructive criticism and ideas back to the Board from their areas (Adcock 1986, 158).

The practice of appointing state secretaries continued until the early 1940s. In December, 1935, a three-day conference was held in Anderson with these representatives as participants. They were invited to share their views and suggest ways of improving the services of the BCEHM. This conference was very positive and productive. The group developed a three-year plan regarding the future of the work and program of the BCEHM. Their goals included these: in church erection, make $250,000 available in new loans; in home missions, start a work in Alaska, put M. F. Tafolla in evangelistic work, and build a building for Hispanic work in Los Angeles; in state evangelism, wherever a state is strong enough for starting a new church, do so in cooperation with the board; in radio, try to work toward having a national radio program; in men's work, set up a men's program as soon as possible; in special projects, respond to Hispanic needs in Los Angeles and help raise fifteen thousand dollars for a new work in Washington, D.C.; in the church service department, prepare bylaws for congregations and state organizations, and publish booklets on finance and church finance (YB 1936, 7-8). Each goal suggested by these state representatives was taken seriously by the board. Most of them were eventually adopted.

This particular conference represented a turning point for the board and its program for the rest of the decade. The focus of concern and activity began to be on new opportunities and possibilities rather than on retrenchment and holding the line as it had been forced to do because of the depression.

In the 1935 annual meeting there was discussion of the input from the board-appointed state secretaries and the value of this kind of process. It appears that there was a first-time corporate awakening to the fact that there were no lay representatives on the BCEHM. The members voted to recommend that lay representatives ought to be on all general church boards (GB 12 June 1935). Considering the fact that all Church of God national organizations were totally clergy dominated, this was a bold action to take.

1936—1940:

For several years, Bess Cupples Wells had been trying to get a Church of God congregation started in Alaska, where she had moved in 1921. In 1934 the board sent Adcock to explore options for missionary work there. The trip convinced him and the board that Alaska was a ripe and ready field. They voted to send a pastor.

In 1935, D. W. and Mae Patterson answered the call and moved to Anchorage. In 1936 the board purchased property, and George and Marie Geiwitz moved there to help. The Pattersons then moved into the Matanuska Valley to start a work in Palmer, where he also started a radio program. The Alaska field continued to open, and congregations were established in Fairbanks, Kodiak, and Juneau. Other early leaders of the Church of God in Alaska included Wendell and Mignonne Byrd, Herman and Mazie Beyer, Lewis (son of Marie and George) and Hazel Geiwitz, and James and Alice Austin.

In Los Angeles in 1936, the board helped erect a mission church where A. T. Maciel served in a Spanish-speaking neighborhood. It was dedicated in 1937. Some of the funds were contributed by the National Woman's Home and Foreign Missionary Society.

There was a heavy flood in Wheeling, West Virginia, in the spring of 1936. A letter from pastor W. O. Boggess came with the sad news, and told of the extreme suffering of members of the congregation who lost everything in the flood. He said he did not see, under the circumstances, how they could make their building loan payments. The board responded by giving the congregation a six-month moratorium on their loan payments, and a donation of the six-months' interest. This act of compassion was well received by the church and by others who heard of it.

A Men's Work Committee made up of board members J. T. Wilson, John H. Kane, and E. F. Adcock was appointed in 1936. They met and discussed the need for a men's organization and suggested how such a group might be organized in the Church of God. The board liked the concept and approved it. However, a national men's organization did not materialize until 1942.

A desire for a new congregation of the Church of God in the nation's capitol was a persistent request from as early as 1933. This request came from pastors of Maryland, Pennsylvania, and New York. They were very insistent, and would not take no for an answer. The board responded, saying it saw the need and that the idea appeared to be a sound one, but with present involvement in other places, could not take on a new project. The minutes show that Otto F. Linn, L. T. Flynt, Walter Ott, and J. S. Reynolds were the four most persistent leaders calling for board action. In 1934 the board agreed to help with the purchase of a lot. Four years later, the lot was determined unsuitable; it was sold and another location was purchased. A primary reason which finally caused the board to become a willing partner in this areawide endeavor was the going of Esther Boyer to pastor a small Church of God group in the city. She was recognized as an able leader, and the congregation had excellent lay leadership.

From 1938 to 1942 the project was promoted and funds from across the church were raised. It was unfortunate that it was often promoted as a project to establish the first congregation of the Church of God in the nation's capitol. In reality, a thriving African-American congregation of the Church of God had been there for years. It was not until many years later that a president of the BCEHM, Marvin Hartman, visited the congregation and offered an official apology for this unfortunate error.

Funds were raised and a fine church building was dedicated on March 22, 1942. Adcock says of the project:

> In the time National Memorial Church was built, it was a sizable achievement. Out of weakness the local group rose up to do great things in a hurry-up campaign, the Church of God folk responded with new generosity. Architect and contractor both gave of their skills and love for the house of God (Adcock 1986, 149).

At the annual board meeting in June, 1936, action was taken to seek official Canadian participation with the BCEHM. It was voted to ask Canada to name a Church Extension Committee of three to work with the BCEHM and to ask Robert Abel to sit as a representative of Canada in its annual meetings.

R. L. Berry met with the board in its annual meeting in Anderson, June 9, 1937. He was a creative person, always thinking of new and better ways for the church to work. He was highly committed to cooperation at the local, state, and national levels. In this meeting he proposed "state evangelism on a cooperative plan." The national board, on invitation, would enter into local or state church extension projects and help with support to make them more effective. No action was taken on the suggestion, but later, in the 1940s, this seed idea became the basis for a new and controversial program. The next year Berry would again meet with and put pressure on the board to seek fifty thousand dollars from the church for special evangelism and church planting projects. A committee of three was appointed to work on these ideas.

From its earliest days, the board had fostered the dream of work among America's first true citizens, the Native Americans. Lack of experience, funds, and leadership delayed the dream until a Sunday in March, 1939, when this vision found concrete expression in two widely separated locations. J. Frank Shaw, pastor at nearby Everett, Washington, met with a small group of local people in the central hall of the Tulalip Indian Reservation in northwestern Washington State. This was the beginning of the national church's work with the mission there.

On that same March Sunday, mission work was launched on the Pine Ridge Reservation at Wounded Knee, South Dakota, in the home of Robert Fast Horse, when a group of students from Gordon Bible School led a prayer service. They were invited to return. The next year, Herbert Petersen became the first pastor. This Church of God start among native Americans came during the last year of the decade of depression. Over the next forty years, Church of God work among native Americans spread to Toppenish, Washington; Lapwai, Idaho; Crow Agency, Montana; Alliance and Scottsbluff, Nebraska; Park Hill, Oklahoma; and Klagetoh, Arizona.

The Decade's Impact on the Board

Difficult situations can make or break an individual. They can have the same effect on institutions. With only eight years of experience as an institution, and with a new executive leader of only two years, the board was forced by the Great Depression to mature very quickly.

The early policies that were established relative to its lending and cash reserve position proved to be very sound, and helped hold the small ship steady during the economic tidal wave.

The decade helped to require of the board a wide range of flexibility in lending, evangelism, and missions work. It had to learn the importance and creative use of volunteers faster than it probably would have otherwise.

An overall lesson well learned was the great importance of teamship and partnership with the church, other national agencies, state organizations, and the host of individuals who held steady in the crisis and remained staunch supporters in the darkest days.

The board began the decade with a young two-member staff, with little experience or knowledge of the vastness of its assignment. The end of the decade found a much more seasoned board and staff who had learned well from a crash course in life at the raw edges.

Chapter 4

Broadening Ministries

(1940–1949)

Just as it was certain that the world was recovering from the Great Depression, it found itself in the second world war. The political world map for the next forty-five years was drawn by the events of the decade of the 1940s. From the war there emerged two world superpowers—the United States and the Soviet Union. Both held themselves and the rest of the world deadlocked in a cold war for more than four decades.

World War I produced the League of Nations, and World War II provided the setting for the United Nations, but perhaps the most far-reaching change of this decade was ushered in when the United States dropped the first atomic bomb in human history over Hiroshima, Japan, on August 6, 1945. The second atomic bomb was dropped on Nagasaki three days later. From that time forward, international politics would be conducted under the cloud of the bomb. The nuclear age was born. The United States moved from its position of isolationism to a foreign policy based on fear of Soviet expansion.

Also in this decade, Mao Tse-tung emerged victorious in the long civil war in China; Nationalist China retreated to Taiwan; India and Pakistan gained independence from Britain; the nation of Israel was formed by taking over

Palestine; Korean independence was recognized by the United Nations, and South Korea became a republic.

The still new medium of television was fast becoming a presence in the homes of America, bringing information and entertainment, and changing the leisure-time habits of Americans. It would be some years before TV was widely used by the churches.

At Home During the War

During the years when the United States was at war, the federal government set up several restrictive actions for its citizens at home. These included a price law freezing wages, rents, and farm prices. There was rationing of gasoline, oil, meats, fats, cheese, and other food items. All building materials were also frozen and restricted for military use only.

Building up a war machine for four or more years of combat requires a national commitment on the part of government and those governed. In order to build stockpiles of supplies needed for the war effort, defense areas were located across the nation at strategic places—near the sources of raw materials, near existing manufacturing or industrial areas, or near labor sources. There was a massive movement of the population from one part of the nation to another to work in defense plants. People were drawn across state lines and from one coast to the other. This often split families. Often housing was not adequate. Temporary housing facilities, usually of very poor construction, were quickly built. These events and conditions eventually resulted in the demoralization of the religious, social and educational life of many individuals, families and communities.

Internal Church Strife

Any war, in any nation, at any time, is disruptive to the lives of its citizens. World War II, because of its length and the massive destruction it caused, was no exception.

In addition to the usual tensions caused by war, the Church of God was having some internal personal and institutional tensions of her own at this point in her development. The recorded minutes of the General Ministerial Assembly, as well as the minutes of the various national agencies, give insights into this troublesome and disruptive time.

There was a growing feeling of discontent across the church. This discontent, particularly among a group of ministers, expressed itself in a variety of ways. There was some decrease in general giving to the overall causes of the church. Letters of criticism were being received by various national agencies from pastors, raising questions which generally pointed to an erosion of trust and confidence in the agencies and their leadership. Some pastors and other leaders felt left out of the decision-making process of the church.

Feelings were developing that those in church positions in Anderson had more power than was necessary to do their work. It seemed to some that those serving on national boards and agencies represented a power bloc, and many felt they had no say in the programs of the church. One common practice at that time helped feed this feeling. From the establishment of the national agencies—1909 through 1923 and into the 1940s—many persons served on more than one board at the same time. It was not uncommon for a head of an agency also to serve on the executive committee of one or two other agencies. This was often done in an effort to save traveling costs. However, in the 1940s this was beginning to give the appearance of a closed system at the national level.

In 1944, at the annual Indiana State Ministers' Assembly, a sermon was preached entitled "Watchman on the Walls." Earl Slacum, a pastor from Muncie, Indiana, was the speaker. His charges were that there had been a departure from the faith and a concentration of power in the national agencies. This was the beginning of a seven-year period of extreme agitation in the Church of God. (For details of this specific period, see Smith 1980, 326-335.)

The Board of Church Extension and Home Missions found itself singled out in the charges. That very year I. K. Dawson had joined the staff as secretary of Evangelism. He had just written a booklet entitled *Working Together in an Enlarged Program of State Evangelism*. This booklet was cited by those dissenting as a prime example of agency power and apostasy. Slacum attacked this approach to church extension as the plan of a "man-made organization in Anderson." He later began publishing a paper, *The Watchman on the Walls*.

The seeds of discord and unrest were sown for two years before the General Ministerial Assembly, in 1946, appointed a special committee to check into the allegations. It was the Committee on Research and Improvement, made up of seven members. After a year of investigation, the committee reported to the assembly that most of the personal charges had no basis in fact. They found no one in the national agencies living out of harmony with the movement, and no out-of-line teaching in the agencies or the college. However, the committee did ask that the assembly reappoint and enlarge the committee to conduct a study of the national structure and organization of the church and its agencies. This was done, and the new group was called the Committee on Revision and Planning.

Getting Adequate Church Buildings

A new decade was beginning. There were signs that recovery from the depression was well under way. In the church building ministry, it was noticed that more and more congregations were ahead of schedule with their loan payments. The payoff of most church mortgages was ahead of schedule. This was a sure sign that more members of the congregations were employed and family income was coming up: a welcomed trend!

As family incomes increased and as congregations faced up to their mission and ministry, the need to either enlarge or replace church building facilities became increasingly more apparent. Requests for church building loans began to arrive at the board faster than invested funds were available. These requests came from urban as well as rural congregations—from African-American as well as Anglo congregations. A new churchwide appeal for loan funds was made. It was successful in increasing the board's lending funds.

Six of the loans made in 1941 were to African-American congregations in the cities. This was a sign of growth of Church of God urban African-American congregations. This trend increased in the years ahead. The financial records reveal also that the board made several loans to the National Association of the Church of God at West Middlesex, Pennsylvania, for campground expansion.

Because of local and national discrimination, income of African-Americans was only about half that of Anglos in the 1940s. For this reason, and because of institutional racism, most financial institutions were very reluctant to make loans to congregations made up primarily of African-Americans. Under such circumstances, the BCEHM proved to be a real ally. Adcock shares the following insights:

> A fair percentage of the early loans of the Board were made to black congregations. . . . They had great faith, great eagerness and a willingness to go all out in their effort to get the building they needed. No one in the Board's loan experience had better credit than our black churches did. . . . The first loan of more than $25,000 to one congregation was made to the Detroit congregation where Raymond Jackson was pastor. . . . Many of these early loans were paid off in less than their allotted time (Adcock 1986, 51).

After the nation entered World War II, the government's War Production Board stopped or greatly delayed all building projects. All building materials were declared off limits for civilian use. For the first time in its life, the board found itself with adequate loan funds, but no market because of this government freeze. It was paying the investors interest on their investments, but no church loans were possible.

Hundreds of Church of God congregations at that time did not have parsonages for their pastors. In this decade there was a growing awareness by congregations that they should provide such housing. Although the war was on, there were houses already built and for sale in many communities which could be purchased for parsonages. Announcements were sent out that the BCEHM had funds available for that purpose. Soon congregations began to apply for board loans for parsonages. In 1943 alone, the board assisted fifty-eight congregations to purchase parsonages—with a total of $127,350 loaned. In the remaining years of the war, such loans continued to be made.

By 1944, as an increasing number of congregations were outgrowing their facilities, the board worked with them in purchasing adequate acreage for building sites. Also, the board encouraged congregations to build up their reserve funds so that, when the war was over, they would have the funds for building. In addition it approved a general plan to encourage congregations to get an experienced architect to help with their building plans. To encourage this action, it was voted to make "conservative loans to help pay for architects' fees, if needed (GB June 1942)."

After the war, church building did boom. According to the Church of God yearbook, the value of local church property increased from $7,050,000 in 1944 to $43,476,530 in 1954.

Evangelism through Cooperative Church Extension

Evangelism was seen as a key emphasis for this decade.

The board's approach to evangelism had consistently been by way of new church development—the starting and developing of new congregations. With a little more than fifteen years' experience in church extension, new insights had been gained. The church was developing at the state and district levels. It was becoming more difficult for a national agency to start and support local projects across the nation. The board did not have adequate staff for the growing needs in church extension. Of the first six or eight new church projects the board had started, most had difficulty in reaching a self-sufficient status. It was thought that part of the problem might be a lack of local or district support and encouragement. Several of these new congregations were seen as national projects, not local ones.

Back in 1937, R. L. Berry had appeared before the board and promoted the idea of national and state teamship in church extension. This idea had been discussed and experimented with in limited ways. The war years had delayed the process some, but in 1944 the decision was made to form a Department of Evangelism. I. K. Dawson accepted the invitation to serve as the secretary of this new department. The objective was to focus on a more cooperative process across the church for evangelism and starting new churches.

The Church of God congregations in each state were encouraged to form a state evangelism board. Shortly after joining the staff, Dawson wrote a booklet which briefly outlined the plan and its purpose—*Working Together in an Enlarged Program of State Evangelism*. The state and the national board would work together in this exciting field of church extension evangelism. As an example of how it might work, the booklet suggested that the state employ an evangelist who would be the state staff person to help start, develop, and encourage new congregations. The national agency's role was to cooperate by offering seasoned counsel and budget assistance.

At first, the plan met with above average favor in most

states. There were the usual questions and uncertainty that are often raised about any new idea or plan of action. Unfortunately, the plan was introduced in the year of the Slacum controversy. For the next two or three years the board had to spend considerable time correcting misconceptions and answering to direct charges made against the plan. It became dubbed the "Dawson Plan" and, unfortunately, there were personal attacks on the man, rather than on the plan.

But the board stood firm. It realized that the concept was one whose time had come. There was growing support for cooperative evangelism. The board sent special mailings to the pastors and ministers trying to keep the discussion on the intent and purpose of the plan. All legitimate criticism was handled with respect and thoroughness. The General Ministerial Assembly's Committee on Research and Improvement investigated and reported that it found no theological or doctrinal problems with the cooperative evangelism proposal.

On June 8, 1948, a group of twenty-two representatives from state evangelism boards met with the BCEHM in its annual meeting. A full day was given to the consideration of the concept of cooperative evangelism and the new Department of Evangelism. The discussion was open and unhurried. Time was spent on the primary objectives—namely, the need to establish strong self-supporting congregations and how best to go about this task. Throughout the discussion, the state leaders were reminded that the issue was the evangelistic mission of the Church of God, not just of the board. The meeting resulted in the development of a list of eight guidelines regarding state and national cooperative work in evangelism (GB June 1948, C).

The twenty-two leaders expressed their appreciation for the constructive meeting. They felt that this approach would result in getting more new congregations started. This positive reaction helped convince the board that cooperative evangelism was the approach for the future.

The cooperative sponsorship of evangelism projects began to increase toward the end of the decade. This new approach was used wisely in 1946-1949 along with the traditional methods of evangelism. The board, working with state and local congregations, sponsored Edgar and Inez Busch as they went to ten new congregations to hold revivals and conduct training conferences. This experiment achieved good results locally, and helped illustrate how the method could be adapted to all situations.

In 1949 eighty state leaders met in Anderson for a three-day institute on evangelism. The agenda included working on the role of the state and the role of the national in Extension Evangelism. How to avoid overlap and how to help both groups get closer together in their planning were the key topics of discussion.

The basic concepts hammered out during this decade became the basis for the board's church extension program for the years ahead. Dawson resigned in 1948 to accept a pastorate in Everett, Washington, but not until he had seen the basic acceptance of the cooperative method of starting and developing Church of God congregations.

Radio Evangelism

Scattered throughout the board minutes from the late 1920s until the decade of the forties are references to the importance of radio as an approach to evangelism. In 1934 the board experimented briefly with a monthly radio broadcast; there was discussion of the purchase of a radio station. A radio committee, made up of members of the board, met annually throughout the thirties to explore the role of radio and evangelism. It was not until the 1940s, however, that a viable plan was worked out to launch the Church of God into national radio broadcasting.

Since joining the staff, I. K. Dawson had taken a keen interest in a national radio program. He explored various options. In the July 11, 1946, board of directors meeting

Dawson explained the approach that was being considered. It would be a weekly, thirty-minute transcribed program, sent to local stations. Richard Meischke, a student at Anderson College with a job at a local radio station, was interested in being the director. Dale Oldham, pastor of Park Place Church of God in Anderson, was being considered as the preacher. Music would be provided by Anderson College. Estimated cost was ten thousand dollars for the first year.

On July 25, 1946, the directors voted unanimously in favor of the plan as submitted. It was to be administered through the Department of Evangelism of the BCEHM (DIR 11, 25 July 1946). The program was launched on January 5, 1947, as *The Christian Brotherhood Hour of the Church of God*. In his first written report to the board in 1947, Richard Meischke, director of CBH, wrote the following:

> At the regular radio conference during Camp Meeting in 1946, it was decided unanimously by those present that something concrete should be done relevant to a national radio program of the Church of God. This matter was discussed with the Board of Church Extension and Home Missions which decided to begin a program of this type as soon as possible. Having been asked to accept the duties of managing director, I began my work under the Department of Evangelism August 1, 1946.
>
> The program was scheduled to begin on the air the Sunday of January 5, 1947. By this time enthusiastic response was already coming from ministers, laymen, and from radio executives who appreciated the idea of having a national program which could be broadcast over any local station. From nineteen stations which carried the program the first week, the Radio Log lengthened to fifty stations within a few weeks time (GB 11 June 1947, F).

The program met with wide success, but problems of financial deficits were chronic. After the first month of broadcasting, at the February 2, 1947, meeting of the directors, the radio committee reported, "We are trying to raise $5,000 to continue the broadcast until June over forty-three stations."

Changes had to be made regarding production and distribution, but on the whole, these were handled without any program interruption. A later report noted:

> Even now the Christian Brotherhood Hour is little more than two years old. The phenomenal expansion of this phase of our work testifies to the great vision of our people, who see in radio the marvelous medium through which we may meet and accept the challenge of the Great Commission (YB 1949, 12).

In spite of the success of the CBH program, there were some unrelenting personal disagreements between the radio staff and the board's executive. These differences had to do with office procedures and management. According to the board of directors minutes of December 18, 1951, these personal differences reached a crisis. At the close of the meeting, the radio staff appeared and presented this written statement:

> As of today the Christian Brotherhood Hour is a separate and distinct organization independent of other Boards and taking its stand before the General Assembly of the Church of God. . . . Furthermore, the name of the organization shall be known as Christian Brotherhood Hour, Inc. (DIR 18 December 1951).

Later that same night the office radio files were secretly removed from the BCEHM building.

This presented the board with its first serious internal problem and was the primary agenda item in directors' minutes over the next six months. The board's position seemed to be open to some structural change to accommodate the radio program. However, the method used by the radio staff was the point of greatest concern and disagreement from the board's perspective.

In the June, 1952, General Ministerial Assembly meeting a plan was accepted authorizing the creation of a temporary commission to sponsor radio work. By June, 1954, the Commission of Radio and Television was authorized as a permanent structure of the church (GMA June 1954).

Men's Brotherhood

To organize some type of national men's organization was on the board's agenda for several years. It appointed three of its members to see what could be done. There had been various attempts in the 1930s at getting groups of men together for a meal and some discussion of their interests and needs. Finally, in 1943, several lay leaders had a meeting under the board's sponsorship and elected officers. A national convention during the Anderson camp meeting was planned, but did not materialize because the meeting was canceled due to the war.

The May 23, 1944, directors' minutes record that an announcement was made asking all board members to be present at a dinner to be held in June for the purpose of organizing a men's group, to be called *The Men's Brotherhood*. The next month, the general board agreed that funds should be budgeted (amount not specified) to help launch the program of men's work. "This would be considered a loan to the brotherhood to be paid back as definite projects are launched (GB 13 June 1944)."

A. P. Gregory was selected by the brotherhood leaders to serve as their executive secretary, subject to the board's ratification. On July 13, 1944, the board ratified Gregory. By December, 1945, he reported fifty-two active groups of *The Men's Brotherhood* and fifty more congregations interested in organizing a local group as soon as a staff visit could be arranged.

On the second anniversary of the brotherhood, there were seventy-nine active groups in twenty-five states with 1,550 members. Later that year, Gregory resigned due to ill health. The staff responsibility was assigned to I. K. Dawson, who was busily involved in getting the radio program under way. An attempt was made to strengthen the brotherhood's identity and organization by having it unite around the radio program as its major project. This did not work because of the lack of a feeling of ownership in the project and insufficient budget.

After Dawson's departure from the staff in 1948, his position was not filled for two years because of a lack of funding. The brotherhood's primary activity for several years was an annual men's dinner at the Anderson camp meeting. Hopes for reviving and putting new purpose into a men's group did not surface again until 1958.

An Expanding Home Missions Outreach

By the late 1930s, there was an increase in the church's concern for those who were bypassed by the mainstream of society. This mission-at-home interest gained greater momentum in the war years. The church was beginning to respond more generously with financial gifts for home missions work. With this increase in interest, and with more opportunities for home missions ministries, in 1943 the board added a staff person to head up this department. T. Franklin Miller, pastor of the Boston, Massachusetts congregation, was invited to join the staff as secretary of Home Missions. "Voted, to employ T. F. Miller full time with the office as soon as a successor can be found for him in the New England work (DIR 4 January 1943)."

When Miller arrived in Anderson, his home missions task included making an appraisal of what was already in operation and which current opportunities to address first. He brought to the task an educational approach. The church needed to be made aware of the many home missions opportunities. From 1944 a steady flow of study materials, filmstrips and slides told of the work the church was doing and gave information on new openings for missions work.

Mission In Defense Communities

Because of the mass movement of people during the war to defense areas of the nation, there was a great need for weekday church school in these places. Mae McAlpine was sent by the board to assume a full-time position in the Dayton, Ohio, defense area. She worked with the local church council in weekday religious education until 1948. Her salary was largely underwritten by the National Woman's Missionary Society. Eloise Butler served for two years in a similar program near Denver, Colorado. Both of these ladies were highly praised for their creative and effective ministries. Letters of appreciation were received by the BCEHM from local churches of the area expressing thanks for this ministry. Arthur Eikamp served for one year in a defense community area in the East while attending Yale Divinity School.

Agricultural Migrant Ministry

Agricultural migrants tour the nation each year, cultivating and gathering the crops—tomatoes, berries, and other vegetables and fruits—for America's tables. It came to the board's attention in the late 1930s and early 1940s that there was an urgent need for church workers to be assigned to migrant farm worker camps. The volunteers had a wide variety of tasks including vacation Bible school, special religious classes, and youth and family activities. In 1942 the BCEHM, working with the Home Missions Council of North America, helped sponsor Arthur Eikamp as the first Church of God person in a migrant ministry. He spent part time and often full time for the next five years working in the migrant stream from Arkansas, to Ohio, Indiana, Michigan, and the New England area.

The board's migrant ministry was made possible each summer from 1943 through 1947 because of student volunteers. Persons giving their summers to this mission work in Indiana, Ohio, Arkansas, and Michigan included Wilma Reeder, Ronald Joiner, Fern Brunner, Phyllis Matzigkeit, Janice Bradley, and others. Nora Angus was on the staff of the board at this time, and she served on the Indiana Migrant Workers' Council and kept the staff and board informed of this vital need.

Ministry In Japanese-American Internment Camps

At the outbreak of World War II, there were approximately 125,000 first generation Japanese-Americans and their children in the United States. They were successful in business and various professions; some had served in the U.S. military, but the day after the bombing of Pearl Harbor, harsh action was taken against them. The following is Adcock's account of this shameful action by our nation:

> The Governor and Attorney General of California, working through sheriffs and district attorneys, took drastic action against these Japanese-Americans. Without incidents of misbehavior on their part, these people were dismissed from their civil service jobs. Doctors and lawyers had their licenses revoked. Commercial fishermen were refused access to their boats, and some were not permitted to do business in any form.
>
> This was unfair and disgraceful treatment of a segment of American citizens. The national policy which was quickly pressed into action was an affront to local American citizens and a violation of the very principles we declared to be fighting for.
>
> The national government reacted quickly and intern-

> ment camps were set up. The peaceful migration of Japanese-Americans was carried out. They were given forty-eight hours to respond to government orders. They must dispose of their homes, furniture, and businesses. They were permitted to take with them only what they could carry in their hand luggage. Investments and bank accounts were forfeited. There could be no protest or even an appeal.
>
> Copies of the "Civilian Exclusion Order" affecting persons of Japanese ancestry were tacked to doors like quarantine notices. Very small children were tagged, crowded into army trucks and jeered by army and civilians who were watching. They were housed temporarily at a race track like Santa Anita, a brewery in Washington state, and in horse stalls or other quick temporary quarters.
>
> As soon as resettlement centers could be built, these prisoners of war in their own country were moved into them. The camps were on federal land in very remote and often inhospitable places. . . . Each camp was surrounded with powerful search lights.
>
> For three years these internees lived peaceably and tried to keep up life as best they could under such strained and ugly circumstances (Adcock 1986, 117-18).

The board discussed what its responsibility was regarding this most difficult situation. Funds were very limited, the cause was very unpopular and emotionally charged, but it was felt this was part of the board's mission field. There was some investigation as to the needs of the people and what the federal government would permit. Under the board's sponsorship, workers were sent to these centers from 1944 to 1947 to offer various community activities including recreation, family activities, and vacation Bible schools. Some of the workers involved in this ministry were Mae Johnson, Eva Joy Smith, Mrs. S. J. Lane, and Dorothy Harriman.

Missions In Appalachia

Mentioned in the charter of the board is the responsibility for "mountaineers." A variety of approaches was used to discover needs of the region and how to respond. Several ministers in the southeast asked for and got the backing of the BCEHM for special evangelistic outreach in Tennessee, Kentucky, and North Carolina. Boyd Conner spent several years in the 1940s working in Appalachia. With the board's help, he started a small church in Spill Corn, North Carolina.

In the first three months that T. Franklin Miller was secretary of the Home Missions Department, he contacted Naomi Randall to become acquainted with her teaching and evangelistic work in the mountains of Kentucky. A school teacher with a master's degree, she had taught in small mountain communities of Tennessee and Kentucky. On November 2, 1943, Miller reported to the directors on his Kentucky trip. It was a very favorable report, with the suggestion that the board find some way to help in this new field of labor. It was voted to commit $250, to match $250 from the National Woman's Missionary Society. The board also agreed to a plan of having Randall give a year's time to this work and to promote it at camp meetings and conventions.

Naomi Randall had dedicated her life to the economic, social, and spiritual improvement of the lives of the people of Appalachia. While teaching in a one-room school, she met Mr. and Mrs. Lee Francis, who had started a congregation at Yellow Rock, Kentucky. They teamed up and were the key motivators for the spread of the gospel in that mountain region.

In 1944 Randall agreed to devote part of her time to the BCEHM Department of Home Missions. She became a full-time staff member in 1945. In the 1940s, mountain congregations were started in Kentucky near Beattyville, at Blaines Branch, Miller's Creek, Pine Crest (formerly Yellow Rock),

Morris Creek, and Athol.

The youth of the Church of God of Kansas heard of the home mission possibilities in Kentucky and of Naomi Randall's dream of a youth center in that area. In 1945, they gave the one thousand dollars needed to purchase twenty acres of land. This is the site known today as Pine Crest. Here the board, under Randall's leadership, set up a center for children, youth, and families. It also was to serve as a prayer retreat center.

This mission station has had a powerful and positive witness for Christ for more than forty-five years. Literally dozens of leaders—pastors, educators, and lay volunteers have served in a wide variety of ways to make the gospel real in this mountain region. Among the key leaders who worked with Randall and BCEHM in developing this effective ministry were Robert and Alma Sperow, Willard and Glenna Armey, Simon and Mae Robinson, and Gene and Ruth Morton (For more details, see Vickie Rice, ed., 1988 *The Pine Crest Story*. Anderson, Indiana: BCEHM).

An Expanding Ministry to Native Americans

Church of God work among native Americans began to expand in the 1940s. Much of the mission work was first sparked by burdened individuals—persons like J. Frank Shaw, who felt led of God to try to make a difference in the lives of native Americans in Tulalip and Toppenish, Washington. Other initiators of native mission work in this decade included: James and Grace Kole, at Lapwai, Idaho, among the Nez Perce; Wiley and LaVaughn Hall with Vern Pickard, at Park Hill, Oklahoma, among the Cherokee; Harold and Laurena Wright, inspired by A. J. Stuart, at Crow Agency, Montana; Mr. and Mrs. Herbert Peterson among the Oglala Sioux at Wounded Knee, Nebraska; and Adam and Marjory Williams, at Tulalip. Adam was the first native worker in the Church of God. His mother was a Nanaimo and his father was a Swinomish. All of these pioneers served with meager financial help. The board gave what support it could, but it was years before more adequate support could be provided.

Outreach in Mexico

Board support of Hispanic work in this decade was limited primarily to the patriarch of Church of God Spanish leaders, M. F. Tafolla, in San Antonio and Somerset, Texas, and to A. T. and Ruby Dee Maciel at the Belvedere Church in Los Angeles, California. Mrs. Maciel was an orphan. This experience gave her a burden to help children. They set up a Hispanic children's home, El Hogar Feliz, with the board's assistance, in 1942. Virginia Stage served as a helper in this home from 1943 to 1945.

A. E. Velez, from northern Mexico, visited California and became acquainted with the Church of God. He returned to Mexico to preach in several villages. By the end of 1947, fifteen groups were meeting in private homes; none had church facilities. The BCEHM sent D. W. Patterson, A. T. Maciel, and Ellsworth Palmer in 1948 to survey the field of Mexico and to help develop plans for mission work there. Within the next two years, small congregations were established at San Antonio de las Alazanas, Jame, and Derramadero. The board provided funds to help them secure modest buildings.

Home Missions Expansion

Home missions expansion in Alaska for the 1940s was centered primarily in Anchorage. Under the pioneer leaders, D. W. and Mae Patterson, a special program was developed for United States servicemen. It focused on ministering to their loneliness and homesickness. The Pattersons were succeeded by James and Alice Austin in 1947. The Austins gave creative leadership to the state for ten years. Other leaders arriving in the 1940s included Herman and Mazie Beyer at Juneau, and John and Blanche Marshall at Kodiak.

An opportunity came for some special evangelism work among African-Americans. The board negotiated to secure the services of Hattie Downer for ten weeks of youth evangelism work in South Carolina in the summer of 1947. This was the beginning of a long relationship with Hattie Downer and the board in home missions work. Emery Williams served with the board in evangelistic work among African-Americans and in interracial settings in the 1940s and 1950s.

Broadening Board Membership—Women and Canada

The issue of board membership and representation was discussed again in 1945. There came a realization that no women were serving on the board. Minutes of the general board meeting, held on December 12, 1945, read:

> It was the opinion of the Board that as soon as a vacancy on the Board appears, two women should be nominated so as to elect one of them as a representative on the Board, and that it should be the policy to have one or more women representatives from that time on.

The next vacancy occurred in 1947, and Naomi Randall was elected.

The BCEHM had been trying to devise a better working relationship with Canada. Early in the decade, word from western Canada came, asking that a minister from their region be elected to membership on the BCEHM. Plans to accomplish this were made. In 1949, H. C. Heffren, from Alberta, Canada, was elected as the first Canadian representative.

Other Items in Brief

Nora Hunter and Laymen Loan Funds. At the beginning of this decade, an effort was made to raise some special gift funds for a revolving loan fund in home missions work. On the occasion of the seventieth birthday of Nora Hunter, founder of the Woman's Missionary Society, the board made an appeal to the church to give in her honor to establish the Nora Hunter Fund. The sum of seven thousand dollars was received in 1944. A year later, laymen of the Church of God made a gift of ten thousand dollars to help establish a Laymen Loan Fund. Eventually these two funds with a total of over twenty thousand dollars were combined into one permanent loan fund. It is used for low-interest loans to home missionaries to purchase automobiles and major appliances.

New Office Building. From its beginning, the board had occupied office space in the Gospel Trumpet Company building. In the 1940s things were getting crowded and space was at a premium. A. T. Rowe, general manager of the Gospel Trumpet Company, kept urging the board to find other quarters. In 1946 and 1947, with the help of O. E. Howard, a builder, and others, the board built a two-story brick veneer office building on the campground. This was its office home for about eighteen years.

Interchurch Cooperation. In the first year of this decade the board became a member of the Home Missions Council of North America. This relationship allowed the board to be effective in agricultural migrant work, ministry to defense areas, and in the Japanese relocation centers. In addition, two staff persons were named to attend the *Federal Council of Churches* meetings as observers, and to serve as members on its Committee on Evangelism. The board also became a member of the *International Bureau of Architecture*. This organization offered valuable service to the staff, who were inexperienced in church architectural affairs. It was instrumental in motivating the board to gear up for a major thrust in church architecture in the 1950s.

Internal Affairs

T. Franklin Miller resigned his position with the board to join the staff of the national Board of Christian Education in July, 1945. He did continue to assist, however, with some promotional work in home missions for the remainder of the year.

Earl Martin asked not to be renominated as the president of the board in 1947. He had served in that position for twenty years. The board elected W. H. Hunt as president that June. By the fall, because of the need for additional staff help, Hunt was asked to serve full time, which he did until 1956.

J. C. Thompson, a pastor in Michigan, was invited to join the staff in February, 1949, to replace W. E. Monk, who was in poor health. Thompson was to serve as field secretary in the area of annuity planning and wills.

Irwin Scheller came as the board's bookkeeper in 1949, and that same year W. E. Reed was elected to membership on the executive committee. The board instructed the staff to devote more time and study to how best to assist rural and small town congregations.

Summary of Decade.

This decade saw the board being forced by events, massive needs, and overwhelming opportunities, to broaden the scope and performance of home missions work. These opportunities, particularly in home missions and evangelism, called for more staff. The board decided that they needed staff members who could specialize in areas of work, rather than generalists relating to all the areas of work.

Work across denominational lines had been a pattern of the BCEHM from the beginning, but the 1940s gave staff and board members ample opportunity to be participants in this broader national arena of church life and work. These relationships were very beneficial to the board and the church. Much was learned as well as contributed in this interchurch work.

Tensions and controversy consumed a lot of time and energy, but the debates over the radio sponsorship issue and the cooperative evangelism methodology brought keen insights, deepened commitment and resolve. The cooperative evangelism concepts and methodology hammered out in this decade became the cornerstone of the board's primary church extension ministry.

The decade also saw the broadening of the board's program geographically. Canadian representation on the general board helped position it for direct feedback regarding the needs in that great nation. Also, the decade saw the beginning of the board's ministry in Mexico.

This was a decade filled with variety and promise, as well as occasions of fulfillment in the life of the church and the Board of Church Extension and Home Missions.

Chapter 5

Restructuring for Ministry and Mission

(1950-1959)

World War II had been over only five years, but peace seemed to elude the world. This decade saw war between North and South Korea with United States involvement, the French war in Vietnam, conflict in the Suez Canal, and the Hungarian uprising. The United States made and tested the first hydrogen bomb and the Soviet Union developed its own nuclear capability. In Africa there was deep unrest as independence movements began to challenge the assumptions of colonial rule.

Here at home the civil rights movement began to be a force. Demands for racial integration grew louder in the South. The Supreme Court outlawed racial discrimination in the public schools of America in 1954. In September, 1957, a federal court order decreed that nine African-American students should be admitted to previously segregated Central High School in Little Rock, Arkansas. Governor Orville Faubus called the state National Guard to bar the students from entering. President Eisenhower sent in one thousand army paratroopers, and the students were allowed to enter.

Senator Joseph McCarthy went on a crusade, which soon turned into a witch hunt, against persons from all walks of life in this country whom he suspected were communists or communist sympathizers. He was censured by his fellow senators in December of 1954. Before the end of the decade, Joseph Stalin died and was succeeded by Nikita Khrushchev; dictator Batista was driven from power in Cuba by Fidel Castro. In Britain, Winston Churchill resigned as prime minister and was succeeded by Anthony Eden.

Microbiologist Jonas Salk introduced the first successful poliomyelitis vaccine in 1953. Alaska became the forty-ninth state on July 6, 1958, and Hawaii became the fiftieth state on March 19, 1959.

Mid-Century—Time to Refocus

The decade of the forties had many issues, in addition to the war, to divert the attention of the Church of God. The internal charges that had been made against the agencies of Anderson, along with other events, put the church in a defensive mode. Many felt that the church was facing new frontiers and needed to look at its organization and also to focus on a new vision and sense of mission.

In 1949, forty Church of God leaders from local, state, and national levels met for a few days to discuss the key opportunities and needs of the church at this moment in history. They concluded that the coming decade of the fifties, the mid-century mark, would be an appropriate time to rally the church to refocus on its central mission. It was decided that the key areas of special need and concern for the church were missions, evangelism, stewardship, education, spiritual life, and doctrinal understanding. These basic ideas were presented to a group of one hundred leaders in the June, 1949, Anderson camp meeting. A third meeting of about fifty persons was held to further refine the proposals. By year's end, a five-year program had been planned which would include all national agencies, state organizations, and local congregations in a concentrated effort to help the entire church gain momentum in its mission and ministry for the coming new half-century (Smith 1980, 343). The major theme was *Go, Make Disciples*. The effort was called the Mid-Century Evangelistic Advance and was to cover the years from 1950 through 1955.

There was a specific emphasis for each of the five years: achieving deeper levels of religious living; releasing the potential power of the local church; evangelizing the larger community; evangelizing the world community; and strengthening the Christian fellowship. Many booklets and materials were written. Pastors were recruited from districts across the states and provinces to train leaders and to promote the program.

The Church of God yearbooks for 1950 and 1955 give some indication that the massive effort had an impact across the church. There were an estimated 96,749 persons in 1,932 congregations in 1950. The 1955 totals reveal 121,655 persons in 2,141 congregations.

Another event of a similar nature took place at the same time. It was the Mid-Century Building Campaign. This effort was carried out by men of the church. Everett Hartung, an outstanding layman residing in Anderson, was the key leader in this endeavor. Lester Crose, a staff member of the Missionary Board assigned to this project, recalls:

> The goal was to raise two million dollars, primarily for special capital fund needs demonstrated by the Missionary Board of the Church of God, the Board of Church Extension and Home Missions, Anderson College, Pacific Bible College (now Warner Pacific College), and the international campgrounds in Anderson. There were included some non-capital fund needs for the Board of Christian Education and the Board of Pensions. Men of the Movement rallied around the slogan, "We Build for the New Age." . . . Enthusiasm ran high. Never before in the history of the Reformation Movement had such a sum of money been raised. What the women of the church had done during the

Great Depression its men were now doing to help the movement with capital funds at this important time when the Church of God was beginning to regain its momentum following World War II. . . . Over five hundred thousand dollars was ultimately made available for overseas missions (Crose 1981, 100-101).

Driving Forces for Organizational Change

The Board of Church Extension and Home Missions was heavily involved in the planning and carrying out of the Mid-Century Evangelistic Advance. Much staff time and energy was devoted to this churchwide effort. But 1947 to 1953 was a troublesome time for the board. A build-up of expectations, misunderstandings, frustrations and poor communications resulted in a number of events and incidents.

The early charges of the Slacum agitation against the national agencies, though proven false, left some scars. The *Christian Brotherhood Hour* administrative sponsorship issue was a thorny one. During the struggle to resolve this, some of the charges made were very personal. Though a General Ministerial Assembly appointed committee found no substance to these personal charges leveled against the board's chief executive, the process of investigation raised doubts in the minds of some, and left painful memories for board members and staff.

There was the widespread feeling across the church at this time that some structural and organizational changes needed to be explored in the way the church and the agencies did their work. This was a primary force in bringing about some agency changes—broader representation, limited terms of board membership, and limited individual membership to one agency at a time. A Commission on Revision and Planning was set up to focus on just what organizational changes might be needed and how to go about effecting these changes.

Board of Church Extension and Home Missions minutes reveal that in 1947-48 some members of the board had engaged in serious discussion on whether some other forms of organization might serve the needs of the church better. Questions were raised as to whether the causes of home missions and evangelism would be enhanced if separated from church finance. This was debated, and the consensus was that it would weaken both home missions and evangelism, as well as church finance, to separate them. The matter was dropped.

The issue of separating home missions from the board was again raised by the Commission on Revision and Planning. The proposal was that there be a "consolidation of both Home and Foreign Missionary work, under the administration of one board," but no specific plan was included in the proposal. This was thoroughly discussed by the BCEHM in its January, 1954, meeting. The discussion concluded with this resolution:

> Resolved, That we go on record to express our desire to see the Board of Church Extension and Home Missions continue to operate the Home Missions Department until a better plan of operation can be found (GB 20 January 1954, 18).

At the June, 1954, general board meeting, C. W. Hatch, of the Executive Council, met with the board. He reported that the Commission of Revision and Planning would have no further recommendation to make to the General Ministerial Assembly regarding the merger of missions.

A year later, no mention or reference was made in the minutes of the assembly or BCEHM on the merger issue. In part this was because there was no clear-cut plan or rationale as to how this would further the cause of missions. Some viewed it as a return to the past. Originally, home and foreign missions had been the responsibility of the Missionary Board.

After World War II and into the 1950s, requests from congregations, states, and district organizations for help from the board put a heavy strain on its highly centralized structure of organization. The chief executive officer was held responsible for every program decision. He was the key decision maker in the granting of loans, home missions work, evangelism projects, and other program matters. The weight of decision making and lack of adequate staff pushed for some new approaches.

Most, but not all board members agreed that a plan must be developed to broaden and spread the leadership responsibilities. By 1953, after thirty-two years of serving the church, the board decided there was a need for strong specialized leadership. It was not realistic to expect one executive or central staff person to be an expert in all fields.

The guiding question was, What organizational structure will help improve the delivery of services to the church? After considering many options, it became clear that the board must departmentalize and provide skilled staff members for each of its departments. Four departments of work were established: home missions, evangelism, church finance, and architecture.

The attempt had been made in the previous decade to specialize the board ministries. I. K. Dawson was invited to help form a Department of Evangelism. T. F. Miller was invited to give shape and substance to a Department of Home Missions. These attempts were only partially successful. The shortage of funds for program and the need of broader structural change postponed the departmentalization until the 1950s.

W. E. Reed Assigned Evangelism

No staff person was assigned the work of evangelism and church extension from 1948 to 1950. This was primarily due to the lack of funds, and exacerbated by the attacks on the board's 1945 plan of cooperative evangelism. In late 1949, the minutes of the board of directors reveal that staff help in evangeliam was considered essential. A two-day conference on evangelism with state leaders underlined this need. The time was ripe for board action in evangelism.

Within a few weeks after the conference, W. E. Reed, who was serving as a member of the board of directors, was invited to join the staff as secretary of evangelism. Reed responded that he would accept the assignment if he would first be allowed to help start a new congregation in Kennett, Missouri. He stated that if he were to be working with Church of God state leaders in starting and developing new congregations, he needed some on-the-job training. The board agreed to this arrangement.

While he was in Kennett, he spent one week a month in the Anderson office. He was assigned the task of seeking state financial support, since it was the state leaders who requested this help. He was also the Board's representative on the Mid-Century Evangelistic Advance planning and work committee. A special mailing was sent to the church, announcing the board's staffing of a Department of Evangelism. The church leaders' responses were favorable and enthusiastic.

During his first year on the staff, Reed sought and received feedback from every state where the Church of God had congregations. There were helpful suggestions on how to set up a department of evangelism, and comments on the need for a state/national revolving loan fund to help states with building needs. This was in keeping with the board's practice of being sensitive to the requests for service from local and state leaders. The suggestions were incorporated into the purpose and scope of the renewed church extension program.

A Change in Executive Leadership

With the winds of change blowing across the entire church, board members continued to search for areas in the board's program and services where improvement was necessary. The key strategy surfaced again and again in board minutes regarding any proposed change, "Study the issue and show how any proposed change would improve the board's service to the church."

In the June 10, 1953, annual meeting of the board, the Committee on Revision of the Bylaws made its recommendation to set up the four departments referred to above. This was voted by the board. Next came discussion of the specialization of staff and its implications for the chief executive officer. Finally, the hard decision was reached to name a new chief executive. E. F. Adcock, who had been the only full-time chief executive officer the board had ever had, was asked to accept a change in assignment. He was asked to devote his time to the responsibilities of treasurer and head of the Department of Church Finance. William E. Reed was elected chief executive of the board, with the title of General Secretary. He was ratified by the General Ministerial Assembly that same week.

As is often the case in vigorous disagreements among leaders, debate and discussion became personal. This was the case regarding the issue of how best to manage and administer the church's national radio program. This came up in the 1952 assembly. The executive of the board had been attacked by some members of the assembly who raised questions about rumors that funds intended for the radio broadcast had been mismanaged. The assembly appointed an investigating committee to look into this and other charges. After a year's investigation, the committee reported in the June, 1953, General Ministerial Assembly that the charges were false. They found no evidence of mismanagement of funds or improper conduct as had been rumored.

The rules of the assembly require each agency chief executive to be ratified by the assembly. This rule does not apply to other agency officers. Adcock was thankful that the investigating committee found him innocent of all charges, but he felt that some ministers of the assembly still had doubts about him. Against the advice of friends and assembly officers, he asked that his name be submitted for ratification as treasurer of the Board of Church Extension and Home Missions. He stated that, although he had been officially cleared of all charges, he did not want any feelings about him to hinder or reflect on the work of the board. His name appeared on the ballot the next day. It was a bold and courageous act on his part. He was ratified by a fifty-three percent vote of the assembly—312 votes for ratification, and 269 against. This act of courage and openness helped to overcome the feelings of uneasiness and suspicion some had regarding his leadership. He served ten more years as treasurer of the board. After his retirement, Adcock served as director of development for Warner Pacific College (1963-1965), and then for nine years as executive secretary for the Church of God Association of Northern California.

Planning and Building the House of God

During the 1950s, the board was involved with hundreds of congregations seeking loans for new church building facilities. It observed the evolution from storefront facilities and the feeling that buildings were not very important because Christ would return soon, to a desire for adequate permanent worship facilities. As pastors and congregational building committees came to the board, they brought plans and sketches for the building they hoped to build. These sketches were often very meager and occasionally crude. The prevailing feeling had been that architects cost too much money, so more often than not they were avoided.

It became increasingly evident that more congregations needed to study and identify their mission before they built. The rush to get a building before proper study was done often resulted in costly mistakes. This became a growing concern of the board and its staff. The desire was to help churches see the building process as a spiritual activity. Each congregation was urged to spend some time discussing and reflecting on the question, What should the house of God be like?

Many articles were written by the staff for the various church publications on the how, what, and why of building the house of God. A recurring theme was that the building should reflect the beliefs of the church, and that the building itself is primarily a tool for the mission God has assigned the congregation.

From 1950 to 1952, the board worked with John S. Kane in his preparation for becoming licensed as an architect. In 1953 the board established a Department of Architecture with John Kane as its director. Two assignments were: to provide better planning for church buildings through advisory services, and to encourage congregations to employ church architects. Draftsmen were employed, and preliminary plans were provided to scores of congregations. Elmer Hutchinson, Warren Pope, and Forrest Spiers were among early draftsmen and workers in this new department. Kenneth F. Ritchhart, a licensed engineer, was added to the architectural staff in 1954.

To educate the church on the importance of wise planning for buildings is a long process. This is particularly true when you also have to overcome negative attitudes about cost and affordability of architects, but the board's new architectural advisory service caught on rather quickly with the church. Within a few years the department was being called on for complete plan service, help in remodeling, and master plan designs for congregations, state youth camps, and campgrounds.

From 1953 to 1959, the Department of Architecture constantly fought the battle of red ink. Finally, in 1959, in a move to economize, Architecture was merged with the Department of Church Finance and renamed the Department of Church Building. Over the years offering this service to the church became more complicated. Pressure was being put on the staff architect to become licensed in each state where the board did business. This was a costly and nearly impossible task. There were now a number of church architects the church could call. It was noted that in the eighteen years the BCEHM offered the service, the church had come to see the wisdom of the use of architectural planning. Finally, the board decided to discontinue its architectural service, and in 1971 John Kane left the employment of the board to start his own private service.

Town and Country Ministry

The Church of God had a strong rural and small town focus. In 1950 the majority of its congregations were still located in rural areas and small towns of ten thousand and less population. In 1942 the board appointed three of its members to serve as a Rural Life Committee. Mack Caldwell was the key member who carried a burden for the committee. He discovered evidence that congregations and pastors in these areas were feeling forgotten or left out. The board broadened its Town and Country Committee in 1950 to include five pastors in an effort to learn more about the life and work of the rural churches.

Since the board did not have adequate staff for much of its work, it depended on its Town and Country Committee to oversee this program. The committee was responsible for leading rural conferences and institutes. It also conducted churchwide studies to determine the needs of town and country Church of God congregations. In 1955 the committee recommended that the board devote more staff time to this area of work.

W. E. Reed, who was serving not only as chief executive officer of the board but also as secretary of evangelism and convener of the Town and Country Committee, wrote the following in his report to the general board in January, 1956:

> Sixty percent of the congregations of the Church of God are located in small towns and in the open country. Scores of these churches are suffering from lack of capable leadership and from an inadequate program of evangelism. Since these churches are so vital to the future growth of the Church of God, it would seem advisable that the Board of Church Extension and Home Missions take immediate steps to further develop its Town and Country program.
>
> For the efficient development of this area of the Board's work, it would seem essential that some person of deep spiritual concern and satisfactory educational training be chosen to serve as director of this work. The person selected should be qualified to teach in the School of Theology and to meet with the approval of the faculty of the school. His work could well be divided between teaching in the School of Theology and doing general field work for the strengthening of small town and open country churches. . . . It is the viewpoint of the General Secretary that this area of work should continue to be related to the Department of Evangelism. The person chosen to serve in this capacity would bear considerable responsibility in the development of an adequate program of evangelism for town and country churches (GB January 1956, 3).

Six months later, in the board's annual meeting in Anderson, the general secretary reported,

> On June 1, 1956, Louis P. Meyer began his work with the Board of Church Extension and Home Missions as Director of Town and Country Church work. He will spend part of his time teaching in the School of Theology and the remaining amount of his time doing field work in behalf of small town and open country churches (GB 13 June 1956).

For the rest of the decade and into the 1960s, the board

sponsored programs tailored for town and country pastors and congregations. Over the next nine years, 312 pastors participated in the board's Town And Country Reading Course. Thirty pastors received scholarships to attend training classes and institutes, set up to assist them in discovering how to interpret community needs and where to find resources for small towns and rural communities. Over eighteen land-grant universities, colleges, and seminaries offered these options for town and country leaders.

In the fall of 1956, the Town and Country Committee was enlarged to fifteen pastors from across the U.S. and Canada; its executive committee was Louis P. Meyer, Marvin Tate, Revere Cook, Ray Bringham, Mack Caldwell, and W. E. Reed. The next year, the president of the board appointed forty-two additional pastors to serve as town and country contact persons between the states and the BCEHM. They served by keeping the board informed of front line needs and by reporting news stories for the board's *Rural Fellowship Dispatch*, a bimonthly newsletter.

From 1959 to 1960, one hundred and thirty congregations enrolled in the board's churchwide program—Town and Country Church of the Year. The program sought to improve the witness for Christ in working for a better church, a better community and a better world: 118 congregations finished the program and received special certificates of participation.

First place honors went to: Royal Chapel, North Carolina (John Mowery pastor); Ashland, Kansas (Eddie Downey pastor); and Piggott, Arkansas (Estel Triplett pastor). The program brought encouragement and a sense of importance to the congregations of rural and small town United States and Canada.

Church Building Campaigns

The decade of the fifties saw a rapid rise in church attendance across America. Building materials were again rationed during the Korean War. This resulted in a backlog of need for new and better church buildings.

By 1955 it was realized that inflated costs of land and rising costs of building materials were having a serious impact on the church. The increase in attendance put pressure on the growing congregations to build larger facilities. In the effort to do this, some congregations were extending themselves beyond their financial limits. To address this problem, the board set up a program to help congregations raise their own building funds.

It was called Church Building Campaigns. Cecil J. Brown joined the board staff as director of this new ministry on August 1, 1956. He had worked with the Mid-Century Building Fund project until it concluded its work in 1955. For the board's new effort he helped to tailor a three-year program of pledging for the local church. His first year on the BCEHM staff was spent developing written materials and manuals for this successful venture.

Ralph Phile was added to the staff as an associate director of Church Building Campaigns in 1957. Others who have assisted with this successful ministry through the years include James Austin, J. Lloyd Brown, Elmer Wolford, Elmer Case, J. L. Hatchell, Cecil Watson, George Blackwell, Jr., A. J. Bugg, and Rodney Bargerstock.

This special service met with wide success from the beginning. In its first five years, Church Building Campaigns assisted 104 congregations in raising $3,539,500 for new church facilities. This was a great asset, as congregations raised a third or more of their needed funds, permitting them to borrow less. By 1990 this ministry helped congregations raise over $100,000,000 in pledges for capital improvements.

A New Department of Evangelism

The 1953 decision of the board to restructure the program and staff took most of the decade to carry out. For a year or so, some departments were not staffed due to lack of budget. The two staff officers—general secretary and treasurer—had to double as department heads of evangelism, home missions, and church building.

As stated earlier, the board's primary focus in evangelism was church extension—starting and developing new churches. The question began to be raised in this decade as to what helps in evangelism the BCEHM had for congregations which were established and self-supporting.

In the annual meeting of the board in June, 1957, the members voted to ask Louis P. Meyer to assume the full-time leadership of the Department of Evangelism. The concern was that this department help the church broaden its concepts of evangelism and become much more intentional and creative in living out the gospel. Under the newly-structured Department of Evangelism was placed the responsibility for church extension cooperative projects, town and country work, men's work, and urban concerns.

One of the first actions of the new department in 1957 was to sponsor a churchwide Simultaneous Evangelistic Endeavor (SEE) for the month of October, to encourage congregations to focus on communitywide evangelism campaigns. It was an attempt to focus the church's attention on unity in evangelism. The method was the old and tested practice of revival. A manual was prepared to introduce some newer approaches to evangelism. Six hundred and thirty congregations participated, and asked that the experience be repeated.

The second SEE Campaign in 1959 focused on the Church of God around the world. Most of the church's national agencies helped to plan this event. Eight hundred and fifty congregations in the United States and Canada participated, plus two hundred Church of God congregations overseas.

Toward the end of the decade, the board, with suggestions and help from state church extension committees, began to upgrade the procedures and process for properly starting and developing congregations. Applications for assistance in beginning new congregations were developed, and a new plan for five-year maximum budget support from the BCEHM for cooperative projects was worked out with the states (GB June 1959).

Men's Work

For most of this decade, the Department of Evangelism worked with the executive committee of MEN of the Church of God to develop monthly program outlines for about four hundred local men's groups. The interest in and concern for this approach to men's work began to decline by 1957.

In 1959 A. Wayne Johnson, who had retired from the army, decided to attend seminary in Anderson. He joined the BCEHM staff that August as director of men's work, and was assigned to the Department of Evangelism. For the next nine years the board, through Johnson, helped to coordinate national men's work. This included writing a manual for men's work and a quarterly newsletter, helping to organize local and state men's groups, developing literature for men in the armed services, structuring a national committee to assume more responsibility for the organization, and opening conversations with the National Association of Church of God Men.

Don Ritchey, an active layman from Findlay, Ohio, accepted the presidency of MEN of the Church of God International in 1962. Ritchey helped set up an active executive committee which assumed the primary responsibility for men's work. They set up their office in Findlay, Ohio. The national board's role changed from sponsorship to consultation. Johnson terminated his services with the board in June, 1968.

Home Missions in the 1950s

The responsibilities for the Department of Home Missions

in this decade were shared by W. E. Reed and Naomi Randall. This was a part of the departmentalization process set in motion by the board in 1953.

Naomi Randall reported to the general board in 1954 that sixty-one persons were receiving full or partial financial support from the board in home missions. Another twenty-seven were donating their time to various phases of home missions ministries. That year there was a total of thirty-seven mission stations and thirty-four church buildings or places of worship. In Mexico there were eleven national workers ministering to people's needs (GB 19 January 1954).

This was an active and expansive decade for Church of God home missions. The board began its support of Mother Ivory Downer and her daughter Hattie in 1950 in Brooklyn, in innercity mission work. The focus at the Williamsburg mission was primarily children. This was the start of a long and faithful witness for Christ in a difficult place of service. Hattie Downer continued serving there with board assistance until her retirement in 1987. The Williamsburg mission continues today to make a significant difference in the life of its community.

Simon and Mae Johnson Robinson accepted the pastorate at Pine Crest, Kentucky in 1950. Five years later, Simon assumed additional responsibilities at the youth center, and established a woodcraft shop. He taught carpentry skills to single young men and fathers of the area. This helped improve the economic life of a number of the families and the community.

In this decade Ballard Johnson, Malcolm McDonald, Willard and Glenna Armey, and Forest and Margaret Drake served the little mountain church at Blaines Branch, Kentucky. Bob and Alma Sperow pastored at Miller's Creek, Kentucky from 1947 until 1967.

Native American work found Lee and Belledene Baker, Boyd and Beulah Kole, Judson and Ethel Masters serving at Crow Agency, Montana; Earl and Esther Bailey, Harry and Eula Martin, Ivyl and Florence Salisbury, at Alliance, and

Mr. and Mrs. Paul Thorsen at Gordon, Nebraska; and James and Grace Kole at Lapwai, Idaho. Toppenish, Washington, workers included J. Frank and Susan Shaw, Elmer and Jean Hossler, the Noble LaVelles, the Warren Kinions, John and Edna Miller, and Louis and Gladys Mitten. Adam and Marjory Williams continued at Tulalip, Washington. The Wounded Knee, South Dakota, mission was served by Norman and Annabelle Hause, Earl and Esther Bailey, and Ivyl Salisbury. It was noted in 1957 that Leroy and Lucille Falling were doing an effective job in mission work in their public school work among the Navajo people in Arizona.

The new state of Alaska received financial assistance for leadership from the board. The children's home, started in Palmer, was moved to Fairbanks. Leaders helping there included Mr. and Mrs. Sanford Davis, Chester and Esther Cantley, Lewis and Hazel Geiwitz (also served at Sutton), and the Maxwell Baileys. Leadership assistance in Anchorage First Church was given by James and Alice Austin, Jarrell and Irene Frazee, Arley and Clora Skinner, and Paul and Mary Ruth Kendall. Anchorage Community Church was assisted in leadership by Ervin and Gayle Cultice, Wesley and Jean Lancaster (also served at Palmer), and Larry and Maxine Lautaret. The Fairbanks church was led by Russell Wilson and later by Fred and Evelyn Mamaloff, who also served at Juneau and Kodiac in the decade. The BCEHM gave some financial assistance to the John Marshalls for their ministry at Sutton and Kodiak.

Special mission ministries among African-Americans in the South were made possible by the board's financial support of Isom and Ola Crockett in Mississippi, and Horace Germany for special educational outreach in Mississippi. Germany's efforts to develop a trade school based on dairy farming received modest support from the board until the decision to develop Bay Ridge Christian College took the project out of the scope of the board's charter.

BCEHM outreach to Hispanic people picked up momentum in this decade. Monthly financial grants for pastoral support were the primary form of help. Assistance was given to Los Angeles, Belvedere congregation: Maurice and Dondeena Caldwell (1949-1954), Samuel and Dora Colunga (1954-1959), and Fidel and Sally Zamarano (1959). Financial grants for pastoral leadership were made to the Corpus Christi, Texas, congregation for pastors L. O. Ramos and Adolfo and Phyllis Pesquera. Albuquerque, New Mexico, Hispanic leadership included Samuel Colunga, George and Marie Geiwitz, Gregorio and Josefina Castaneda, William and Evangeline Westlake, Albert and Irene Bentley, and Lewis and Hazel Geiwitz. The San Antonio, Texas, Hispanic congregation where the Geiwitzes, Castanedas, and others worked, also received assistance.

The work in Mexico under the board's administration started in the 1940s. The need for training leadership for the dozen or more congregations of the Church of God was keenly felt. Several special trips and studies were made on how to approach this. It was finally decided that a Bible training school needed to be established. In 1954 Maurice and Doneena Caldwell were invited to become directors and teachers at La Buena Tierra in Saltillo, Mexico. They did this until 1962, when the board invited Maurice to serve as secretary of the Department of Home Missions. Others who served as teachers at La Buena Tierra were Adolfo and Phyllis Pesquera, the Albert Bentleys, the James Hamiltons, Amelia Valdez, Raymond and Elna Mae Hastings, Ronald and Ruth Shotton, George and Marie Geiwitz, Calvin and Myrlene Pitts, Jolene Sommers (Lopez), Joe Lapp, and Luz Gonzales.

Loyd Butler served as the board's Hispanic field director for northern Mexico from 1953 to 1956.

Intrachurch Missions

Periodically, suggestions came from various leaders and groups within the church for more unity in mission endeavors. In 1943 a resolution came from the state of Wisconsin suggesting that all national publications be merged. Part of the reason for this request was to conserve paper during the war. Although no official action was taken on the Wisconsin request, all publications were cut back during those war years.

Publications. In 1948 serious conversations began between the Board of Church Extension and Home Missions, the Missionary Board, and the National Woman's Missionary Society on the possibilities of combining their missions publications: *The Pioneer, Missionary Outlook,* and *Friends of Missions.* By 1951 they were merged into one publication, *Church of God MISSIONS Magazine.* This magazine has had a wide influence in informing the Church of God about its total mission work at home and around the world. Years later, Warner Press and the Board of Christian Education each accepted the invitation to name a consultant to the joint Missions Education Committee, which manages the financial affairs of the magazine.

World Missions Conventions. The decade of the fifties saw increased interest of the church in missions work. The three missions agencies worked very effectively together to inform the church as to mission opportunities for the rest of the century. A series of five world missions conventions were conducted from 1955 through 1963. These were planned by the Missions Education Committee. They were held in Dayton, Ohio, in September, 1955; Wichita, Kansas, in September, 1957; and Oakland, California, in August, 1959. An extensive evaluation of these conventions revealed that primarily the same mission-minded people were attending each convention. In 1961 the missions convention was conducted in three cities in the East and three cities in the West. A fifth convention was held in 1963 in the new Warner Auditorium in Anderson. The last attempt at this joint educational approach was made with simultaneous meetings in eight cities in the United States and Canada.

Pioneer Memorial Loan Fund

From its beginning the BCEHM had needed a loan fund it owned (not borrowed funds) to help new and struggling congregations get facilities at a very low rate of interest—just enough to help the board cover clerical and legal expenses.

The Pioneer Memorial Loan Fund got its start in 1951, when an aged Christian in northern California sent a contribution of $250 to the board with the request that its use be made perpetual in helping to establish congregations of the Church of God. This fund grew to a balance exceeding $800,000 by 1990, and has assisted hundreds of new congregations to get facilities.

Interchurch Cooperation

In 1950 the National Council of Churches of Christ was formed. That same year the complete Revised Standard Version of the Bible was published. Considerable controversy arose over both. The board received several inquiries as to its relationship with the National Council of Churches. In response to earlier unrest and to these inquiries, the Board of Church Extension and Home Missions adopted a position statement entitled "The Church of God and Interdenominational Agencies" in its June, 1951 annual meeting. It gave a brief history of the relationship of national Church of God agencies to interdenominational organizations. It stated that for twelve years the Board of Church Extension and Home Missions had been affiliated with the Home Missions Council of North America, and with the Church Building and Architectural Bureau, and other interchurch organizations. In part it said:

> The attitude and general policy of this Board has been one of cooperation with interdenominational agencies in common fields of interest and service, but

> without organizational commitments or obligations of any kind. This relationship between the Board and interdenominational agencies is similar to that of local congregations where the minister is a member of the ministerial fellowship of the city. To do less, we believe, would be crippling in some areas of the Board's work and would fall short of the general doctrine of the Church of God to acknowledge and cooperate with a true Christian work wherever found, but not depend upon organizational forms or commitments for bringing about the unity for which we stand (GB June 1951, K).

The minutes note that the board "endorsed the article and recommended its distribution among our brethren as they call for such a statement."

Internal Affairs

Victor J. Gritzmacher joined the staff as a member of the Finance Department in March, 1958. He served as a loan consultant to help congregations understand the lending options of the board and how they might apply for a loan. He served in several capacities with the board, including secretary of the Department of Church Building and secretary of investments and development.

Nora Angus was named as the board's recording secretary (1956) and assistant treasurer (1959).

Gene W. Newberry was elected president of the general board in June, 1956. He chaired the meetings of the directors, executive committee, and general board for the next seventeen years. Roy Creamer, a layman from Alexandria, Indiana, was elected vice president of the board in 1957 and served in that capacity for eleven years.

Need for Additional Office Space. In 1957 W. E. Reed noted at the board's annual meeting that space in the office building on the campground was far too small for the expanding staff and program of the board. Requests for extra land on the campground to enlarge the building were turned down. After a study of future needs, property at the corner of Third Street and Nursery Road in Anderson was purchased. In 1959 the first New Office Building Committee was appointed. Further study of requirements, zoning, and the acquiring of additional property for expansion took five years.

$100,000 Profit. In the late 1930s, the board acquired an office building on Main Street in downtown Anderson through an estate, as an investment property. It was sold in the 1950s for $100,000 profit. This helped the board offset most of the deficit built up during the depression.

Deaths During the Decade. These board members and home missions persons died during this decade: W. E. Monk (1950), J. T. Wilson (1954), W. H. Hunt and D. W. Patterson (1957).

Summary of Decade

This decade began with another war, the Korean War. This had its impact again on the board's church building loan program.

The psychology of entering into the last half of the twentieth century provided strong motivation for the expanded ministry of the board in the 1950s. This expansion was also encouraged by probing questions concerning the future needs of church and society and what organizational form could best achieve God's plan and purpose. The decisions of the board to develop program departments and staff them to carry out specialized ministries and to change executive leadership assignments helped to make program expansion possible.

The events of the decade, the church's trust and counsel,

and the enlarged, newly organized staff resulted in three new program thrusts: town and country ministry, architectural advisory service, and church building campaigns. The fully staffed Department of Home Missions helped the board expand its ministry and service in native American, Hispanic, and Alaskan work. The newly restructured Department of Evangelism, with a full-time staff person assigned exclusively to its work, resulted in an expanded program in evangelism, church development, and state and national cooperative evangelism.

It was also a decade of increased national agency cooperation in the Mid-Century Evangelistic Advance, and in cooperative missions ministries.

(Full captions can be found beginning on page 280.)

1 Open Air Meeting, 1951

2 Russell R. Byrum, 1926.

3 W. E. Monk, 1935.

4 First 4 CEOs, BCEHM.

5 BCEHM Office, 1934.

(Full captions can be found beginning on page 280.)

1 Earl Martin, 1938

2 Omaha Church of God

3 Russell R. Byrum, 1971

4 Executive Committee, 1939

5 General Board, 1939

(Full captions can be found beginning on page 280.)

Executive Committee, 1964

Board and Staff, 1971

Board and Staff, 1980

Board and Staff, 1990

(Full captions can be found beginning on page 280.)

1 Dedication service, 1966
2 New building, 1966
3 BCEHM building, 1946
4 Dedication service, 1966

5 Office worship, 1954

6 Staff meeting, 1955

(Full captions can be found beginning on page 280.)

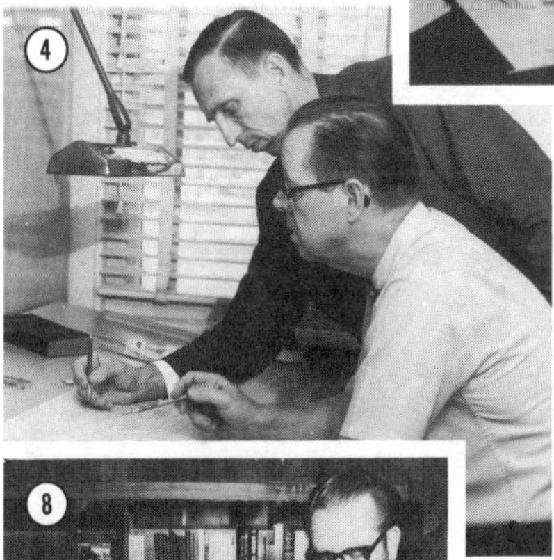

1 Richard Lee Meischke, 1946.
2 Nora Angus, 1940.
3 Edward L. Foggs, 1970.
4 Kane, Hutchinson, 1956.
5 Nilah Meier/Youngman, 1975.
6 Leroy Falling, 1983.
7 J. Perry Grubbs, 1988.
8 Reed, Hartman, 1970.
9 Program staff, 1975.

(Full captions can be found beginning on page 280.)

1 Palmer, Alaska, 1949.

2 Mae, D. W. Patterson, 1940.

3 Alaska Pastors, 1954.

4 Wendell, Mignonne Byrd, 1937.

5 J. Frank Shaw, 1952.

6 Navajo leaders, 1976.

7 James, Alice Austin, 1952.

8 Indian Council, 1974.

9 Indian Council, 1981.

(Full captions can be found beginning on page 280.)

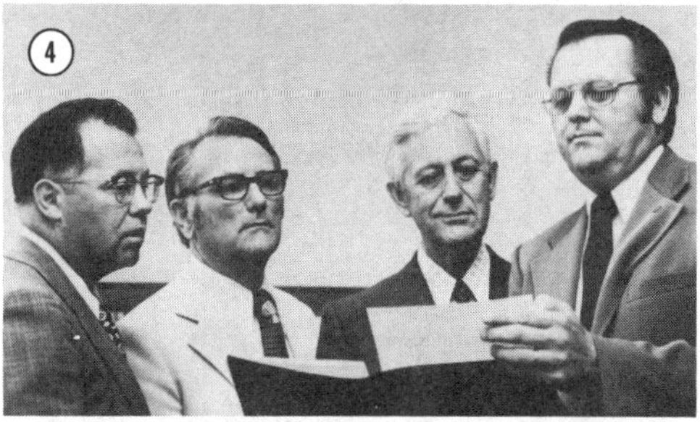

1 Toccoa, GA, 1924.

2 Warsaw, IN, 1937.

3 Clark, Snowden, 1951.

4 $1 million investment, 1973.

5 Spanish leaders, 1975.

6 Tafolla celebration, 1947.

7 David Cotto, 1989.

8 Hispanic youth, 1978.

(Full captions can be found beginning on page 280.)

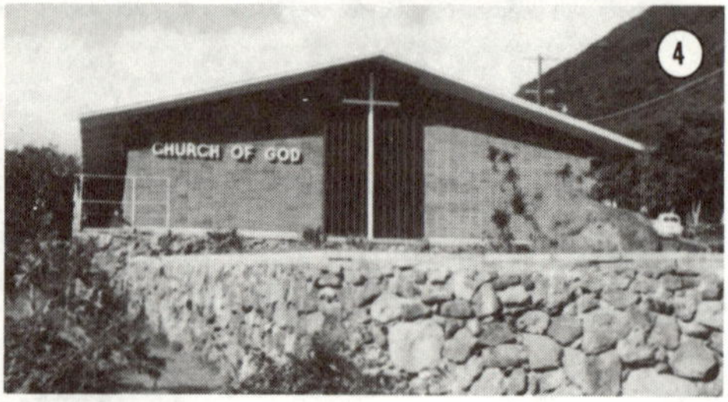

1 Korean pastors in US, 1984.

2 Haitian leaders, 1983.

3 Hashem Sweis, family, 1979.

4 Honolulu Church of God, 1974.

5 Korean children, 1983.

6 Ivory Downer, 1970.

7 Hattie Downer, 1960.

8 Pinecrest, 1979.

(Full captions can be found beginning on page 280.)

1 Hope Hill, 1978.

2 Hope Hill trustees, 1975.

3 Town & Country pastors, 1957.

4 "Church & Community," 1962.

5 Paul, Lana Sanders, 1975.

6 Men's Committee, 1965

7 "Pastoring in City," 1975.

8 State Coordinators, 1971.

Chapter 6

A Time of Unrest

(1960-1969)

In this decade the United States and the rest of the world saw the pace of change quicken in family, cultural, social, and international affairs. Many felt that their world was becoming barely recognizable. The rapid expansion of technology made many new options possible. Some of the more dramatic areas of this new technology were in space travel and exploration, and in the development of heart transplant surgery.

The decade of the 1960s saw the last vestiges of world empires disappear in Africa as Britain, France, and Belgium relinquished their colonial interests to the massive tide of black nationalism. These racial winds of equality, freedom, and individual rights were loudly echoed in the United States. Under Martin Luther King, Jr., the civil rights movement struggled for recognition against the personal and institutional forces of inertia and prejudice.

In 1963 the African-American civil rights campaign gained momentum. On August 25th, over 200,000 African-American and Anglo civil rights supporters from all across the nation marched to Washington, D.C., to urge the nation's lawmakers to pass legislation guaranteeing to all citizens of the United States their personal freedoms. It was here that Martin Luther King, Jr., made his now famous *I Have a Dream* speech, a speech which helped to mirror the Bill of Rights for all Americans.

Civil rights workers marched throughout the South, dramatizing opposition to the system of second-class citizenship. President Kennedy nationalized the Alabama National Guard when Governor George Wallace tried to prevent two African-American students from enrolling at the University of Alabama at Tuscaloosa.

In September, 1963, a bomb killed four African-American schoolgirls in Birmingham. Two months later, on November 22, President John F. Kennedy was assassinated in Dallas, Texas. Vice President Lyndon B. Johnson became president of the United States.

In a matter of months a vital piece of legislation, the United States Civil Rights Act of 1964, became law. In many ways, more progress was made in the struggle for racial equality in the United States from 1962 to 1968 than in the entire preceding generation. This legislation was far-reaching in raising the hopes and dreams of all racial and ethnic groups in America. It was part of a global trade wind carrying hope of freedom, equality, and equal opportunity to oppressed and neglected people around the world.

But it takes more than a new piece of legislation to correct centuries of personal and institutional racism. Personal hopes were raised, but poverty and squalor continued to be a reality in all major metropolitan areas. The pressures to attain more of the promised freedoms built up, unchecked. Soon there were rebellions and riots in Watts, Los Angeles, Detroit, New York City, Chicago, and other large urban areas. It was a time of deep unrest.

Another major segment of the American population was raising serious questions about equality and personal freedom at this time. Although the struggle for the liberation of women had been going on for many years, it gained great momentum in this decade. It was not until 1920 that the women of this nation were given the right to vote. Now, forty years later, freedom and the rights of all human beings was a key topic and concern from Africa to America. Women from all walks of life and all economic strata began to unite. Their concern centered around equality and liberation from past social practices and expectations. The cry now was equal pay for equal work, and the full rights of citizenship. It was a time of unrest.

A third cause of the seething social and human unrest of the sixties was the Vietnam War. In just over twenty years, the United States involved itself in its third military conflict. World War II ended in 1945, the Korean War was in the early 1950s; now, in 1964, and throughout the rest of the decade, America was to be embroiled in Vietnam. This was one of the most unpopular military conflicts in American history. The government's long involvement deeply divided the nation.

Still other historical events occurred during the decade: the Berlin wall was built; Arab-Israeli conflict changed the map of that area in just six days; Soviet and American programs competed in the space race; the decade began with the first man in space and ended with the first man on the moon; satellite-enhanced worldwide communication made possible a television audience of five hundred million people to watch the moon walk; satellites also created a massive worldwide youth culture as music of the Rolling Stones, the Doors, and other groups came to be symbols of their young audiences' rejection of parental values; sexual and social taboos were greatly eroded by the manufacture of the contraceptive pill and the widespread use of marijuana and other drugs.

This decade saw: Kenya become a republic; Nelson Mandela imprisoned in South Africa; the death of Winston Churchill in 1965; Martin Luther King, Jr. given the Nobel Peace Prize in 1964, and his assassination in 1965; Senator Robert Kennedy gunned down at the age of forty-two on June 5, 1968; massive anti-Vietnam War demonstrations in 1960; and the first flight of the Boeing 747 jumbo jet carrying over three hundred passengers.

The sixties were years of massive contrasts, of deep and increasing unrest; a decade with an unrelenting pace of change, constantly challenging the church to carry out its ministry without blueprint or precedent from the past; a decade when each year presented new territory without maps or guidelines.

Evangelism in Times of Change and Unrest

During this decade, reports of the board's president to the General Assembly of the Church of God and the books of minutes of this agency reveal the beginning of a broader concept of and concern for evangelism.

The 1960 census revealed many changes in the population. People were moving at an increasing rate to urban and suburban areas. Science and technology were gaining influence and power in the nation's system of values and priorities. Complete new towns were on the drawing board in Virginia, Maryland, and other places, to be developed as social experiments. The board was faced with the exciting challenge of how to carry out its chartered assignment in the midst of unrest, uncertainty, and unequaled opportunity.

The decade began with the staff of the board working hard at getting a focus on the societal changes and directions. Seminars conducted by the U.S. Census Bureau were attended. Staff also sought input from the leadership of the church on the priorities to be set and the approach to be taken in evangelism for the future.

The secretary of the Department of Evangelism was assigned the responsibility of setting up a national consultation on evangelism, hosted by the board. Leaders from all national agencies of the church, pastors, evangelists, lay leaders, and district leaders met for a three-day discussion. The purpose was to get key leaders of the church to concentrate their thoughts on evangelism in a time of change: to consider whether the Church of God had been retarded in its evangelistic outreach because of too narrow a concept of evangelism; to focus more on the why (purpose) of evangelism rather than the how (methods); to discuss the role of the laity in the evangelistic task of the church, and to help each participant acquire a broader understanding of the nature and task of evangelism.

The consultation was held in New Albany, Indiana, November 7-10, 1960. Fifty-one leaders from twenty states and each national agency participated in the presenting of papers, panel discussions, and open dialogue. This was a most significant event in the life of the board and its Department of Evangelism, as well as the church.

This event encouraged the board and staff to make evangelism a major priority for the 1960s. Up until this time, most of the board's focus on evangelism was at the point of new church development or church extension. The consultation raised the question of what the board had to offer in the area of evangelism for the hundreds of established Church of God congregations.

Preliminary studies were done by staff on how pastors and leaders of the Church of God viewed or defined evangelism. It was determined that congregations which held annual or semi-annual revivals or gave altar calls after Sunday services were considered evangelistic congregations. The staff developed materials and designed other educational approaches to help pastors and congregations see evangelism as more than the methods used, and to understand that the goal of evangelism is not only to make converts, but also to produce mature Christians. The materials of the board stressed that evangelism involved Christian obedience in daily life, and the participation of the Christian community in the church's mission in the world.

Church and Community Committee

The board had an active Town and Country Church Committee for many years. In the 1950s and 1960s there was a steady movement of people to urban and metropolitan areas. Staff saw ministry in both urban and rural areas as connected, and felt the two ought to be addressed as a whole. It was also felt that the deep unrest of the 1960s needed to be addressed from the perspective of the church's evangelistic task. New and bold ways needed to be found to communicate the gospel.

By 1962, in an effort to pick up some of the concerns raised by the 1960 National Consultation on Evangelism, and to unite rural and urban ministry planning as a single task, a Church and Community Committee was named. The assigned task was broad in scope, as stated in a *Vital Christianity* news item:

> A new Church and Community Committee has been named to serve with the Department of Evangelism of the Board of Church Extension and Home Missions. The eight pastors on the committee will study and experiment with new methods and approaches in evangelism in their various communities.
>
> Chosen for the different kinds of communities in which their church is located and for their insights in evangelism the pastors are: Don Collins, Pittsburgh, Pennsylvania; James Massey, Detroit, Michigan; Edgar Williams, Chicago, Illinois; Dale Lehman, New Boston, Ohio; Wilbur Skaggs, Seattle, Washington; John Conley, Morehead, Kentucky; Leroy Fulton, Drexel, North Carolina; and Jack Anderson, St. Louis, Missouri.
>
> The Committee will act in an advisory capacity to the Department of Evangelism to give a cross section of their views and thinking regarding the needs of the church. They will seek to develop more effective ways of Christian witness in the changing communities and especially in the trend to urbanization. They will help aid the local congregation in interpreting and understanding its evangelistic task in its community.
>
> The new committee will meet annually, and will read much of the material published in the Protestant field on evangelism. They will discuss study papers and set up experimental projects by which they will seek to find more effective methods of communicating the

gospel to the non-Christian world.

Louis P. Meyer, Secretary of the Department of Evangelism, explained that the committee will act as an evangelistic vanguard, in their work. They will help the Department and the Church discover ways of returning the primary task of evangelism back to the laity (VC 16 December 1962).

The Church and Community Committee served from 1963 through 1968. The membership varied, but its purpose remained the same.

The eight members of the committee, plus twenty-two other pastors, each chose a special group or setting for experimentation with how best to witness for Christ. Some evangelism experiments were conducted by pastors and congregations that were adjacent to university campuses, others chose to work in such areas as evangelism and the elderly, sharing the gospel in ski lodges, in shopping malls, and with delinquent youth.

Other areas included were: searching for ways to relate each Christian more directly to daily witnessing; broadening the concept of evangelism and bringing it into sharper focus in the organization and life of the congregation; renewing the church through mass evangelism. With thirty pastors and congregations in twenty states working on a variety of experiments throughout the decade, evangelism received increased attention across the church. Other pastors were inspired to find more effective ways and settings for communicating the good news of the gospel in their own communities.

A controlled study was conducted by staff over eighteen months, from July, 1963, through December, 1964. The objective was to determine how effective the Church of God was in reaching persons not related to the church. Where were the points of contact for new people? Why are people attracted to our congregations? And why are other persons dropping out?

Fifty-five Church of God congregations, with memberships ranging from fifteen to three hundred members and representing the major geographical areas of the nation were participants in the study. Each quarter, each congregation reported on persons who became active in some phase of their church life during that quarter. The report also noted persons who had dropped out of the local church program.

The study helped each participating congregation gain insights regarding the strengths and weaknesses of their evangelistic obedience to the gospel. The quarterly reports revealed that for the test period six hundred new persons had become active in the congregations, while four hundred had stopped attending. Sixty-seven percent of those who left did so because they were leaving the city or community. This gave a helpful insight that the church must learn to adapt its evangelistic lifestyle to serve people on the move. In that decade, twenty percent of the U.S. population changed addresses each year (BCEHM New Persons).

It was clear that an aggressive and more inclusive approach to evangelism was necessary. The annual report of the Department of Evangelism for 1964 gives this insight:

> As a department, we feel our obedience to Christ and our assignment by the Church includes more than just responding to requests from congregations for service. There is a prophetic element to our work. The Department's role includes: (1) guiding the Church in establishing a firm biblical base for evangelism; (2) alerting the Church to the new shapes of society today, and offering some guidance in interpreting these trends and changes in light of the gospel; (3) urging the Church to train itself to discover God at work in His world, and to join in His action of redemption; (4) challenging each congregation to structure itself to train its laity for the ministry of reconciliation;

(5) stressing the need for each congregation to dare to trust the Holy Spirit, and be mature enough to take the risk of obedience; and (6) urging the Church to learn to interpret redemption and reconciliation in terms of society, as well as the individual (AR 1964, 1).

For three years the Church and Community Committee worked faithfully with the board staff in evaluating society in a time of unrest and rebellion. The desire was to intensify the sense of mission and the spirit of evangelistic urgency throughout the Church of God. In the annual meetings of the committee in 1963 and 1964, the decision was reached to suggest to the board that 1965-66 be designated as Emphasis Evangelism Year throughout the church.

The board endorsed the proposal and invited all other national agencies to participate. The General Ministerial Assembly passed a resolution approving Emphasis Evangelism as a churchwide thrust. The theme for the year was, God Calls the Church To: Care . . . Serve . . . Witness. A 110-page Emphasis Evangelism Resource Book was sent to each registered congregation. The first sixteen weeks of the emphasis were devoted to biblical studies on the nature of evangelism. There were four sessions each on the nature of the church, the evangelistic mission of the church, the world as the object of God's mission, and God's call to the laity to do the work of evangelism.

Then these biblical insights were applied to the organizational life of each congregation in light of the needs of the community where each served. Over eight hundred congregations participated in this program. The records reveal that permission to use or adapt Emphasis Evangelism materials was sought by other church groups, including the Churches of God of North America, the Lutheran Church of America, the United Methodist Church, the Nazarene Church, and the Society of Friends.

For the rest of the decade, the biblical perspectives developed for Emphasis Evangelism served as the theological basis for the board's efforts in program development in evangelism. A follow-up study of the congregations who participated suggests that this was the most effective churchwide evangelism program the board had ever sponsored. The objective of broadening the church's perspective on evangelism was partially reached.

Evangelism Through New Church Development

The changing times and social unrest of the decade also caused the board to take a new look at its primary assignment of church extension. With the changes in community structure, the growth of urban areas, and the realization that the Church of God had not been very effective in large cities, it was felt that the staff should come up with a more comprehensive plan for starting new churches.

In an effort to render more effective service to the states and districts in new church development, the board voted to add an additional staff person as assistant secretary of the Department of Evangelism. The job description reveals the board's interest and determination to serve the states and provinces:

> The Assistant Secretary of the Department of Evangelism shall have these responsibilities: his primary task will be the area of new church development, to find ways of establishing new congregations through strategic evangelism; he will help sharpen the Board's interest, role, policy and program in the area of extension evangelism and conservation; he will be the liaison person between the Board and state or area extension committees and work with them in developing an approach to churching America; he shall serve as an extension consultant, and be the Board's point of contact in new church extension projects; and he shall seek to interpret to the church at large the urgent need for a more adequate program of church exten-

sion and development in light of our current population boom (AR 1960, 2).

Isham (Joe) Crane accepted this assignment and joined the staff on August 1, 1960. The first year was spent in visiting most state and district church extension boards and committees to learn what type of help they were needing. Based on this study of needs, the staff developed a format for in-service training for area church extension committees, called Extension Evangelism Workshops. These involved two-and-a-half to three days of intensive work. They were designed to engage a state or area evangelism committee in developing a long-range plan of conservation and new church development for its region. The staff would guide the state committee members in discovering the latest population statistics and trends, mobility rate, economic growth or decline, and other socio-economic factors that affected the lives and movement of the people in their state.

In an Extension Evangelism Workshop the state committee would also study the history, growth, and development of the Church of God in the state for the past thirty years. Such a workshop did not offer a packaged program. Rather, it was designed to introduce state committees to the basics for setting up their own processes of planning, establishing procedures, and setting goals.

An average of six workshops a year were conducted in this decade. It was one of the most effective church planning services the BCEHM offered. Because of the frequent turnover of the membership of state church extension committees, the staff was called back several times to the same state to repeat these training experiences.

Staff time was also devoted to the visitation of new church extension projects. Twenty or more projects were visited each year to offer encouragement, counsel and suggestions on how to become a self-supporting congregation. Monthly reports were received from new projects receiving national and state budget support. Criteria were developed also for assisting new projects to become self-supporting in three to five years.

Training experiences for the pastors of new church projects and their spouses were set up in the 1960s, often on an interchurch basis. It was an experience in confidence building, sharing of insights, and receiving helps for their unique needs as leaders of new church projects.

If new church development were to be carried on primarily by metropolitan, district, and state organizations, it was felt that the leaders of these areas should be involved as advisors to BCEHM staff. To assist in charting a clearer path for this work, the board appointed a seven-member New Church Development Committee. Its assignment included: calling the attention of the church to the unique opportunities for new church development; creating closer ties with and serving as liaison to state and area church extension committees; and helping to plan and initiate a more comprehensive and intensive church development program. The committee held its first meeting in January, 1967 (GB 1966).

The Urban Frontier Challenge

Although Americans had been moving to metropolitan areas of America for several decades, many church leaders and others did not become aware of this phenomenon until the 1960s. The rural-to-urban shift had been accelerating at an increasing rate from 1940, as the 1960 U.S. census forcefully documented. This, coupled with the social unrest across the land, brought home to church leaders across denominations that the church in America had the challenge of a new frontier on its hands.

The board allowed the secretary of the Department of Evangelism to attend a 1960 summer postgraduate seminar on urban planning at Wayne State University in Detroit. The heads of the city planning departments of Chicago and

Detroit were the leaders of the two-week event. It was a type of crash course for church and community institutional leaders. Very helpful demographic and statistical information was shared. The underlying plea was for better planning on the part of all urban social, religious, educational, and political institutions to prepare for better living in the cities of the land.

The board sponsored the first urban conferences to be held at the Anderson international convention in June, 1961, on Urban Life and the Church. These annual conferences continued throughout the decade.

As civil and social unrest increased, church leaders from across the nation felt increased pressure to help the church in America respond more creatively and redemptively. On November 20, 1961, a consultation on the urban crisis was held on the Bethany Seminary campus in Chicago. Over sixty leaders from more than twenty national church staffs attended. The discussions revealed that no church body was adequately addressing the new urban frontier of America, either at the local congregational level or at the college and seminary training level.

It was decided to invite all national home missions boards who cared to participate to join in a new venture of urban training. The focus was to be on pastors and lay leaders serving in urban areas. Training events were set up for one month, three months, and six months. It was called the Urban Training Center for Christian Mission (UTC). Its prospectus described its purpose this way.

> The Center is to be headquarters for study and demonstration, for reflection and involvement, for implementing the relationship between the gospel and urban culture. It is to be a demonstration school, an urban laboratory, concerned for injecting the Christian way of life into the urban community so that the church may fill its rightful role in this vast segment of contemporary society (UTC 12).

Fourteen national home missions boards formed the first Urban Training Center board of directors. In order to get this experiment set up as quickly as possible, funding was sought from various foundations. The Ford Foundation was the first to respond. It granted $250,000 over a three-year period to help with start-up costs. UTC held its first classes in the fall of 1962. After a year of operations, the UTC board of directors named James Parks Morton as director. He was the inspired, charismatic leader of this interchurch project for ten years. His sense of daring and ability to interpret and relate the gospel to the urban culture made this experiment a most successful one.

The directors of BCEHM voted to participate as a full member of the new training center. They committed five hundred dollars for 1963, and promised to increase their support to two thousand dollars by 1968. The board appointed Louis P. Meyer to be its representative on the UTC board. He served as an officer of its board of directors from 1965 through 1970 (DIR December 1966).

In its ten years of operations, UTC allowed the sponsoring churches the opportunity to use the Chicago area as an urban laboratory. The Church of God had twenty-four pastors who benefited from this rewarding ecumenical training opportunity.

Board Establishes Urban Ministries

As the evidence of the urbanization of America mounted at an alarming rate, the board and staff struggled with how to respond: first, to comprehend this phenomenon; second, to learn what responses would be possible given the limited understanding, budget, and staff.

Pressure for more adequate responses to metropolitan America continued as the decade surged ahead. The staff received requests for help from three congregations in greater Chicago. Each was seeking to be more effective in evangelism. In 1966 the first pilot Urban Ministries Workshop was conducted by staff in Chicago. The design was to get all of the Church of God congregations of the metropolitan area together for two days to discuss their common mission field. A look was taken at the statistical data of the city, the trends, the organizations of the area, and the most critical problems and greatest opportunities. The event was concluded with a covenant agreement called A Declaration of Interdependence. The rationale was that no single congregation could be as effective as a group of congregations responding in service and evangelistic outreach to the needs of the city. Every congregation is needed for a corporate ministry in metropolitan areas.

Within a few months, Church of God congregations of the Detroit metropolitan area asked the staff to help them to increase their evangelistic effectiveness. Staff responded by conducting a second Urban Ministries Workshop. This effort resulted in the Detroit congregations' forming a Greater Detroit Church of God Metropolitan Planning Council to cooperatively face their ministry.

That year in the annual board meeting, the Department of Evangelism reported:

> The pressure from our congregations facing such overwhelming odds and opportunities in metropolitan areas are forcing us to take another look at our budget and program priorities. We are thankful for these breakthroughs, but a massive effort is needed by the entire Board and all of our national agencies if we are to take the crisis seriously. More budget and additional staff are imperative (GB 1967, 2).

The records reveal that a series of meetings on the response of the church to urban America were held by the staff. W. E. Reed invited all agency heads to meet with him and Louis Meyer to discuss the need for joint action in urban affairs. Ideas were shared on the designing of a Church of God urban strategy. All department heads had several meetings to discuss how each department might respond to the urban challenge.

In September, 1967, the board appointed a Metropolitan Task Force to help awaken the church to the urban opportunities, focus more sharply on metropolitan mission and ministry, and structure a better plan and organizational approach to evangelism in metropolitan America. The members of the task force were: Don Collins of Pittsburgh, Pennsylvania; James Massey of Detroit, Michigan; Robert Culp of Toledo, Ohio; David Telfer of Chicago, Illinois; and staff member Louis Meyer. This group refined the Urban Workshop format and drafted a proposal asking the board to create its own urban ministries program.

In his annual report to the General Ministerial Assembly, W. E. Reed sounded the alarm and stated the urgent need for the church to act:

> The fact that seventy American cities were riot-ridden in 1967 is no small cause for concern. If the Church of God has anything to say and do about the present situation, now is the time for the Church to speak and act with corporate strength and wisdom. Because of its assignment to work among minority and ethnic groups of people, to start and develop new churches, and to spearhead the outreach of the Church of God in strategic centers—this Board [Board of Church Extension and Home Missions] cannot escape its responsibility in American society today (AR 1968, 62).

In the May, 1968, annual meeting of the board a formal proposal was presented, requesting that a special Urban Ministries program be set up and staffed by two persons. Because this action required a change in board program and the reallocation of finances, it precipitated a rather vigorous debate.

After all views and cautions were expressed, the board

gave unanimous approval to the proposal to employ immediately a staff person as director of Urban Ministries. The responsibilities of this office would be:

> To research the needs of Church of God congregations in metropolitan areas, to help these congregations become aware of their corporate strengths and resources in fulfilling God's mission in metropolis; to work with the departments of the Board—and with other agencies of the Church of God—in developing a more effective strategy in evangelistic outreach to all peoples living in metropolis; and in developing the best possible stewardship of resources. . . . And also
>
> That the Board authorize the appointment of a second staff person by mid-year 1969, as Field Coordinator of Urban Ministries. The responsibilities of this office would include: working directly with metropolitan areas where the Church of God has five or more congregations in the development and implementation of goals, objectives, structures, programs and financial resources for corporate fulfillment of their mission, and work with the Department of Evangelism and the Director of Urban Ministries in pilot projects resulting from the corporate planning of congregations in metropolitan areas. . . . And
>
> That the Board authorize its President, its Executive Secretary, and the three Department Secretaries to serve as a Standing Committee on Urban Ministries: to counsel the secretary of the Department of Evangelism regarding the future of the work of the Church of God in metropolis; recommend to the General Board plans of action whereby the Board can better fulfill its corporate assignment in city slums . . . in large cities and strategic centers; and review program priorities and budget adjustments as required to maximize effectiveness in offering the resources of the board—financial and leadership—to the tasks of evangelistic and missionary outreach (GB May 1968, G).

Since the most experienced urban leaders of the Church of God at that time were African-American pastors, the proposal requested that the new director of Urban Ministries be selected from this experienced group. However, it took over a year to secure the full-time services of a director of Urban Ministries. In the interim, a contractual agreement was worked out with Melvyn F. Hester, of New York City, to serve as consultant on urban ministries. His major assignment was to direct Urban Workshops and conduct area and regional urban conferences. He had assisted the staff in the designing of this new ministry (DIR 7 October 1968).

Soon leadership was secured to fill the two urban ministries staff positions. This was made financially possible because of a fifteen thousand dollar start-up grant from the Woman's Missionary Society. David A. Telfer was employed as field coordinator of Urban Ministries on January 1, 1969. One year later, Edward L. Foggs became the full-time director of Urban Ministries, and the first African-American staff person of the board. In July, 1975, Richard Goode assumed this position, and in July, 1984, Sethard Beverly was called to serve the board and church in this important ministry. This program emphasis was met with wide favor by pastors and churches in the innercity areas of the nation. It has increased in importance, effectiveness, and acceptance across the church for more than two decades.

Issues of Race Relations and Human Rights

One of the assigned tasks of the board was that of keeping before the church its responsibility to establish a stronger witness among the minorities of America. Throughout its history the board has used a variety of approaches and methods to fulfill this task.

BCEHM minutes of each decade of its existence reveal an ongoing concern and focus of attention on race relations, human rights, and special outreach ministries among various minority and ethnic cultures of the nation. In the general board minutes in 1946, is this notation:

> The officers of the Board reported efforts to increase cooperative work in Negro projects and to enlarge the church's missionary outreach to this great group of people in our land (DIR 14 June 1946, 3).
>
> Through Gabriel Dixon, a member of this Board, and other leaders of our colored work, the Board hopes to develop a strong missionary program for the benefit of the great Negro population of this county (GB 15 June 1946, 6).

The BCEHM appointed from its membership an Interracial Committee. In 1947 the minutes note a suggestion that this committee of this board work with other like committees for an effective presentation to the church re: Negro work (GB 14 June 1947).

The General Ministerial Assembly had an Interracial Commission. Several concerns had been voiced by African-American Church of God leaders regarding racial designations in the Church of God yearbook. In the 1947 meeting of the General Ministerial Assembly, R. Dewitt Howell reported that the Interracial Commission of the GMA had undertaken the following program: 1) to hold regional interracial meetings; 2) to promote interdenominational, inter-racial activities; and 3) to eliminate racial discrimination from the yearbook, camp meetings and other places in our own church programs (GMA 17 June 1947).

Unrest and growing impatience on the part of minorities accelerated in the late 1950s and the 1960s. The General Ministerial Assembly responded by appointing a Study Committee on Race Relations. It was to serve from 1957 to 1962. The more study that was done in the area of civil rights and racial equality in the church, the more it became apparent that the Church of God had not kept up with the times and the demand for racial justice in light of its own message of unity. This became clearer as dialogues between national church agency leaders and African-American leaders took place.

The tragedies and inequities revealed in the early 1960s cried out for some response. The pressure of events, pressure of the gospel, pressure of minorities wanting justice and equality without further delay, and pressure of a bad personal and institutional conscience, converged to evoke action for institutional and behavioral changes.

By 1964 the assembly created a Commission on Social Concerns. The purpose and actions of the newly elected commission were limited. It was a study group. It could raise issues, study them, and recommend action, but it could not do programming or make pronouncements on behalf of the church. Its prerogative was described as "Speaking to the church, but not for the church." Although, in the minds of some, this did not go far enough, it was a start on behalf of the General Ministerial Assembly to position itself for becoming better informed on the social issues of the nation.

In 1963 the Board of Church Extension and Home Missions had received a plot of land in Anderson, Indiana, and developed it as a subdivision for housing. In 1964 it sold one of the lots in this real estate development to an African-American family. This created quite a stir in the city real estate community and among a few of the residents in the subdivision. After much of the original negative reaction had died down, a real estate agent in the community privately expressed words of appreciation to the board for its action. He said that this act had helped to break the racial housing barriers in the city. Now it would be easier for him and other realtors to sell property to other minorities anywhere in the city. The board of directors' minutes suggest that this action was taken because it was right. The conversation with the realtor helped the board to realize the power of its influence in the marketplace on such issues as racial justice and equality.

Even though an agency has in its charter the assignment for keeping before the church the needs of minorities, this does not guarantee or imply that it is itself free of institutional racism. There was a series of dialogues and consultations in the 1960s between the board or staff and African-American leaders which helped to bring about some much-needed changes in the organization and policies of the board.

One such consultation occurred November 4-5, 1965, at the office of the board. It was called, Prayer Retreat and Consultation. Dr. Harry Richardson, president of the Interdenominational Theological Center of Atlanta, was the guest leader. In this meeting these topics were discussed: "Trends for the Next Ten Years," "Theological Implications of the Social Revolution," "Pitfalls to Avoid," and "The Role of the Home Missions Board in the Freedom Movement." This event helped to open the door for some fresh, frank sharing of views and feelings.

There were several of these face-to-face meetings between the board and members of the Church of God Black Caucus. Some of the primary issues brought to the board in these consultations for its consideration and action had to do with the fairness of its loan policies for minority and low income congregations. The board was called upon to refuse loans to congregations seeking to flee a racially changing neighborhood, to make a moral audit of its invested reserve funds, and also to explain why there were so few minority staff members and no African-American leaders serving either as officers or as members of the board of directors. It was also strongly urged that the board make urban ministries its highest program priority.

This series of consultations and the subsequent dialogue were painful at times, but overall brought about greater understanding for both groups. The African-Americans discovered why certain loan policies were in effect and just how the lending program of the board worked, and the board had its consciousness raised as to the views and perspective of minority persons. It saw that it did need to clarify and simplify its loan packet and materials, and that more attention needed to be given to offering additional staff guidance and counsel to minority congregations seeking a loan or general advisory service. The BCEHM did conduct an audit of its invested reserve funds to make sure none was invested in companies or organizations with poor records in human rights.

The dialogues also resulted in speeding up the process of the board's putting into action its plans for a broader representation of board members from the minorities and other underrepresented groups in the church. Since that time, through the nomination and election process, additional minorities have been elected to the board. As of 1990, of the twenty-one members of the board, four were African-American, two Hispanic, and four women. Ten were lay persons. Also, minorities were elected to the board of directors and as officers of the corporation. Today the BCEHM is an agency more representative of the Church of God constituency.

$100,000 Special Project

The expanding program of missionary outreach in the United States and Mexico created an urgent need for capital improvements in the first part of the decade. The board requested that home missions be designated as the recipient of the World Service special project for 1965-1966, for $100,000. The appeal was granted.

Forty thousand dollars was to be used in Mexico toward the erection of three new church buildings and the building of a new dormitory at La Buena Tierra Training School. Twenty thousand dollars was for native Americans at Lapwai, Idaho, Wounded Knee, South Dakota, and Klagetoh, Arizona. Eighteen thousand dollars was for leadership development and for building repair of African-American churches in the South. Twenty thousand dollars was for the urban-rural centers of Brooklyn, New York, and Appalachia, in Kentucky. Of the $100,000 goal, ninety three thousand dollars was received. This gave a great boost to the work of the church in these areas of home missions.

Home Missions Highlights

In an effort to give more staff time to specific needs and opportunities in home mission areas, the board added a full-time secretary of the Home Missions Department. W. E. Reed had been dividing his time between home missions and the chief executive officer responsibilities of the board. Maurice Caldwell joined the staff as secretary of home missions on September 1, 1962.

W. E. Reed and Lester Crose, executive of the Missionary Board, made a tour of Latin America in 1961. They were interested in more cooperative work between the various countries and between the two mission boards. As a result of these efforts, the first Inter-American Conference was held in August, 1962, in Mexico City, under the joint sponsorship of the two boards. It was reported that:

> More than fifty delegates represented our churches in Cuba, Panama, Costa Rica, Guatemala, Mexico, and Southwestern U.S.A. . . . This mission to Latin America is one mission. Our Board and the Missionary Board are working very closely in several areas of common concern including: Cooperative Evangelism, Training of Workers, and Spanish Literature. . . . Latin America is the only part of the world where converts are being made at a higher rate than the growth of population (AR 1962, 2)!

The second Inter-American Conference was held in 1964 in Guatemala.

A sound color film, *Mission to Manuel,* was made in 1962 portraying the board's work in Saltillo. More than two hundred congregations viewed the film. It was an effective tool, telling the story of the mission in Mexico and the training school there.

After five years of Maurice's creative leadership as secretary of the Department of Home Missions, Maurice and Dondeena Caldwell felt burdened to start a Church of God congregation in Mexico City. They went under the board's sponsorship in February, 1967. They were asked to serve also as coordinators of all Spanish work for the department. In June, 1967, Tom A. Smith was called to the staff as secretary of home missions.

Both missionary boards worked very closely together in the decade of the 1960s. The Missionary Board was gearing up for a decade-long thrust into Latin America in the 1970s. There was a series of conversations between the two boards and their staffs concerning the administration of the work in Mexico and La Buena Tiera Training School. A Resolution on Transfer of Mission Administration was presented to the General Assembly on June 18, 1969. It called for the assembly's concurrence in the transfer of the administrative responsibilities for Mexico from the Board of Church Extension and Home Missions to the Missionary Board of the Church of God. The resolution passed unanimously (GA 1969, 24-25.).

Time to Adjust Structure Again

Times of rapid social change sooner or later force organizations and institutions to adjust in some way to the new situation. This was true for the board in this decade.

For several years, some members of the board of directors had been appointed by the general board rather than elected by the regular process. Originally, members who resided in and around Anderson were named to serve in order to save travel expenses. But as the work load of policy decision making increased, and as requirements for the operation of a multimillion dollar institution became more complicated, several elected members of the board felt that too many far-reaching decisions were being made by the board of directors without input from the general board.

In the April, 1966, annual board meeting this issue came sharply into focus. Gene Newberry, chairman of the board, appointed a Planning and Study Committee, and instructed it to review all facets of the issue and come back with specific recommendations for strengthening the board's corporate structure.

The final recommendations adopted by the general board included these: 1) increase the membership of the board from fifteen to twenty-one members; 2) the directors to be ten in number, including the three officers of the board, plus seven elected from the twenty-one board members; 3) the board of directors to meet quarterly; 4) create an executive committee of at least five persons, including the three officers, plus two chosen from the board of directors; 5) set up a nominating committee for filling expired terms of members.

A major objection to this new structure was the cost of bringing six new members to annual board meetings, and the annual cost of holding four meetings of the board of directors. But in the final analysis the prevailing feeling was that these costs were necessary in order for the board to deal responsibly with the enlarged task of policy making and oversight of the growing agency. The plan of restructure was ratified by the General Assembly in June, 1967, and was operational by June, 1968.

A New Office Building

As noted in the previous chapter, growing demands for service increased the need for a larger staff and for more office equipment. The office building located on the campground was very crowded. During this eight-year period, the joke among staff was that the offices were so crowded, one had to step out into the hall to change one's mind!

Since the board was in the information sharing business in relation to the planning of church buildings, the planning of its own office building was seen as a real challenge. Three years of careful study were put into this project. It was felt that the planning of the new building was an opportunity to demonstrate to congregations the importance of studying future needs, and of determining the exact purpose of its mission before a building is built.

Planning for the next decade or more was crucial as far as this project was concerned. Wise planning was aided by good architectural counsel. It was felt strongly that the building should reflect openness and a feeling of welcome to those who would come for a visit or to do business. Johnson and Ritchhart and Associates of Anderson, Indiana, were the architects for the project. They received national recognition for the design and function of this building.

Early in the planning process some board members expressed a concern that other agencies be contacted to join in the projected new building. The general board minutes for April, 1962, record the concern that a new building should include both the Missionary Board and the Woman's Missionary Society, so that the three offices dealing with missions could work more closely together (GB April 1962). Contacts were made with the other two organizations to test their interest in one building with space for all three offices. The timing was not right for either of them, so plans were drawn for the projected needs of the Board of Church Extension and Home Missions.

The major hurdle was the cost of such a venture. This issue was solved through the generous annuity gift of $250,000 by C. C. and Ina Mansfield of Oklahoma. The new office building, 16,600 square feet on two levels, was built without a mortgage. The land was dedicated at Third Street and Nursery Road in Anderson, in June, 1964. Staff moved into the facility in October, 1965, and it was dedicated during the international convention in June, 1966.

Refinement of Advisory Services

As the pace of life quickens, and changes are more rapid, planning and decision making at all levels becomes more complicated. This was certainly true in this decade. Often, congregations and pastors were uncertain how to determine whether to remodel or to build a new structure. In response to this need, the board refined its services in general counseling.

Many congregations found themselves in situations of having to face up to a church building program with no experience or knowledge of how to proceed. There were the issues of how to estimate construction costs, how to deal with complicated building codes, and the legal implications of a building program. Pre-building planning was necessary due to the many local and state building codes and requirements. It was also true because the process of applying for and meeting the requirements of a first mortgage loan was getting more complex. There was need for guidelines to help a congregation follow sound credit rules for a good church loan. During this decade the board made a staff person available for general counseling to help congregations facing these issues.

Other congregations needed help in taking a look at why they were not growing. Was it program? Was it because the present building was too crowded or because there was no place to park? Again, special advisory services were provided by staff.

Architectural Advisory Service was a very popular service of the board. Through the architectural staff members, it helped over fifty congregations in the 1960s.

From the beginning, the board offered general counseling, but in the 1960s it became a more studied, personalized service. From this decade on, the counseling and advisory services of the board were more focused, and tailored for a variety of situations. Through the years these services were called by a variety of names—General Advisory Service, General Counseling, and Church Development Studies but the objective always was to increase the understanding of the pastor and congregation regarding their particular needs. It was an effective ministry. Church building planning and erection greatly improved in this decade. The church got better, more functional facilities for each dollar invested. John W. V. Smith wrote:

> The Church of God also showed considerable growth throughout the period (1963-1972) in terms of property values. Local church property climbed from $73,040,888 in 1963 to $149,144,810 in 1972. Many church building programs were under way during this period to build new and/or expanded facilities (Smith 1980, 380).

The frank and open dialogue with the Black Caucus in this decade brought attention back to the task of simplifying and helping the church understand the services available from the board and how a congregation or state group might avail itself of the services needed.

Conditional Deeding of Church Property

Down through the history of the Church of God, there have been occasions where some independent group got control of local church property. In order to discourage this from happening, the General Assembly established a plan whereby Church of God congregations could conditionally deed their property to the church in case it ever fell into disuse or was threatened by take-over from some outside faction or group. The Board of Church Extension and Home Missions was assigned administrative responsibility for this procedure.

The issue of conditionally deeding property was raised

with each congregation getting a church loan from the board. Because of local autonomy in the Church of God, the BCEHM used only the power of suggestion, never demanding that this be done. This service has been offered for decades. From the 1950s on, the board worked with state and district evangelism committees, urging them to help new congregations to see that the conditional clause was included in the local deed. The plan was promoted more vigorously in the decade of the 1960s and thereafter. The board produced a booklet, *How to Safeguard the Title to Local Church Property,* to explain the concept and procedure to congregations. This plan has been an effective tool in protecting church property.

Other Program Items in Brief

The history of the board in the 1960s as well as in other decades reveals too many events and activities to be written in this digest of its program services, but below is a list of several program events not covered in this chapter.

Laymen Lift Cabinet. In 1961 and 1962, there was growing recognition that the Department of Church Building needed invested dollars for the board's church building loan program. A cabinet of twenty-five lay leaders from a wide geographical area were asked to help. There was an annual meeting for planning and idea exchange over the next three years. The experiment did help to get the board's story out to a wider group in the church. The treasurer of the board retired in 1963, and the Laymen Lift Cabinet was not reappointed after 1964.

New Church Development on a Shoestring. To review the financial records of the board in the area of cooperative evangelism and church extension, one is surprised that so much was accomplished with so little money. Most of the time the board had to limit its monthly budget support to a new church project to only $50.00 per month. This was matched by the state group and the local congregation. Thus a minimum of $150.00 per month was raised for each new project; with wise planning and clear communication among all parties of this cooperative plan, it worked quite well. For the 1960s, the board helped support fifty-eight new congregations with a total expenditure of $135,500. In the first fifty years of the board, 1921-1971, $448,588 was distributed in the form of monthly budget grants to help establish 245 new congregations.

Evangelism Events. In this decade of expanding horizons in evangelism the board helped to sponsor several ecumenical events. In November, 1969, various evangelical groups sponsored their first nationwide Evangelism Festival in Minneapolis, Minnesota. The board provided assistance for forty-four Church of God pastors to attend. The Central Department of Evangelism of the National Council of Churches held the Annual National Conference on Evangelism from 1965 to 1968 at a retreat center in Green Lake, Wisconsin. These conferences explored personal evangelism, evangelism in the public arena, and the various shapes of Christian obedience in times of social upheaval.

The board made scholarships available for several Church of God pastors to attend these enriching and mind-expanding events. Also, the BCEHM participated interdenominationally with a variety of other church groups in trying to discover how to make the gospel relevant in new towns. In Columbia, Maryland, created from the dreams and plans of a developer, the board experimented for several years on how to start congregations in new towns. The new town movement in the United States did not expand much beyond the 1960s and 1970s.

Internal Affairs

Cecil J. Brown resigned from the staff as director of Church Building Campaigns in 1961, and took an assignment with World Service in stewardship. James Austin assumed the role of director, which he held until his retirement in October, 1969. J. L. Brown joined the CBC team in January, 1961, and served in this capacity until his retirement in April, 1971.

W. E. Reed's title of general secretary was changed to executive secretary in 1961, and several shifts in staff responsibilities were made.

Victor Gritzmacher was named as secretary of the Department of Church Building in June, 1962. In 1970 he was assigned a new task as secretary of the Office of Financial Development where he served until he retired in December, 1972.

Elver Adcock retired in September, 1963, after over forty years of continuous service to the board. Nora Angus resigned in May, 1963, after completing twenty-five years with the board.

Tom Kurtz was the board's accountant from December, 1960 until he resigned in July, 1963. Glenn Bair joined the accounting staff in 1961, and served as head of the department from 1963 to 1965. Raymond Troutman came to the board as head of the Accounting Department in December, 1965. He served the board in various capacities until his retirement in 1967. Dorothy Miller joined the department in 1967 in the role of bookkeeper. She served as head of bookkeeping from 1980 until her retirement in 1984. Edgar Barnett, after twenty-five years of service to the BCEHM as a bookkeeper, retired in April, 1965. June Rohrback came into the employment of the board in 1965 as a member of the Accounting Department.

With the heavy increase of work in church loans, Merle Bosworth came to the staff in August, 1963, as loan officer. He served in the Department of Church Building until his untimely death in 1969, caused by a heart attack.

Joann Howard (Smith) became a member of the staff in 1961 as a secretary and worked her way up to the office of secretary of the corporation. She left the employ of the board in September, 1983.

In 1969, Isham (Joe) Crane was assigned from the Department of Evangelism to be the associate secretary of the Department of Church Building. He became secretary of that department in 1970.

Summary of the Decade

Racial, ethnic, social, and institutional unrest were the major driving forces of this decade. Every secular and religious institution was affected by the boiling cauldron of unrest and rising minority expectations. It is the nature of institutions to protect themselves and, as a rule, to prefer the status quo over any major changes, but in the decade of the 1960s the status quo had to give way to change.

In the midst of great social turmoil, if individuals and institutions really listen and react to events from the viewpoint of what is right rather than what has been the past practice, helpful change can take place. Creative responses often come forth in the most disruptive of times.

The decade of the sixties stands as one of the most innovative in the history of the BCEHM. This dynamic decade helped the board broaden its understanding of evangelism and find new ways to respond to the needs of the church and society. Painful struggle with racial and minority confrontations, several years of program budget deficits, and the scramble to adjust institutional structure to meet modern needs, all contributed to a more informed board, staff, and program service. By the end of this decade, the board and other national agencies of the church were more aware of and more effectively responding to some of the real needs of the great metropolitan areas of the land.

The board's changes and enlarged vision were due, in part, to its strategy of using a wide variety of volunteers and advisory people. The appointing of the Church and Community Committee, New Church Development Task

Force, Laymen Lift Committee, Metropolitian Task Force, and others, provided a valuable diversity of feedback on the perceptions and desires of the church, and on what was happening in society.

The basic services of the BCEHM for the next twenty years were heavily influenced by this decade. An enlarged vision and understanding of evangelism and a clearer understanding of the views and needs of the ethnic minorities of the nation served the board and staff well for the years to follow.

Chapter 7

Regulations, Inflation and Team Building

(1970-1979)

For many people the decade of the 1970s was a decade of disillusionment. The rosy idealism of America at the start of the 1960s turned into disenchantment, cynicism, and bitterness. The positive American vision changed radically to the nightmare of Vietnam and Watergate.

On the international scene the East-West détente was quickly silenced by the Soviet invasion of Afghanistan. The peace settlement agreed to by Israel and Egypt did not come to pass because of the revolutionary changes in Iran and utter chaos in Lebanon. The ever-present Palestinian problem helped to fuel international terrorism which, in turn, affected all nations of the globe.

As the decade began, the United States was still deeply entrenched in Vietnam. There was an explosion of refugees from southeast Asia. The United States' withdrawal "without victory" from Vietnam greatly damaged American morale. This national hurt was made worse by the Watergate scandal which swept Richard Nixon from the White House as America's first president in history to resign the presidency.

From a world perspective, the most disturbing development was the ruthless spread of international terrorism.

Political violence is as old as the human race, but the terrorism of the 1970s brought a new level of kidnappings and deaths. Everyday citizens now joined the front line casualties of the undeclared war. This decade witnessed airline hijackings in Jordan and Uganda, and bombings in major city streets by terrorists in Northern Ireland, Britain, Italy, and Canada.

The western democracies were experiencing economic decline and industrial unrest. In 1973 the OPEC cartel radically raised the price of crude oil. This action sent shock waves through the industrialized world. By 1977 fifteen million people were registered as unemployed in the United Kingdom, United States, France, West Germany, Italy, Japan, and Canada. Energy conservation and the search for alternate sources of energy gained momentum.

By 1979 the Shah of Iran was swept from power as the tide of Islamic fundamentalism returned the Ayatollah Khomeini to Tehran. This event marked the beginning of the American hostage crisis.

American morale sank lower when President Jimmy Carter seemed helpless in the face of the hostage crisis. This resulted in a further decline of confidence in America's self-appointed guardianship of the free world.

Other memorable events of this decade included: the U.S. spacecraft Apollo 14 landed on the moon in 1971; President Nixon and Leonid Brezhnev of the U.S.S.R. signed the SALT treaty, limiting and freezing nuclear missile systems in both nations; Nixon met with Mao Tse-tung in China to try to normalize relations between the two nations; in 1973, leaders of the American Indian Movement (AIM) took hostages at Wounded Knee, using the Church of God church building there as its headquarters; 800,000 boat people, mainly Chinese and middle-class Vietnamese, became refugees from the repressive communist regime in South Vietnam; President Carter, Anwar Sadat of Egypt, and Menachem Begin of Israel met for the 1978 Camp David summit; and the worst nuclear accident in United

States history happened in 1979 at Three Mile Island. This event gave a major warning to the nation with respect to relying primarily on nuclear power as a source of electricity.

National and world events reminded humankind that to identify causes of unrest, and to find new paths to peace, one must factor into the equation the part religion plays in the causing of conflict and war as well as its role in resolving conflicts. The civil unrest and war of the 1970s cannot be properly understood without recognizing the religious factor. In Iran, Iraq, Lebanon, Israel, India, Pakistan, Northern Ireland, and many other troubled spots, religion was a causal factor in the conflicts, and the role of religion must be carefully considered if solutions and lasting peace are to be realized.

A New Chief Executive

This decade began for the Board of Church Extension and Home Missions with the task of selecting a new chief executive officer. In 1969, W. E. Reed accepted the invitation to become the executive secretary of the Executive Council of the Church of God, effective in January, 1971. The board started its search process to find a new leader.

The April 28, 1970, general board minutes record that the directors presented the name of Marvin J. Hartman as the nominee to be W. E. Reed's successor. The committee gave its rationale. He had wide experience in national agency work. He had served as a staff secretary in the World Service office, and as a pastor had served for five years on the Division of World Service. He had also served as chairperson of the Executive Council and as a member of the National Budget Committee. W. E. Reed gave his full endorsement of the candidate, stating that Mr. Hartman was "forthright, open, creative, highly respected, and had a good team spirit." There was a motion "to elect Marvin J. Hartman to a five-year term to become executive secretary-treasurer of this board as Dr. Reed's successor, subject to ratification by the General Assembly. Motion carried unanimously." Hartman came to the staff in September, 1970, for a four-month overlap with Reed. He became the board's fourth chief executive on January 1, 1971.

Reorganization

In a changing society, an agency dedicated to serving the needs of the church must be flexible and must frequently modify its organization to enable it to serve effectively. In every decade of the board's history there was some organizational reorganization and/or staff and program adjustment.

By 1968 there was growing awareness that such adjustments were needed. The concern was to adjust to the realities of the times in order to serve the church more helpfully and to utilize the best skills of the current staff. W. E. Reed had asked certain staff members to work with him to draft a plan for staff and program reorganization. Over a period of months, the plan was reviewed by directors and staff. In the April, 1970 general board meeting, the final plan of reorganization was approved:

"Moved (Reid-Heffren) that we adopt the 8-point restructure plan, with the understanding that the executive secretary-treasurer will see that Christian witness development receives high priority and the church at large knows it; with review next year and again the next year. Motion carried unanimously."

The plan of reorganization included several major changes. It called for the merger of two departments—Home Missions and Evangelism—into one Department of Evangelism and Missions. In this department there was to be added a staff person whose special assignment would be Christian witness development.

The plan also called for a new Office of Financial Development. The responsibilities of this office included: the soliciting of gifts for programs of missions and evangelism;

securing investments for the making of church loans; advising in estate planning; and creating promotional materials. V. J. Gritzmacher was assigned this responsibility.

The most innovative part of the restructure was the creation of the first Church of God agency Office of Program Research and Planning. Louis P. Meyer was asked to assume the responsibilities of this office. The minutes note:

> This office has been charged with the following tasks: (a) developing a process of evaluation of existing Board programs; (b) developing a process of input to staff to keep them aware of the sweeping changes of our world; (c) seeing that the process of planning always includes the possibility for new options and new programs; and (d) serving as liaison with states, area leaders and organizations to discover the problems, needs, and opportunities as seen from their perspective (AR 1970, 15).

Then there were many changes of staff responsibilities and a shifting of assignments. Tom Smith was assigned the newly merged Department of Evangelism and Missions. Joe Crane was assigned the administrative duties of the Department of Church Building.

One major hesitancy was expressed by the board. Since this plan had been under study and revision for two years, How did the new chief executive feel about it? Because he had been thoroughly briefed on the plan during the job interview process, Hartman stated that he "considered the new organizational chart [plan] very workable, especially with the team spirit of the staff (GB 28 April 1970, 2)."

Fiftieth Anniversary Celebration

The year after the restructure and the arrival of the new chief executive, the Board of Church Extension and Home

Missions celebrated its fiftieth anniversary. The twelve-month celebration started with the June, 1971, General Assembly of the church in Anderson, Indiana. The June 16 minutes of the General Assembly record these events of the celebration:

> Gene Newberry, [chairman of the board] calling the celebration a "sentimental journey," invited the very first Executive Secretary of the Board of Church Extension and Home Missions, R. R. Byrum, to join him at the front of the auditorium. The Assembly welcomed Mr. Byrum with a warm standing ovation.
>
> Mr. Newberry announced that every Executive Secretary who had served the Board was present in the Assembly, and introduced and called forth Elver Adcock, second Executive Secretary; W. E. Reed, third Executive Secretary; and present Executive Secretary, Marvin J. Hartman.
>
> . . . Marvin Hartman, proceeded to call forward all who have served as a home missionary for the Board, all who have received monthly budget assistance from the Board or serve a church that has received monthly budget assistance, all present Board members, and all who have served as Board members, and all present staff members. He asked those in the Assembly to stand who have benefited by a church loan, architectural advisory service, church building campaign, or loan consultant service. It was a very impressive sight to see the host of people stand to their feet.
>
> Mr. Hartman announced with enthusiasm that "We have, here, something to celebrate, and since what has been accomplished has been done by the Church, it is just and right that we celebrate together."

Arlo F. Newell, chair of the assembly, then offered a prayer of thanksgiving and praise for what the church had accomplished in fifty years of corporate ministry through this board and prayed for continued guidance for the future of this service agency.

Published materials for the celebration reveal that in its first fifty years the board had made seventeen hundred loans for a total of $12,700,000. It is interesting to note that $5,976,757 of this total had been loaned during the decade of the 1960s. At the time of the celebration, the board was servicing 350 church loans, aggregating $4,250,000. In fifty years the church had sent out through this board 173 persons to various homeland mission fields. These workers had helped to establish seven congregations in Alaska, ten native American mission stations, twenty-four congregations and a training school in Mexico. By 1971 staff members had assisted 350 congregations to raise pledges of over $14,475,000 to build new church facilities. In church extension work over these fifty years, the board was instrumental, working with states and districts, in establishing 248 congregations of the Church of God in forty-five states, the District of Columbia, and Canada.

In the annual board meeting of April, 1972, Hartman stated in his report:

> During these fifty years of change, the Church has been working through our Board. We may be tempted to look upon what has been done as insignificant or modest, and it may well be. But to the congregation and the individuals who have been redeemed in that congregation, to the minister and the trustees who have received help in time of need, the service rendered by this Board has not been insignificant. It has been valuable. This Board has been an instrument through which people's lives have been changed by the power of God. This is still our task. It has not changed in spite of the changing times.

There had been serious talk of program cutbacks in 1969 and 1970 because of a shortage of program funds. As could be expected, this had a negative effect on the staff. However, the fiftieth anniversary celebration had helped board members and staff to gain a new perspective on and appreciation for the board's mission. The stimulus of the new decade and the coming of a new chief executive inspired renewed commitment to do an even better job over the next fifty years. There was a sense of expectancy in the air. This can be detected in the opening paragraph of the 1972 annual report of the secretary of Program Research and Planning:

> Times of stress and strain offer us the opportunity either to cower or be courageous: to be evasive or inventive. It is great to be a part of a Board that is attempting to accept the challenge of leadership in these turbulent but tremendous days of opportunity. These are days calling for new ideas to be tested, new strategies to be adopted, new forces to be redeployed and old structures to be loosened to contain the winds of the Spirit.

During the first two years of the decade, five new staff members were added. These new ones needed to be trained and oriented to a teamship ministry. Another dynamic at work became evident in the mid-1960s. As has been mentioned in the previous chapter, some general board members felt they did not have enough say in policy matters and budget priorities. At that time, the general board membership was enlarged to twenty-one and the board of directors to ten members. The organizational structure had been improved, but still needed was a well-orchestrated planning unit, including the general board, directors, and program staff. Teamship became one of the new executive secretary-treasurer's highest priorities for the decade. The following paragraph appeared in his 1972 annual report to the general board:

> For the past two years one of our highest goals has been to develop a sense of teamship—not only among

staff members but also between staff and the members of the Board. We believe we should all be mutually supportive of each other's responsibilities; and we are determined to continue to find ways of making this teamship more efficient, supportive, and relevant. We believe we have made progress, in spite of the fact that within the last three years each staff person has had new responsibilities. We are experimenting and discovering new evidence that this is one staff serving the Church. While it is necessary to have clear lines of responsibility in the internal functions of the Board, we seek to project an image of the Board and its staff serving as one unit for the Church.

The task of becoming a harmonious team required a lot of time and effort. The secretary of the Office of Program Research and Planning was asked by the new executive to come up with a rough draft statement on team ministry. This outline was taken as the beginning point, and the entire program staff worked and reworked it for a year, until a final page-and-a-half statement was adopted by the group as their statement. It defined teamship as a feeling and attitude which included a commitment on the part of each staff member to wholeness, teamship, and working together for one board, staff, and program. "Many program services, but one board and one staff," became a basic theme of the decade.

New board members from time to time had expressed the feeling that the magnitude of the board's assignments, financial responsibilities, and expanding program was overwhelming. The general board met only once a year. Some new members said that by the time they had a grasp of the board's scope and work, their terms had expired. To address this need, a planned curriculum, Orientation for New Board Members was developed. Since 1974, every elected board member has received special training for his/her newly-assumed task. The two-day orientation sessions include a study of the board's charter, history, organizational structure, program services, budget, and financial matters. The experience ends with a discussion of the role of the general board, the board of directors, and the meaning of teamship for each individual board member.

Job Goals and Performance

With each new decade the work and services of the board became more demanding on management and staff. This was more obvious in the 1970s. The church's need for more advisory services in the areas of church building, fund raising, evangelism, church extension, and home missions work often exceeded the staff's time and its ability to respond as quickly as needed.

There were times when it appeared the board was operating a curb service operation. The staff and board had always put the needs of the church as a first priority, but sometimes the requests for field service were not central to the BCEHM charter. Early in the decade a policy was developed to have each program staff member set his or her primary performance goals for the year. These goals were reviewed by the responsible department head each summer for the coming program year. All goals were then reviewed and coordinated by the Office of Program Research and Planning and management to avoid overlap.

A Salary Administration Manual was written and adopted by the board. For the rest of the decade and into the 1980s this manual was the basis for all performance reviews and salary adjustments.

One Board Publication

Various newsletters and department publications were mailed to the church from the board in the 1960s. These included: *Evangelism News, The Church Builder, The Rural Fellowship Dispatch, The Home Missions Newsletter,* and others. In 1970 all publications from the board were combined into one quarterly publication, *FOCUS*. This was an effort to tell the board's story more effectively, and to give concrete expression to the newly declared teamship of the BCEHM, its staff, and program. By the end of the decade *FOCUS* was being mailed to thirty thousand Church of God persons.

Staff Sabbaticals

A study of the history of this board reveals that it is like other church-related and not-for-profit organizations. There are seldom, if ever, adequate program funds to meet the demands of the church. This inevitably results in asking the staff to do the best job possible with the limited dollars and time available. Each staff member is given extra assignments because the budget does not permit the employment of new personnel. In the decade of the 1970s the general board began to voice concern that some of the program staff were having to spend too many days out of town. It was felt that too heavy travel commitments robbed the staff of time for personal and professional improvement and for keeping up with the times, the trends of society, and the needs of the church.

A study was conducted. It revealed that program staff members were out of town from seventy-five to 268 days a year. For the rest of the decade, the board annually monitored each staff person's days out of the office. A limit of two hundred days a year per staff member was suggested for out-of-town work.

Studies were made as to what other church groups and not-for-profit organizations were doing to address these concerns. It was decided that one approach to help staff stay alert and on the cutting edge would be to provide the opportunity every five years for qualifying members to take sabbatical leaves. The executive committee of the board reviewed the management proposal for such a policy (EX 8

February 1977). In its annual meeting in April, 1977, the general board voted unanimously for the proposal, and the new staff sabbatical plan became policy (GB 15 April 1977).

Emergency Succession Plan

For several years there had been a concern as to procedure if suddenly, because of health or accident, the president or treasurer could not adequately serve. In 1976 various board members expressed concern that some orderly procedure be developed to handle such an occurrence. The administrative staff drafted a proposal for the board's consideration. In the 1977 annual meeting, the general board discussed and voted the Emergency Plan of Succession of President and Treasurer.

Complicating Regulations

Each decade has its own unique economic pattern. Inflation was a reality of the early 1970s, and inflation increases uncertainty. This is particularly true for an organization charged with the responsibility of making church building loans. To provide and service first mortgage loans for ten to fifteen years per loan with funds the church people invest for only one to five years creates a vulnerability gap. The risk factor increases as inflation increases. The disparity between the interest rates the board pays to investors and what it charges the congregations becomes very real and often complex. More and more time in quarterly directors' meetings and annual board meetings was devoted to the financial aspects of the board's work.

Then a totally new regulation was imposed on the board by the states in which it did business. In the early part of the decade two or three religious groups or organizations had taken money invested with them and used it for operations. When the investors wanted to withdraw their money, it was not available. The securities commissions in each of the states where this happened rightfully forced these groups to make restitution. Soon states across the nation began forcing all religious organizations to register and meet certain requirements. The state of Indiana enacted a law requiring all religious groups within its borders to comply with the security regulations.

In resistance to this added burden, the issue of the separation of church and state was raised by some church groups. The BCEHM explored all options. It had been in business over fifty years and had never defaulted in honoring any investor's request to withdraw funds, including interest. It would be a very costly procedure to comply in every state where the board did business, but the argument finally hinged on the issue of ethics. Although the board had a good record in sound business and in honoring the trust church people had placed in it, this was the law of the state; as a responsible organization, the board felt that it ought to comply. The executive committee voted to work out an orderly, deliberate plan for compliance in Indiana and in other states (EX 17 November 1976).

This decision was reported to the General Assembly of the Church of God with this brief statement by the president of the board:

> Recent laws enacted in Indiana and many other states make it necessary for not-for-profit organizations selling securities (notes) either to have an approved registration or an approved exemption. The Board of Church Extension and Home Missions has gone on record instructing management to comply with the laws of each state regarding security matters. We are in process of registering in those states where registration is required and where the Board does business (AR 1978, 60).

The process of registration took several years. Each state has different laws and regulations of compliance. In most states, registration has to be repeated each year. This process added considerable cost to the board's annual operations. Because of its stringent requirements, the cost for securities registration in one state exceeded fifty thousand dollars. The process of annual securities registration forced the adding of a budget line item of thirty-five thousand dollars or more in the board's annual budget. Each year the regulations require that a financial prospectus be printed for each state where the board does business and provided to each prospective investor.

The registration requirement lessened the board's control of its decision-making process. When the board registers each year with a division of the Office of the Secretary of State of Indiana, that office approves the range of interest rates the board can pay on money Church of God people invest for that year. One year, during the time of spiraling interest rates, the board had asked for approval of a range of five percent to fifteen percent for new investments. For some reason the Division of Securities set the ceiling at twelve percent. Before the year was over, nationwide rates soared to nineteen percent. In three months time, board depositors had withdrawn over two million dollars because the board's top twelve percent rate was not competitive. This action created a very serious cash flow problem. The board had to go to its line of credit with the local bank and pay twenty percent interest. Finally, a second trip to the state securities office resulted in the needed change in the ceiling interest rate. But the damage had been done, and it took more than two years to recover from the financial loss.

Gains on Sale of Securities

Through the years individuals have made cash donations to the board for special missions and programs of church extension and evangelism. Some of the donations were in the form of blue chip stocks. Often these stocks would appreciate in price and dividends. For example, an individual once gave the board one hundred shares of stock valued at twenty-five dollars a share at the time of the gift, for a gift of twenty-five hundred dollars. This stock was kept by the board in its reserve account. In a few years there were a couple of stock splits, and the value of the stock had risen to over four hundred dollars a share!

In the 1950s and 1960s, the board had in its reserve account a good portfolio of stocks. Some of these had been given to the board through annuity agreements, and a small percentage of the board's own reserve funds had been placed in equities for diversification. It was a common practice, at the end of the fiscal year, to use some of the gains realized on certain equities (current market value over original cost) to help cover some operational deficits. This gave the board another option for funds to cover year-end deficits of twenty-five thousand dollars to ninety thousand dollars.

The inflation of the 1970s and 1980s, the state securities compliance regulations, the rising interest rates, and the lack of performance of the board's equity reserve funds, made management of the board's fiscal affairs more difficult. Not only were the equity portfolio earnings down at this time, but a change in accounting procedures also added other complications. The value of a stock portfolio on the board's accounts had to be, not the original purchase price, but the price quote at the last business day of the year. This greatly diminished the option of realizing gains on sale of securities. This regulation also had a negative influence on the budget and program of the board.

Right Actions with Negative Impact

As has been discussed in a previous chapter, the board agreed to pass the administration of the Church of God work in Mexico to the Missionary Board. This move seemed right, and had the approval of both boards and the General Assembly of the church.

This action, however right and proper, had a negative financial impact. For years the board had carried on its books the price it had paid for the properties and buildings in Mexico. Now that Mexico was assigned to another agency of the church, the BCEHM felt it was not proper to ask that agency to pay for the value of the property, so the board had to write off $142,000 for the book value of the Mexican property. This created a deficit in budget operations. In the April 27, 1971, general board minutes, is this statement:

> With reference to the defensive retrenchment pledge of last year, executive salaries were cut back by redeployment of staff, and mission station expenses were reduced due to the transfer of Mexico. . . . The general operating deficit is all from the Mexico property transfer.

The work of the board in Alaska for twenty years had resulted in eight congregations, a children's home, and many special ministries. From 1970 to 1979, the Alaskan congregations increased their membership by 86 percent.

The cost of living and building in that region has always been high. In order to get congregations established, the board assumed financial responsibility and title to some of the church properties. Over the years some of the congregations began to grow in numbers and financial stability. Self-supporting congregations had been the board's goal from the beginning, so the issue was how to turn over to the congregations of Alaska the titles to their properties without asking them to purchase them from the board. It was decided that the only course of action was to grant them the titles and have the board absorb the loss. The April 27, 1973, annual board minutes record that all properties in Alaska were deeded back to the local churches.

Thus another proper and appropriate action had a negative impact on the board's cost of operations.

The Interest Rate Adjustment Clause

There were indications in the late 1960s that the interest rate on money borrowed and loaned was becoming more volatile. The president of the board and the executive committee sought the best legal and financial advice on what could be done to protect the church, the board, and the congregations borrowing building funds, in times of rapidly fluctuating interest rates and inflation.

In March, 1969, the board adopted a policy which gave it the option of including an interest adjustment clause in the contract of newly negotiated first mortgage loans to congregations. This adjustment clause was to be used only as an emergency measure. It was devised to achieve safeguards in times of volatile interest rate changes. The clause stated that under conditions previously agreed to by both the congregation and the board, the interest on the mortgage could be increased up to the agreed-upon amount. In its spring meeting of 1972, the general board voted to include the interest adjustment clause in all mortgages (GB 24-25 April 1972). The clause was used in 1972 for the first time since it was established in 1969, and, because of inflation, was used four more times in the 1970s.

Understandably the adjustment clause was not popular with the congregations. Indeed, according to the minutes of the board, it was a key public relations problem in the later 1970s and early 1980s. Many staff visits were made to congregations to help them understand the issues involved. Beyond question, this clause was a great help to the board in weathering some of the most severe inflationary times in its history.

The president's annual report in 1971 gave a preamble to the board's financial battles for the decade and into the 1980s.

> This has not been an easy year for the staff of the Board since we determined to face honestly and realistically the problems incurred by rising inflationary costs and the plateau of donated funds to the work of the Board. The dollar increases we have received from World Service have not been enough to keep up with inflated costs. . . . In the immediate future we shall have to face the problem of a financial write-off of properties for many of our home missions stations, as well as transferring many of our state revolving loan funds to state ownership (AR 1971, 5).

Although the BCEHM did receive an increase each year from the church's giving through World Service, it was never adequate to cover the spiraling cost of operations of existing mission stations and other program ministries.

The Mission Outreach Endowment Fund

In 1969 there had been discussions by the president and administrative staff concerning how to increase gift income for missions and evangelism. The obvious fact was that the board had either to find a way to get more gift dollars or drastically cut its program services. In 1970 the Office of Program Research and Planning came up with a preliminary suggestion for establishing an endowment program fund. The president and administrative staff worked on the concept for several months.

In the October 8, 1971, board of directors meeting, a formal proposal was made by management. The proposal called for the establishment of a Board of Church Extension and Home Missions fund to be known as the Mission Outreach Endowment Fund. The earnings generated by the fund would be for "restricted use for program money in the area of missions, evangelism, and church extension, with special emphasis on venture and exploratory ministries." The program fund was further "to encourage congregations to think of new ways to perform their mission and ministry, and to encourage Christian servanthood." Grants from the fund would be available for new ministries, congregational and district mission outreach, evangelism projects, urban ministries, seed or risk money to generate other local funds, and for ministries in new and difficult places. The directors voted unanimously to establish this new Mission Outreach Endowment Fund (MOE Fund).

In the 1960s, a couple of special friends of the board, Art and Polly Bruner from St. Paul, Indiana, had worked out an annuity agreement with the board. They had given real estate and some blue chip stock to the board. At their deaths in 1971, there was a $134,000 residue in the account. In their memory, the directors voted to place this money as the first major contribution to the Mission Outreach Endowment Fund. In this way the Bruners' gift would never be spent, but would serve as an investment to earn funds for various mission ministries of the church.

The endowment built up slowly. At the end of 1971, the fund's first year, there was $140,957 in the endowment. By 1982, the corporate balance of the MOE Fund had reached $509,154. At the close of the 1980s, the fund had a corpus of over $1,000,000.

In its first twelve years, the fund made program grants of $327,192 to fifty-eight separate ministries. The grants from the MOE Fund were usually in one of three categories: outreach ministries by congregations to meet some special social need; home missions and ethnic ministries outreach, such as Haitian, Hispanic, Arabic, and Native American work; and new church development, to help meet pressing needs when World Service income was insufficient.

The Mission Outreach Endowment Fund did not solve the board's need for a stronger financial base for program services. However, it bought some time and allowed a variety of special ministries and mission development which would otherwise have not been possible. It continues to be a primary source for increasing the board's program ministry funds for supplementing home missions and evangelism needs of the church.

Mission USA

Other attempts were made to find adequate program funds for home missions and evangelism. In 1971, the board joined with other national agencies in getting a special project passed by the General Assembly, authorizing World Service to raise $200,000 above the regular national budget. It was called Mission USA, and was a two-year thrust. The goal included ninety thousand dollars for student scholarships for disadvantaged youth administered through Church of God colleges. The Board of Christian Education was to administer thirty-five thousand dollars for continuing education for pastoral development, schools of stewardship, and training for youth ministry. Then the Board of Church Extension and Home Missions was to administer seventy-five thousand dollars primarily in new and difficult fields of mission, pastoral assistance for urban and inner-city churches, and for strengthening congregations in racially changing neighborhoods.

The Mission USA project was very helpful for getting funds for the board's newly launched Urban Ministries program. The annual reports 1973 booklet gives this summary:

> Funds received by the Board of Church Extension and Home Missions have been used to help in many different areas. Some of the congregations receiving help have been in Chicago, Illinois; Columbia, Maryland; Decatur, Illinois; Denver, Colorado; Detroit, Michigan; Houston, Texas; Miami, Florida; and Toledo, Ohio. Also, Metropolitan Workshops were held in Houston, Texas; Anderson, Indiana; Seattle, Washington; Milwaukee, Wisconsin; and Oakland-San Francisco, California (AR 1973, 68).

Million for Missions

The pressure for program dollars, fueled by spiraling inflation, increased each year of the 1970s. The Missionary Board had opportunity to open new mission fields in Asia in the 1980s and to continue the growing mission outreach in Latin America. Here at home there was the recognition that the Church of God needed to put forth a strong effort to reach the rapidly increasing Hispanic communities in our nation. The chief executives of the two boards, Donald Johnson and Marvin Hartman, got together to explore how additional funds could be secured for these opportunities. It was decided to request that the two missions boards be designated as the recipients of a three-year World Service special project and that one million dollars, over and above the regular Church of God giving to World Service, be raised for missions at home and abroad.

The formal proposal was submitted to the National Budget Committee on February 13, 1976. The opening paragraph reads as follows:

> The Missionary Board of the Church of God and the Board of Church Extension and Home Missions make a unique, new, and we think exciting, proposal to the Budget Committee. We propose a joint world-wide missions Special Project over a three-year period to raise $1,000,000 for missions, climaxing in a Victory Celebration at the Church of God Centennial Ceremonies [in 1980].

The General Assembly in session on June 15, 1977, approved the Million for Missions (MFM) special project. The home board was to receive twenty-five percent ($250,000) of the total. The raising of funds for MFM began on July 1, 1977.

These funds offered another source of "over and above" money for the missions and evangelism programs of the church here at home. Approximately $92,000 went to help establish and work with eleven Hispanic congregations; $34,500 to assist in ministries in Hawaii; $30,000 for urban and ethnic ministries; $23,600 for native ministries; and $12,000 for special training ministries in the rural South.

Personal Evangelism

The attempt to expand the board's program helps for the church in evangelism beyond new church development began in the mid-1960s with Emphasis Evangelism. By 1970 there was a demand by the members of the board that more program assistance in personal evangelism should be offered to the church. In their annual spring meeting, when the board members voted for the restructure plan, they did so with the understanding that "Christian witness development would receive high priority."

Charles R. Tarr was brought to the staff in 1971 as director of Witness Evangelism. The assignment was to motivate the congregations of the Church of God to place personal evangelism as a top priority. The focus was to train both pastors and lay people to become better equipped to share their personal faith with others.

The Executive Council sponsored the 1970 consultation of two hundred local, state, and national Church of God leaders from the United States and Canada. The purpose of the meeting was "to find clear direction for the church in the 1970s" (EX Council 1970). In a report of the consultation, the section on evangelism says in part, "The need for a practical program of personal evangelism is most crucial. . . . The decade of the seventies is the time that we MUST get the church involved in a program of personal evangelism that will get us moving (AR 1970, 27)."

This emphasis was carried out largely through the regular church publications, books, and specially written materials. The primary method to increase awareness of the need for witness evangelism and how to do it was through Personal

Evangelism Clinics held in various sections of the nation, where three or more congregations would come together for special training. By the end of 1974, 521 pastors and associate pastors, plus 999 lay leaders, had attended one or more of these clinics. This proved to be one of the most effective training tools of the board for encouraging and equipping the church in witness evangelism.

The decade also began with the 1970 General Assembly of the Church of God voting, as requested by the BCEHM, to endorse participation in Key '73, an ecumenical, nationwide evangelism effort. Leaders from twenty or more denominations had worked and planned for three years for this mass effort to get the church members of America to put personal evangelism first in their lives and work. 1971 was the Year of Presentation to the churches of America. 1972 was the Year of Preparation, and 1973 the Year of Penetration. The event did help to get personal evangelism higher on the agenda of many thousands of congregations. Nine hundred Church of God congregations did participate. The event got many denominational groups working together who had never done so before.

In the summer of 1975, Charles Tarr left the staff to return to a pastorate. Charles R. Shumate was invited to continue the work of Witness Evangelism.

Although the Personal Evangelism Clinic was the major witness evangelism thrust of the board throughout the 1970s, the approach was revised and improved upon. By 1976, a new approach was used. It was called a H.E.L.P. Clinic (How To Enlist Leadership Program). The focus was more on being and doing than on learning methods and techniques. A one-day mini clinic was developed for congregations needing a refresher course in witness evangelism. Then, in 1979, a new tool was added. It was called TELL Witness Program (Training for Evangelistic Lifestyle Leadership). Eight training video cartridges and a user's guide were developed for training leaders on how to share personal faith more readily and easily in daily life.

To feed and keep the spirit of personal evangelism alive and before the church, an evangelism reading course was conducted each year for four years. More than four hundred pastors and their associates benefited from this plan. Toward the end of the decade, the Evangelism/Missions Department of the board also offered special help in strategy and training for youth evangelism.

A need was expressed by several full-time evangelists for help and moral support in their work. They wanted a structured setting for sharing and reflecting on their special calling. The board responded with seminars geared to meet some of these needs. A staff person was made available to meet with them annually and help process their concerns. These efforts resulted, in 1979, in the forming of the Association of Evangelists of the Church of God.

Home Missions Activities

There was a growing awareness in this decade that more decentralization was needed in home missions ministries. The BCEHM sought help from the state organizations regarding administrative responsibility for minority ministries in their regions. Congregations also were encouraged to be more aware of and responsive to home missions opportunities in their communities.

Example: A congregation wrote stating that they had determined there were several thousand Hispanic neighbors in their metropolitan area. The letter requested that the board find some way to reach and minister to them. A series of letters was exchanged between the pastor and the Department of Evangelism/Missions. The staff's response was that the congregation was better able to respond than the national board. However, the board would serve as consultant and resource for the congregation.

In the articles and reports on home missions throughout this decade, such phrases as "Mission on Location," "Mission at Home," and "Doorstep Missions" frequently appear.

Mission Discovery Weekend Workshops were conducted to help congregations reach out in their neighborhoods and communities. The attempt was made to get the state organizations where existing home missions projects were located—Native American Missions, Pine Crest Youth Center, Hispanic projects—to enter into partnership with the board in each project. Moral support, encouragement, and a variety of other helps could best be given by the local area. The entire decade was used to educate the church to understand that home missions responsibilities are not just a national concern and obligation. More can be accomplished when each congregation discovers God's mission to all people in its own neighborhood.

Focus on Hispanics

From its beginning the BCEHM had been involved in Hispanic work and ministry. There was a rapid increase of Hispanics in the United States population, beginning in the 1960s. It was realized that the Church of God could and should be doing much more to reach this vibrant and growing population. Nilah Meier was asked to help with this promising aspect of home missions work. She joined the staff in July, 1975, as director of Hispanic Ministries. The responsibilities of the assignment included: serving as advisor and consultant to the Spanish American Concilio of the Church of God; stimulating cooperative ventures with other Church of God agencies for Hispanic Americans; helping to put Hispanic concerns on state and district agendas; building up scholarship possibilities for Hispanic youth; translating and fostering the development of resource materials in Spanish; enlisting leaders and setting up seminars and workshops for Hispanic congregations on family life, stewardship, counseling, and Church of God history and doctrine. This new ministry was made financially possible for the first two years by a start-up program grant from WOMEN OF THE CHURCH OF GOD.

The addition of a staff person with the exclusive task of working with and in behalf of Hispanic Ministries proved to be the right move at the right time. More and stronger Hispanic congregations were established, more leaders were trained, and more books and materials of the Church of God were translated into Spanish. It also made the church aware of the special gifts and leadership abilities of Hispanics. By the early 1980s, Hispanic leaders had been elected as members of all the national boards and agencies.

Hunger in America

In this decade the Church of God began to take more seriously its responsibility for persons at home and overseas who were hungry. World Service, in 1975, began to receive funds from the church to meet some of the hunger needs of the world. The two missions boards were asked to administer the distribution of these funds. The BCEHM appointed a hunger committee from members of its staff to supervise distribution. A range of fifteen thousand dollars to thirty thousand dollars was received annually and distributed by the board.

In 1976, WOMEN OF THE CHURCH OF GOD granted five thousand dollars to the board to supplement the diets of pregnant women, children, and sick and elderly on a Navajo Reservation. Staff was sent to meet with Navajo school and health officials to determine their nutritional needs. Over a two-year period of time, special nutrition kits, prepared by WOMEN OF THE CHURCH OF GOD in New Mexico, were delivered every two weeks by the Klagetoh congregation. This experience helped the Hunger Committee learn the importance and wisdom of getting input from the persons being served by the hunger program.

Annually, beginning in 1976, the world hunger funds which the board administers have been used in twenty or more home mission stations and through individual congregations to help some of the malnourished of the land. Part of the hunger funds were used to encourage long-range projects and to seek solutions by fostering self-help industries and projects. For almost two decades this ministry, made possible by the giving of the church, has brought life and hope to thousands of persons and continues to do so.

Reaching Out to Arabs in USA

In 1978 the door of opportunity opened rather quickly for an Arab Exploration Outreach Ministry of the Church of God. Hashem Sweis began work in Yonkers, New York, and Jacob Kakish began his work in Detroit, Michigan. Both found secular jobs and used their weekends to make contacts in their communities—meeting people and responding to their needs, teaching English classes, and conducting home Bible studies. For more than twelve years these ministries have been successful in reaching Arabic people. The Detroit outreach resulted in the establishment of an Arabic-speaking congregation with Kakish as pastor. A grant from WOMEN OF THE CHURCH OF GOD allowed the beginning of these two outreach ministries.

Native American Council Organized

Church of God work among Native Americans has been a long and slow process. There were successes, but the greatest need was for native leadership. In 1974, at the Klagetoh, Arizona, Shelter Mission, the first Native American Caucus was held. This meeting laid the groundwork for the Indian American Council of the Church of God, which was formed in May, 1977, at Crow Agency, Montana.

The following goals set by the council were recorded in the minutes of the caucus: to help with recruitment and training of native ministers; to plan for new congregations; to encourage program development in existing congregations; to plan meetings for mutual enrichment and inspiration; and to generally assist with planning for the Indian ministries of the BCEHM. [These phrases are taken from the minutes of that caucus.]

Training events were set up on various reservations to help achieve the goal of increasing the knowledge and leadership skills of the native people. One model for training was established in 1975 by the Native American Leadership Development Seminar held in Portland, Oregon.

More progress was made from 1974 to 1990 in Church of God Native American work than in the previous thirty years. In 1975, nine native young people from our mission churches were enrolled in Church of God colleges. New native congregations were established, and an effective Native American and Aleut outreach ministry was begun in Alaska under the effective leadership of Fred and Evelyn Mamaloff.

Hope Hill Children's Home

Hope Hill Children's Home was founded in 1961 in Hope, Kentucky, by Ruby and Robert Kitchen. It was founded on the belief that all children have the right to experience the warmth of a loving family, the caring of a Christian community, and to be nurtured and guided through difficult times.

After ten years of operation by a group of Church of God leaders serving as trustees of the home, they began to express a concern for safeguarding the property and program for the Church of God. In 1972 the trustees of Hope Hill Children's Home, Inc. wrote to the Executive Council of the Church of God asking for its counsel. The conclusion was reached that the national agency best suited to work with the home's trustees on this matter was the Board of Church Extension and Home Missions. There were many visits and discussions on the best way to approach and handle this issue. The following is an excerpt from a news release giving details of the transfer:

> After several years of conversation between officials of Hope Hill Children's Home and members of the Board of Church Extension and Home Missions, the Board of Trustees of Hope Hill Children's Home voted unanimously to make a gift of the home to the Church of God. The trustees decided that the Board of Church Extension and Home Missions was the proper agency to receive this gift on behalf of the Church. . . . Brother Willard Wilcox, Chairman of the Board of Trustees, reports the reason for the gift of the Home to the Board is to preserve it perpetually for the Church of God and to make it possible for the entire Church of God to join in this ministry. . . . The home is located ten miles southeast of Mt Sterling, Kentucky, on a 185-acre campus. It is totally debt free and provides an opportunity for an unique Christian ministry for the Church of God (BCEHM *Focus* 1974 Summer, 1).

Paul and Lana Sanders became the directors of Hope Hill Children's Home, Inc. in the summer of 1974. They helped the home to give caring, creative service. Hundreds of children, young people, and families have received loving Christian care. Most of the children in child care programs across the nation are not orphaned; ninety-seven percent have parents who are living. Many of the children who come under the care of Hope Hill have been victims of alcoholism, drug abuse, desertion, or family violence. In his 1974 annual report, the president wrote:

> This new kind of ministry will offer us challenges in the future. A great many of today's children are hurting, and certainly the healing of some of these hurts is one of the significant ministries of the church today (AR 1974, 6).

Retiree Housing Exploration

It was evident, even before the late 1960's and early 1970s, that Americans were living longer. By the 1980s, the fastest-growing age category, on a percentage basis, was Americans eighty-five years of age and older. Questions were being raised as to the role of the church in this area of American life. Housing and health care for the elderly became a topic of frequent discussion and concern. The federal Department of Housing and Urban Development (HUD) was seeking responsible sponsors to build and manage federally subsidized housing.

The June 21, 1971, minutes of the board of directors of the BCEHM record that the Executive Council of the Church of God requested that the board explore the federal HUD plan of church sponsorship for housing.

Explorations by the staff were made and special seminars were attended. By the time the study was completed, the federal government had frozen all funds for this type of housing. This changed the picture of retiree housing, but the need still existed. The records of the board reveal that each year from 1975 to 1978, it received a dozen or more inquiries from congregations wanting to learn the requirements for sponsorship of retiree housing, or from couples and individuals wishing to retire in a Church of God sponsored housing project.

This matter was a topic of discussion and study by the board for two years. In the annual meeting in April, 1977, board members voted to affirm retiree housing as an appropriate ministry for the church, and declared its intent to enter this field of ministry. They ordered that a financial feasibility study be made, and went on record that, if the study revealed the soundness of such a project, the directors be empowered to proceed with construction.

A national church retiree housing firm, the American Baptist Service Corporation, was employed to do the study and to serve as consultant to the board. Land was located for the proposed project, but additional land was needed in order to meet zoning requirements. The agency which had sold the original tract for the proposed housing project refused to sell additional acreage. Thus ended this particular venture. The executive committee voted "to put this project on the back burner for the present time (EX 27 April 1978)."

The need for board-sponsored retiree housing was discussed again in the early 1980s. Serious exploration was conducted, but no project ever materialized.

State Revolving Loan Funds

From 1950 to 1953, when the church had its Mid-Century Advance Campaign, some funds came to the BCEHM for its work. At the time, the board decided that it should help Church of God state organizations develop funding for church extension. The board made the offer to match dollar for dollar, up to one thousand dollars, any state organization that would set up a loan fund with the board. Many availed themselves of this offer. By 1972 the states were employing their own full-time leadership and wanted to administer their own church extension funds, and to withdraw them from the board. Finally, authorization was given to phase out of this program of twenty years and to allow an annual withdrawal of up to thirty thousand dollars of state revolving loan funds (GB 25 April 1978).

Genuine State/National Teamship

The board's concern for the church's state organizations expressed itself in many ways through the years. In the decade of the 1970s, this relationship came to full stature as both the states and the national agency realized the strengths and rewards of partnership and cooperative ministry.

In January, 1971, the president of the board and five

other staff members met for two days with twelve full-time state coordinators at Deer Valley Ranch, Nathrop, Colorado, to explore mutual concerns, discuss state and national goals, and improve lines of communication. The experience met with such favor that the state executives requested the board to name a staff liaison to meet annually with them and help with their planning and corporate work. The meeting ended with an invitation to each state coordinator to be an observer at the next annual meeting of the BCEHM in April, 1971. For more than twenty-five years the board has hosted a breakfast during the International Convention each year for state executives and area assembly leaders.

Louis Meyer was designated as liaison to the state executives. Isham (Joe) Crane became responsible for this assignment in the 1980s. A special news sheet, *PLUG IN,* was developed to give state leaders advance information of program plans, changes in mortgage rates, and other vital news of the board. This relationship continued for most of two decades, with staff persons of the BCEHM serving as consultants and resource persons to state staffs. A deep sense of appreciation and an unusual level of trust developed in these relationships. An example: The state leaders once asked for and received permission to meet with one of the divisions of the Executive Council to present their views and ask for more representation in the decision-making process. At this meeting they requested that the BCEHM staff liaison sit on their side of the table to help them express their perspectives on the issues being discussed.

Joint Strategy and Action Committee—JSAC

In the late 1960s, home missions executives from seven national church groups met together to form a voluntary Joint Strategy and Action Committee (JSAC). Its purpose was to enable national home missions agencies of a wide variety of church groups to develop common goals and strategies and to identify areas appropriate for joint action.

JSAC met twice a year. It had a variety of task forces, made up of staff members from the cooperating denominations. These task forces were centered around staff program assignments in ministries such as urban, non-metropolitan, church development, responsible living, Native American, Asian American, Hispanic, and others. The BCEHM staff was actively involved with JSAC and its task forces from 1972 until 1989, serving as officers and as chairs of several task forces. According to the testimony of board staff, JSAC was one of the most helpful ecumenical groups for practical work and missions action.

Volunteers Task Force of the Church of God

In 1978 the staff began a study of how to develop a process whereby Church of God people could volunteer their time and skills for Christian service in the United States and Canada. By 1979 the Volunteers Task Force of the Church of God was formed. It was made up of a staff representative from the Board of Church Extension and Home Missions, the Board of Christian Education, the Missionary Board, Anderson University Tri-S, WOMEN OF THE CHURCH OF GOD, Church of God MEN International, and a state coordinator. The winter 1979 issue of *FOCUS* states:

> The purpose of the Task Force was to coordinate the work of volunteer ministries of the Church of God. It is a united, cooperative, coordinated effort of the state organizations and national agencies of the Church to foster and encourage volunteerism as a needed ministry at all levels of the life and work of the Church—local, district, state and national.

The group tried to identify areas of need, and to discover

persons with skills and a willingness to serve, at their own expense, as volunteers. The group used the logo SERV, which stood for "service by volunteers."

The task force met with some success over the next eight years. There were volunteers who worked at several home missions stations, and in a variety of other settings. Adolph Dreger served without pay as director of SERV for four years. The major problem of the venture was that each sponsoring agency was short of program funds and could not commit budget support to the program.

Potpourri of Program Matters

Termination of Architectural Services. After eighteen years of architectural advisory services offered by the board, with John S. Kane as staff architect, the directors, in their October 8, 1971, meeting, voted to terminate this service. Kane had submitted his letter of resignation from the staff position in order to open his own architectural business. Since the board began offering this service in the early 1950s, over five hundred congregations had been assisted with architectural advisory service. The directors passed a resolution of commendation and thanks to Kane for his faithful and creative service to the church and recommending him and his talents to the Church of God across the country.

Seventy-Three Pianos Received. In 1962 O. C. Lewis, a long-time board member and businessman in Sikeston, Missouri, indicated that he and Mrs. Lewis would like to make pianos available to the BCEHM for new congregations and home missions stations. Over the next thirteen years, this committed couple donated seventy-three new pianos. During the June, 1975, Anderson International Convention, the Lewises were honored at a luncheon by the board and given a plaque commemorating the event (BCEHM *Focus* 1975 Fall, 4).

Pastor's Home Equity Plan. The board, in its annual meeting on April 25, 1972, voted to approve a plan to assure adequate housing for pastors during their retirement years. The congregation would agree to pay a certain amount annually in the pastor's name to the board, according to a schedule worked out by the pastor, congregation, and board. The board served as the depository for the funds. This plan met with limited success.

Limitation of Board Members' Terms. In 1972 the general board adopted a policy to limit its board members' terms to two full consecutive five-year terms. The policy states that a former member is not eligible for renomination until he or she has been off the board for at least a full year. Years later, a similar policy was adopted by the General Assembly of the Church of God for all national agencies.

BCEHM Assumes Administrative Responsibility for Hawaii. Since Hawaii had become one of the states of the nation, the Missionary Board offered to transfer its administrative responsibility for Hawaii to the Board of Church Extension and Home Missions. After meeting with the leaders of the church in Hawaii, the board voted in its annual meeting in April, 1970, "to accept transfer of the work in Hawaii."

Church Development Studies This became a valued program ministry of the board during the seventies. These studies were for congregations needing to build, expand, buy property, relocate, merge and/or add staff for their expanding programs. Ten to twenty of these studies were conducted each year. In an effort to help congregations do a better job of preparing to build, and to help them have the information necessary when they applied for a loan from the board, a new staff position was established in 1977. George D. Blackwell was assigned the responsibility of the Office of Building Advisory Services.

Disciples of Christ Respond to Critical Need for Loan Funds. The decade began with a number of congregations having approved loans, but with the board's not having enough funds to lend. A special appeal was made through the Office of Financial Development, and in twelve months more than one million dollars of new investments were received by the board for first mortgage loans. This relieved the pressure for funds briefly. By 1973, the shortage of loan funds became critical again. The board's friends and colleagues of the Board of Church Extension of the Disciples of Christ in Indianapolis, Indiana, deposited one million dollars of their funds for three years with the board to help provide loan funds for Church of God congregations.

From 1970 to 1979 the board advanced 551 church loans, for a total of $22,527,275. The staff conducted 337 church building fund campaigns for Church of God congregations, helping them raise $26,046,525 in three-year pledges.

In its annual meeting of April, 1979, the board drafted a resolution and sent it to the General Assembly of the Church of God, recommending that a representative assembly with lay delegates be established. The resolution passed the board by a unanimous vote, but did not meet with much favor in the assembly.

Internal Affairs

Early in this decade, the General Assembly established a policy which prohibited national agency staff persons from serving as trustees or board members of other agencies. This action forced the retirement of Gene Newberry as president of BCEHM, because he was also serving as dean of the School of Theology. In an average week the board has a dozen or more legal documents which have to be signed by the president. This was one reason for an Anderson resident's serving as president. In its spring meeting of 1972, a solution was worked out by changing the title of the board's chief executive officer from executive secretary to president, and changing the title of the one who chairs all the official board meetings from president to chairperson of the board.

Toward the end of the decade, action was taken by the board to relieve the office of president from so many administrative details and to broaden the decision-making and management operation. The responsibility of treasurer was separated from the office of president, and a vice president was named to assume more responsibility in program development, evaluation, and staff performance. The president was asked to give more time to long-range planning and financial and gift development for the ministries of the board.

The major urban ministries services were in the form of Metropolitan Mission Workshops and Leadership/Ministry Development Workshops. Most every major metropolitan area where the Church of God had three or more congregations benefited from one or more of these workshops. Eighty-nine congregations had direct involvement in some phase of urban ministries.

In 1972 Felix Flores became the first Hispanic to be elected as a member of the board. By 1990 two of the twenty-one board members were Hispanic. Lawrence P. Wyatt became chairperson of the board in July, 1974, the first African-American to be elected to this position. He chaired the board until his membership expired in June, 1983.

Program staff persons joining the board in this decade included: Paul J. Smith (1970) as director of Loan Services; J. L. Hatchel (1971), Elmer Case (1972), Cecil W. Watson (1975), and Andrew Jack Bugg (1979) as directors of Church Building Campaigns; Forest F. Carlson (1974) as financial development secretary; Edward L. Foggs (1970) and Richard A. Goode (1975) as directors of Urban Ministries.

Staff resignations and retirements for the ten-year period include: Victor J. Gritzmacher retired in 1972; Elmer Hutchinson retired in 1973; Ralph Phile resigned to go to work for Warner Press in 1972; J. Lloyd Brown resigned to go into his own business in 1971; John S. Kane left in 1971 to go into private service; Charles Tarr resigned in 1975 to return to the pastorate; Edward L. Foggs resigned in 1975 to become associate secretary of the Executive Council; and Elmer Case left in 1976 for health reasons.

The board established a branch office in Denver, Colorado, in 1971. David A. Telfer was sent there as coordinator of Metropolitan Missions, with responsibilities for Hispanic and Native American work in the midwest and western states. He served there until his resignation in 1977, to take the pastorate of the Aina Haina Church in Hawaii. In Hawaii, he took assignments from the board regarding a long-range plan for the development of that state. He returned to the staff in 1980 as secretary of the Department of Home Missions.

Deaths of former staff which occurred in this decade included: A. Wayne Johnson, J. C. Thompson, J. Lloyd Brown, and Adam Williams.

Summary of the Decade

This decade witnessed several major changes in program and in the way the board did its business. Some of these changes came about, in part, because of external conditions and regulations. Other changes seem to have been due to the growing maturity of the board and staff.

The events of this decade—the oil embargo, inflation, rising interest rates, and state security compliance—made it clear that the process of providing church building loans for Church of God congregations had become much more complicated and costly. It was no longer a simple operation between the board and Church of God investors. In some ways it was a new world in which church business was to be conducted.

On the program front it was a decade of expanded ministries. The urban ministries thrust became a reality and brought hope, insight, and new coalitions for ministry. Hope Hill Children's Home enlarged the board's and the church's sensitivity and opportunity for ministry to needy and neglected children. An awareness of the hungry and unfortunate ones in the nation resulted in the church's hunger program. These events aroused in some the need to get personally involved, resulting in the Church of God volunteer program, SERV. The board's ministry was also expanded through the gain of the administrative responsibility for Hawaii.

One of the most intense and sustained program ministries of the board for the decade of the 1970s was personal evangelism. For fifty years, the board's primary evangelistic focus had been the starting and developing of new congregations. There were several programmatic explorations in evangelism in the 1960s, but in this decade Christian witness development/personal evangelism became a major ministry.

In home missions the focus was largely on mission's being local. "Home missions begins at home" was the motto of the decade. This focus was carried out by the BCEHM's stressing local control and responsibility for missions stations and projects. Many deeds to mission property were returned to the mission congregations. The formation of the American Indian Council of the Church of God in 1974 and the adjustments in the Spanish American Concilio were attempts to help each group become indigenous and control their own affairs. There was a definite shift from survival goals to goals of program development and growth.

The long working relationship with state leaders reached a deeper level of partnership. Mutual trust and confidence increased, resulting in a close planning and working relationship.

Internally, the orientation training for new board members resulted in improved understanding and wiser policy formation. The forming of the first national Church of God agency Office of Program Research and Planning was an indication that the BCEHM did not intend to do business as usual, but was open to the future. The enactment of a program staff sabbatical policy said in a tangible way that the board realized the value and worth of staff members to its ministry to the church.

This decade ushered in the complications of external controls, the challenge of diversity in ethnic ministries, and divergencies within the church as well as society. These presented continuing challenges to the board, its management, and staff.

Chapter 8

A Broader Economic Base for An Extended Ministry

(1980-1990)

On the eighteenth of May, 1980, Mount St. Helens volcano in the state of Washington erupted. It was a spectacular explosion which spewed volcanic ash for several days. This ash soared miles up into the atmosphere and was carried around the globe by the jet stream. The sky over Japan and other nations of the world was darkened for several days because of this eruption in the United States.

This incident was a dramatic introduction to the decade of the 1980s. It graphically depicted the interconnectedness of the world. It was an irrefutable example that the globe is one community, intricately interrelated. Though the explosion took place in one nation, the fallout affected all the earth, regardless of political or national boundaries.

For many years, such issues as nuclear waste, depletion of the ozone layer, heating of the earth's environment, and pollution of the world's water supply were concerns of a wide variety of environmental groups. Events of the 1980s helped inject these issues into the political mainstream of many nations.

A second dramatic and far more tragic event of the decade helped to put environmentalism and ecology on the world's political agenda. It was the world's worst nuclear accident, which occurred at Chernobyl in the Soviet Union in 1986. The nuclear fallout of this tragedy took many lives and left many areas in Europe contaminated with radioactivity.

This event informed people that the environmental crisis is no respecter of nations or boundaries. By the end of the decade there were other disturbing reminders. The rise in skin cancer, the increasing pollution of water and air, as well as other related ills, became indisputable evidence that these issues must be addressed. Preserving the environment became a matter of life or death for human beings and all species, for nature, and for the entire planet. It was a time which witnessed progression on the critical issue of arms control. The INF treaty was signed—the world's first agreement ever—to eliminate an entire category of offensive nuclear weapons.

This also was a decade of radical change in the atmosphere of superpower relations. From talk of "evil empire" to talk of peaceful co-existence—changes took place from 1980 to 1988 in four face-to-face talks between Mikhail Gorbachev of the Soviet Union and Ronald Reagan of the United States. Gorbachev rose rapidly to power as head of the Soviet republics in 1985. He quickly added two new words and concepts to the world's vocabulary—glasnost (openness), and perestroika (reconstruction). These two concepts helped to bring about some radical changes in the Soviet Union and eastern Europe.

This decade saw the continuation of personal violence. President Reagan was shot by a would-be assassin, John Hinckley, in March 1981. Two months later, Pope John Paul III was wounded in Vatican City by a young Turk. In October of this same year President Anwar Sadat was assassinated by Islamic fundamentalists in Egypt at an annual military parade. In 1984 Prime Minister Indira Gandhi of India was assassinated in New Delhi by Sikh members of her bodyguard.

Violence also continued between nations. There was the Falklands Conflict between Great Britain and Argentina in 1982. South Africa's apartheid policy created struggle within that nation and around the world. The eight-year war between Iran and Iraq, and the invasions by the United States of both Grenada and Panama took place in this ten-year time period. Constant violence in Lebanon and other parts of the Middle East went on throughout the decade. It spilled over into the 1990s with Iraq's invasion and take-over of Kuwait. This brought the United States and other nations, through the United Nations, into the conflict to free Kuwait.

In 1983 the United States made AIDS (Acquired Immune Deficiency Syndrome) a top health priority when it was learned how rapidly this dreaded disease was spreading. According to the Center for Disease Control in Atlanta, Georgia, there were 161,073 AIDS cases in this country from June, 1981 through December, 1990. The center reports that 100,777 of these people died as a result of this disease by the end of 1990. This vital issue will doubtless require the best sustained efforts of religious groups, educational systems, medical research, and governmental agencies for years to come.

In spite of the repeated cycles of violence at the personal, national, and world levels, there were many signs of the birth of new hope in the 1980s. There were signs of new approaches to world issues and a glimmer of a hope that perhaps world leaders were beginning to search more diligently for ways other than war to settle regional and international disputes. The radical change in the Soviet Union, the tearing down of the Berlin Wall without a shot being fired, the signing of the U.S.-Soviet agreement on prohibiting nuclear offensive weapons, are but three signs of this spirit of hope and of finding another way to deal with ecological issues and with each other.

A New Decade—and the Next Hundred Years

The decade began for the Church of God with the celebration of its one hundredth anniversary. All national agencies participated in the churchwide celebration in a variety of ways. The Board of Church Extension and Home Missions prepared a special filmstrip and cassette tape entitled *New Every Morning* on its own sixty-year history. It had a wide exposure across the church, and several hundred congregations bought the filmstrip.

In its annual meeting in April, 1980, the board passed a Declaration of Commitment which staff and management had carefully worked out. It was a declaration of renewed commitment to the task assigned the board for the years ahead. In part the document reads:

> We will follow with joyful devotion and loyalty the biblical mandates of our Christian faith. . . . We will be faithful stewards of our own personal and corporate resources, and those of the earth, for all belongs to God. . . . We will be thinking in terms of the future, seeking to serve at the cutting edge of both the church and society. . . . We will support the strength of diversity, affirming the value of cultural richness and ethnic uniqueness. . . . We will keep before the Church the need for every believer to find ways daily to share their faith in word and deed. . . . We will be part of the struggle to remove economic, social and racial injustice. . . . We will be immersed in Christian hope, moving toward the day when human and spiritual values predominate in our world.

Every board and staff member signed the document, which had been written on parchment. The signed copy of the declaration was framed and hung in the foyer of the board's office building.

A Broader Economic Base

The rising cost of living due to inflation and the rapidly fluctuating interest rates which began in the 1970s, continued into the 1980s. The decade began with interest rates going up to eighteen percent; inflation for the first year of the decade was 12.4 percent. Favorable interest rates shifted from the usual higher rates paid on long-term investments to higher rates offered on short-term investments. This had a heavy impact on the Board of Church Extension and Home Missions and its church building loan program. Along with the nation's savings and loan institutions and banks, the board found considerable difficulty servicing eight- to fifteen-year church building loans with short-term investments. Partially responding to this condition, Marvin Hartman, president of the board, read a paper giving his insight into what was happening.

> Many of the factors with which we deal are not directly controllable by this Board, nor its staff. . . . I believe the Board of Church Extension and Home Missions has financial strength and breadth of personnel to meet the challenge of the 1980s. We are prepared to attack the problems we face with creativity, with trust, and with resolve. . . . Inflation is the mad dog that keeps snipping at our heels. . . . The balancing of the budget will not grow any easier in the near future (GB 24 April 1981, 3-4).

Through the years, the board estimated that it needed a 2.5 to 3 percent interest spread in its lending ministry. The goal was to net at least 2.5 percent more income than costs in order to cover the total price of getting the funds and paying for the many advisory services requested by the church. A study of the minutes and annual reports reveals that this was a difficult and often illusive goal. Frequently, the spread per year was only 1.5 percent, which did not adequately cover the costs of services.

An insight into the board's mood and persistent struggle at this time is given by a report of the president at the board of directors meeting October 13, 1983, which stated in part:

> This Board has been ushered, not without protest, into the mainstream of economic life in our country and in the world. For the majority of its sixty-three years, the Board operated in the warm, comfortable "womb of the Church" and in a not-for-profit "security blanket." We are now in the cold world of economic and financial reality—with the previous comfort of the "Church" and "not-for-profit" gone. We are like other institutions which deal in notes and mortgages (banks and savings and loans), subject to world shifts in interest rates.
>
> While I do not want to be defensive about the financial difficulties, we all need to be reminded of some of the facts regarding the history of the last five years:
>
> The change in securities laws . . . has forced us into added costs in our operations. . . . The change of priorities by the Board's investors, from a position of service and ministry to one directly related to interest rates, has had a major impact on the financial structure of the Board. In the past, persons of the Church of God were motivated to place deposits here based largely on the ministry aspect of what the deposits were going to do, namely, build church buildings for the Church of God. That has diminished drastically. We are not critical of that fact, we only mourn!

These new financial waters had a dramatic effect on all of the board's services and programs. Inflation ate away at the program dollars supporting home missions work among Native Americans, Hispanics, Alaska outreach ministries, and other ethnic outreach. In new church development, evangelism, and church growth, the inflated dollar curtailed many programs and hindered the board's ability to respond to new opportunities for ministry. The modest increases of dollars from the church through World Service for home missions and evangelism allowed little, if any, new outreach. It was getting increasingly more difficult just to maintain the existing program ministries. The president of the board expressed it this way in 1985:

> The demands for money for ministry are inexhaustible. The resources with which we have to work are limited. This year, the fact that the Board ended the year with a modest surplus is the result of hard work and team commitment to do everything within our power to be responsible managers and operate within our given resources. I do not anticipate such future struggles will be quickly resolved or changed overnight. A high priority of management during the next few years must be the dissolving of the general fund deficit accrued during the years of almost uncontrollable interest rates. . . . High on the Board's list of priorities must be maintaining and improving the standard of excellence demonstrated in the Board's servant relationship to the Church. The general fund deficit looms as an irritating problem which must receive high priority. The Board must always seek to operate from a position of financial strength (AR 1985, 10-11).

This vital concern was again a part of the president's annual report to the general board in 1987:

> In 1986, a major policy decision made by the General Board was that in order to continue an effective ministry of services to the Church assigned this Board by the General Assembly, ways must be found to broaden the Board's financial base, refine our budgeting proc-

ess, and get the growing general fund deficit under control.

A Top Priority—Gift Development

Early in the decade the management team, comprised of the officers of the corporation, began to address the financial issues of the board. Of particular concern was the impact a general fund deficit was having on its program and service ministries. After a year of study and analysis, management presented a document to the board of directors in their January, 1983, meeting. It made the argument that in troubled times the tendency was to deal with the problems rather than the opportunities. It pointed out that for almost a decade, because of persistent crises, management and the Board had been forced to give an inordinate amount of time to investments, loans, and escalating interest and loan rates. It further said:

> Opportunities for the Board's work and ministry in Church Extension, Missions, and Evangelism were never greater. The opportunity for new ethnic ministries challenges us with increased pressure. The time is ripe for a church-wide challenge to an aggressive new church extension thrust. Districts and states are seeking our counsel more frequently concerning new church development and mission to minorities. Ways for a more effective response must be found.
>
> We must face our deficit situation squarely, creatively and honestly. However, we must not succumb to a spirit of pessimism or a mentality of retrenchment. We believe we have a God-assigned task and mission as a Board. We strongly feel the ministry assigned this Board is vital to the health and well-being of each congregation of the Church. There is concern, and potentially far greater support throughout the Church for the work assigned us—adequate facilities, missions, evangelism, and church extension.

The document goes on to suggest that if program ministries of the board are to continue and grow, an aggressive effort must be made to broaden the economic base of the entire board:

> We feel that in order to take advantage of these increasing new opportunities for mission and ministry, the Board must be financially healthy and aggressively move to increase our net worth. Continued ministry to the Church in all aspects of the Board's services is primarily dependent upon adequate finances and a strong net worth position. . . . The time has come for us to build up our two permanent funds—The Mission Outreach Endowment Fund and the Pioneer Memorial Loan Fund. This endeavor will not be for the sake of finance or "going after profits," but for the sake of ministry and mission. More net worth is needed in order to perform more effective ministry. . . . We must seek, as soon as possible, a staff person for the specific and exclusive task of Gift Development. We feel an all-out effort in gift development is essential if we are to respond to the challenges and opportunities of this decade in mission, ministry and service (DIR 13 January 1983, I).

The directors and the general board, in April, 1983, adopted this proposal. It became the key priority of the board and management for the remainder of the decade.

As is often the case, it proved easier to make a policy decision than to follow through with the action required. Finding and employing an experienced gift development person took more than two years to accomplish. In the meantime, some staff assignments were shuffled to allow existing staff to focus more on gift development. A consultant was used on a part-time basis for a year. Finally, it was learned that J. Perry Grubbs, one experienced in this area, had resigned his post at Warner Southern College. He accepted the board's invitation and joined the staff as director of advancement in July, 1986.

The pursuit and building of a broader economic base to guarantee an expanded program of services to the church extended into the decade of the 1990s.

A New Permanent Fund

The program responsibilities assigned to the board included many practical, vital ministries which were capable of helping every congregation: evangelism, church planting, and ways to help the church to grow; loans to build new facilities and fund services to pay for them; conditional deeding of church property. These, plus effective work in urban areas, home missions ministries, state work, and a wide range of advisory and consulting services added up to an increasingly popular package of services requested by the church. The demand increased with each passing year.

The board's desire was to deliver its services to the church with as little cost as possible. However, in an effort to do this, the program budget was often overspent. Small fees were attached to certain services, but the fees never covered the actual cost of delivering the services. If the fee were increased to cover the true cost, it often put the service needed beyond the reach of the small congregation.

Recognizing these dilemmas, and as an attempt to help reduce the general fund deficit, the directors voted in 1985 to ask the general board to set up a new permanent fund as an ongoing source of income for operational costs of mission and advisory services (DIR 17 October 1985). The board voted to establish the Ministry Extension Endowment Fund in its April, 1986, meeting (GB 3 April 1986). By the close of the decade, the endowment balance was $175,000.

New Program Thrusts

Before this decade began, plans were underway to expand the board's services and try to economize through such expansion. Management and staff were taking seriously the axiom, Make less do more.

West Coast Office. Various leaders of the Church of God in the western states, over a period of three or more years, asked for some form of agency representation on the West Coast. Staff did a study in 1979 which looked at the need, the advantages, and the cost effectiveness of opening an office there. The president of the board visited three areas of the region and met with pastors and area executives to determine their interest and support of the idea. All leaders were supportive, and a job description was drafted, based on the feedback from the regional leaders.

The BCEHM regional West Coast Office was opened in San Jose, California, late in 1980. Tom A. Smith, secretary of the Department of Home Missions, a native westerner, was asked to assume the assignment of this office. David Telfer was invited to return from a pastorate in Hawaii to become the secretary of the Department of Home Missions.

The objectives for the West Coast Office were: to improve state, national, and regional communications; to encourage cooperative planning and joint development; to discover area needs; to be an advocate for that region; and to pick up some of the staff assignments in fund campaigns, evangelism clinics and field visits in the region.

The office did accomplish most of its goals. Services to the region were increased and improved. Having a staff person in a decentralized office helped to reduce program staff visits from Anderson. Communications between the region and the board improved. But, after five years of operations, and as the board's pernicious budget problem continued, it was determined by the directors that the West Coast Office would have to be closed by the summer of 1986, when Tom Smith would retire from the staff.

Office of Church Extension and State Development. In the 1978 annual meeting of the full-time Church of God state executives, two days were spent in listing the types of specialized services they needed. They addressed their appeal for help to the Board of Church Extension and Home Missions. On October 1, 1980, the board responded by establishing the Office of Church Extension and State Development. Isham (Joe) Crane was asked to switch from his position as secretary of the Department of Church Building to become the director of this new office. Andrew (Jack) Bugg was appointed the new secretary of the Department of Church Building. A report of the Director of the Office of Program Research and Development observes:

> Although most of the services of the board have been focused primarily on the local congregation, some very significant ministries and services have been rendered at the state level. With the increase of state organizations, more and more of the board services in this decade will be focused toward the states. The opening of the new Office of Church Extension and State Development was done in conjunction with the coordinators and executive secretaries of the various states. They have named three of their number to work with board staff over the next three years in the area of church extension, church development and growth, and state development (AR 1980, 31).

Those named were Gale Hetrick of Michigan, Francis Jolliff of Indiana, and Joe Morgan Davis of Tennessee. Originally, Donald Courtney of the national Board of Christian Education served along with Isham (Joe) Crane and Louis Meyer of the BCEHM staff. Later, this group was enlarged to include minorities and representatives from other national agencies.

The responsibilities of the new office were: to develop a more comprehensive and effective process of planning and program development for the local, district, state and national church, related to the starting of new congregations; to assist the smaller congregation to become more adequate for its ministry; to work with district organizations in planning program services for church extension, and for congregational and state development.

This program proved to be a real catalyst in the church for starting new congregations and for church growth. Research revealed that another of the most effective ways of reaching unchurched people with the gospel was through the starting and developing of new congregations. The approach to church growth in this decade was based primarily on this premise.

The board's philosophy and strategy for church planting in the 1980s was stated in a report by the secretary of the Office of Church Extension and State Development:

> There are encouraging signs of renewed interest within the state and district organizations for doing church planting. . . . Our strategy includes three target areas for helping the Church to accept ownership and participate in church planting: the general church agencies, the seminary and Church of God colleges, and local congregations (AR 1981, 39).

Church Extension workshops were held in eighteen district assemblies in just one year. Many more were held across the nation and Canada in the decade. These workshop experiences were tailored to improve the district organizational program, the services to the churches, the cooperation between congregations and the district organization, the securing of adequate finance, and the establishing of guidelines for selecting state coordinators.

A Decade of Church Planting

The State/National Task Force designed a National Strategy for Church Planting. The state coordinators, during their annual meeting in 1983, sent resolutions to the Board of Church Extension and Home Missions, the General Assembly of the Church of God, and World Service, recommending that the church accept the National Strategy of Church Planting for the next two decades.

The goals of the national strategy were: to plant 773 churches in ten years, of which fifteen to twenty-five percent were to be ethnic churches; to ask all state assemblies to cooperate; to ask five hundred congregations each to sponsor a new church in the next ten years; and to encourage individuals with special gifts in church planting to start a new church in this period of time.

In its April, 1984, annual meeting, the board enthusiastically endorsed the National Strategy for Church Planting, and voted to join the state coordinators in recommending that the General Assembly endorse the plan as a major ministry of the Church (GB 25 April 1984). On Wednesday, June 20, 1984, the assembly voted unanimously to endorse the plan. The assembly action changed the name to The National Strategy of Church Planting for the Church of God in North America, to include Canada.

This represented one of the church's most inclusive and concentrated efforts to plant congregations. Church of God organizations in all states and districts were asked to set target goals for the number of new congregations they would sponsor over the ten-year period. The largest congregations were each asked to consider sponsoring a new congregation within a decade. The question asked, "Has your congregation sponsored a new congregation lately? If not, why not?"

To help with the financial needs, a special World Service appeal was set up in 1987. It was called Partners in Planting, and sought to raise $500,000 over a two-year period. By the end of 1989, the Church of God had planted 201 churches. Fifty-nine of these were new ethnic congregations, including thirty-four African-American, thirteen Hispanic, five Asian, three Native American, and four interracial (AR 1989, 57).

By the end of the decade the emphasis was modified and

broadened by the board. Although new church starts were still a primary goal, the focus was enlarged to include many types of church growth and a concern for renewal. In 1989, the department was renamed the Department of Church Growth and Renewal Ministries. Oral Withrow joined the staff in 1989 as vice president and minister for church growth. Charles Shumate became minister for renewal. The goals announced for the newly named department included these: the enlistment, training and strengthening of leadership for church growth; the encouraging of renewal across the church; and the fostering of new church development across the United States and Canada.

Church Growth Leadership Team

Toward the end of the decade, the board selected a Church Growth Leadership Team comprised of two dozen insightful Church of God pastors and state leaders. This leadership team was organized into three focus groups: national planning and strategy, renewal focus, and church planting. The design called for staff to take the information produced by this team and incorporate it into ministries that would produce growth for the Church of God in the United States and Canada.

Biblical Basis for Evangelism

There were many plans, methods, and approaches to church growth and evangelism in this decade. Mass mailings were received by Church of God pastors and leaders from a wide spectrum of evangelical sources. Many of the approaches were based on methods for quick numerical growth. While numerical growth was a desirable goal, the board and staff felt it was important to focus the church's attention on the biblical basis for evangelism and growth as a prerequisite to any program or methodology. The president of the board stated:

I would hope that we as a Church will experience a new wave of durable, biblical, and theologically sound evangelism that emphasizes costly discipleship and life-changing commitment (BCEHM *FOCUS* 1980 Spring, 1).

In 1980, a pilot Biblical Basis for Evangelism conference was held in Dayton, Ohio. The approach proved to be a sound one.

A series of these conferences was held. Hundreds of congregations participated in one or more of these focus events. Each conference began with consideration of the biblical and theological dimensions of the gospel and evangelism. The conferees were helped to redefine their goals and priorities in reference to evangelism and the mission of the church. Each conference included personal sharing by pastors and lay leaders about what God was doing at the local level. The objective was to inspire, teach, and demonstrate that there are many ways to share the news of the gospel. Each conference ended with specific helps for implementing sound, biblically based methods of evangelism and church growth.

In October, 1983, the board sponsored a Special Day of Prayer for the Lost. This simple reminder to pray for the unchurched grew in acceptance across the church throughout the decade. In 1987, the Day of Prayer was expanded to a Month of Prayer. Over seven hundred congregations participated in the month-long emphasis.

A New Vigor in Home Missions

No phase of life, either personal or institutional, can be sustained over many years with equal focus and intensity. This is true of the program services of the board. Although there were ebbs and flows, peaks and valleys, throughout its seventy-year history, the shortages of operational and program funds in the sixties and seventies put undue stress on home missions ministries. Despite continuing hardship in the 1980s, there was renewed commitment by the department staff, driven and fed by a strong, theologically oriented approach to this ministry. The anvil of adversity had brought about a reassessment. The department's annual reports reminded the board and the church that, in spite of hardship and deficient funding, the church's mission in "Jerusalem, Judea, and Samaria" must be carried out.

The spring 1980 issue of *FOCUS* gives this account of the homeland ministry challenge:

> Today we are told that there are over twenty-five million Blacks, approximately twenty million Hispanics, over two million Asians and Orientals, and an estimated one million Arabs living in the United States. We have 14,000 new Far East immigrants arriving on our shores each month. Ethnicity will place a real challenge before the Church in this decade. How can the Church best reach out in Christian love to all people in our society?
>
> In addition to continuing the various home mission centers that have been established in past years, the Board is gearing up to intensify a homeland ministries thrust throughout the entire Church of God. A strong emphasis will be placed on the congregation as God's primary instrument for mission. God calls not only persons, but also congregations. He sends them out to perform His mission in their neighborhoods, communities, and cities.

Native Americans. By the end of the decade, the board had ten Native American mission status ministries. Mission status means that those who serve at a particular mission are employees of the board and receive the majority of their financial support and benefits from the board. The mission status works included four ministries with the Sioux nation at Alliance and Scottsbluff, Nebraska, and at Wounded Knee and Allen, South Dakota; two mission posts with the Navajo nation at Klagetoh, Arizona, and Farmington, New Mexico; one at Crow Agency, Montana, with the Crow Indians; a Nez Perce mission at Lapwai, Idaho; the Tulalip mission at Tulalip, Washington; and the Alaskan Native Ministry at Anchorage, Alaska.

There were also six Native American mission-related ministries. Mission-related refers to ministries which receive minimal financial support from the national board. The ministers and workers are not employees of the board. These ministries included: Anchorage and Bethel, Alaska; Oklahoma City and Park Hill, Oklahoma; Gordon and Winnebago, Nebraska.

The encouraging advance in work among native Americans was due in part to the board's Office of Indian Ministries. Leroy Falling, a Cherokee, long associated with Church of God native mission work, took early retirement from the federal Bureau of Indian Affairs and, in September, 1983, agreed to become the director of Indian Ministries for a modest stipend. The importance of his joining the staff is summed up in the 1983, Department of Home Missions annual report. It said that the coming of Leroy Falling greatly strengthened the board's ministry with Native American churches and provided great promise for an expanding ministry in the future. His wide experience, keen mind, and gentle spirit brought new directions and new programs to the work of the department.

Hispanics. At the close of the 1980s, the board was involved with twenty-four Hispanic congregations and outreach ministries. These were located in Arizona, Texas, California, Florida, Colorado, Ohio, Indiana, and Washington, D.C.

New Ethnic and Immigrant Ministries. This decade brought a challenge to the board through opportunities to reach new ethnic groups in America. The board assisted in getting six Korean congregations started. These were located in: Baltimore, Maryland; Philadelphia, Pennsylvania; Los Angeles, California; Atlanta, Georgia; New York City; and Wichita, Kansas. Arabic language ministries included a congregation in Detroit, Michigan, and some specialized outreach ministries to Arab groups in Yonkers, New York, and Indianapolis, Indiana. The ethnic ministries also included Haitian ministries in Brooklyn, New York, Washington, D.C., and Montreal, Canada. All of these ethnic ministries were in large population centers where the cost of real estate was very high. Because of inflated costs, none of these mission ministries owned their places of worship.

To address this need, varieties of methods were used, including two or more language groups using the same building at different hours, bilingual services, or worship space rented from other church groups. At least fifty congregations or ministries tried the shared-facilities approach. It is logical to assume that ethnic churches can share buildings with Anglo churches. However, the records suggest that this assumption is not always correct or practical.

On October 20, 1989, there was a special review of the board's home missions work, attended by the Department of Home Missions staff, several members of the board of directors, and others with special interest in this area. An overview was given of the current mission thrusts and of the hardships and unique opportunities for mission work in the United States and Canada. A study document prepared for this session concludes with the following statement:

> The biblical mandate, as well as the Board's charter, call us to be involved in ethnic minority ministry in our day. We are called to be on the cutting edge of the Church in terms of evangelism, church planting, and compassionate ministries in ethnic minority communities. We need to find ways to inspire and motivate

the Church at large to broaden its vision of what our total ministry is. The power of the resurrection is available to us and we move ahead in that hope (BCEHM *Home Missions* 1989).

Urban Ministries in the 1980s. Urban Ministries came more into its own as a board and church priority. This was due in part to the fact that although urban areas have many problems they also present many wonderful opportunities for the church, and that networking with other congregations would be more effective in metropolitan ministry than by "going it alone."

The growing attention to urban work was also due to staff development of a biblical theology for metropolitan ministry. It stressed that Christ has called the church to be involved in urban mission, which includes evangelism, compassionate services, minority ministries, and metro church networking. Sethard A. Beverly joined the staff in July, 1984, and he was primarily responsible for this biblical and theological emphasis.

The decade ended with the board's passing an urban ministries resolution titled, Concerning the Urban Mission of the Church of God. It called for the General Assembly to affirm metropolitan/urban areas, in all their pluralism and problems, as proper and fitting places for the Church of God to be on mission (churches, national agencies, and educational institutions), in response to our Lord's command to make disciples of all nations.

The resolution also asked congregations and agencies to respond in creative ways to the urban challenge, and offered suggestions of how the church could move beyond occasional fellowship and unity meetings to develop active ministry networks (AR 1989, 22-24). The resolution was unanimously adopted by the General Assembly on June 21, 1989.

Bridge Building

The 1970s theme, on home missions' being a responsibility of the whole church, carried over into this decade. In 1983, a new program, Bridge Building with Home Missions Churches, was designed to help individual congregations build bridges of cross-cultural understanding with individual home missions projects. Bridge building is accomplished through on-site visits, work camps, prayer covenants, cooperative evangelism, correspondence, and financial support. The bridge building program has proved to be a practical educational experience and has assisted congregations to get outside their familiar economic and cultural realms.

The Year of the Hispanics

The Hispanic outreach of the Church of God continued to grow and mature as leadership was developed to take over the responsibilities of the Concilio and the Spanish-speaking congregations. The population projections were that Hispanic Americans would be the largest minority in the nation by 2020. The BCEHM was concerned with how to alert the church to the growing opportunities for Hispanic work.

In 1984, the staff and the board drafted a resolution which proposed that 1986 be designated and celebrated as the Church of God Year of the Hispanics. The resolution was approved by the board and Executive Council. On June 20, 1984, it was presented to the General Assembly and approved unanimously (AR 1984, 24, 26). The resolution called for 1986 to be a year when the entire church would focus on the Hispanic community, become better acquainted with the culture and language, and recognize the urgency to evangelize and minister in Christian love.

The concilio set goals for itself in church planting, evangelism, leadership training, and stewardship. There was strong cooperation. WOMEN OF THE CHURCH OF GOD pledged fifty thousand dollars for Hispanic ministries and elected four Hispanic women to the WCG board. The Board of Christian Education elected two Hispanic pastors to its board of directors. Warner Press printed a book in Spanish and a series of *Vital Christianity* articles highlighting Hispanic opportunities. Anderson University pledged matching scholarship assistance for Hispanic students, and the School of Theology agreed to hold leadership training seminars for Hispanic pastors. The Mass Communications Board highlighted the Hispanic cause throughout the year. Two Hispanic pastors were named to the International Convention's Program and Music Committee. The convention's theme for 1986 was Cristo el Camino (Christ the Way), and, for the first time, a total of twenty-five Hispanic pastors attended the annual convention in Anderson.

In addition, Hispanic leaders began to recognize and accept their place in the organizational life and work of the church. The special celebration also helped congregations to see Hispanics and other ethnic groups in their own communities as partners in mission.

In 1987 Nilah Meier-Youngman, the first director of Hispanic ministires, resigned to become an adjunct faculty member of Anderson University. Gilbert Davila, upon the invitation of the board, resigned his pastorate in Corpus Christi, Texas, to assume the position.

Transition and Search Committees

In the January, 1985 board of directors meeting, the president shared the fact that, within three years, four staff members would retire: the president, vice president, director of financial development, and secretary of the office of Church Extension and State Development. A Transition Study Committee was appointed to study the program needs of the board and church and determine the type of leaders needed to fill these vacancies.

The committee, chaired by board member Fred Davey, met for in-depth interviews with former and current presidents W. E. Reed and M. J. Hartman and the eight department and administrative heads. Each was asked to submit a paper on the future program needs of the board (GB 10 April 85). The design followed was to space the retirements as far as possible to allow for an orderly process of bringing in new administrative staff persons. The committee proposed to have a new president on the job by January, 1988. This would allow several months of overlap with the retiring president.

In its January, 1986 meeting, the directors named a Presidential Search Committee. Its task was to sift through the data gathered by the Transition Committee and establish a criteria of qualities needed for the chief executive position. It further was to seek input from the church at large. Members of the search committee were Fred Davey, chair, D. R. Troutman, Gale Hency, Joe Salinas, Alex Shumate, Elaine Todd and Wayne King.

Before the committee could meet, President Marvin J. Hartman died unexpectantly of a coronary, on March 12, 1986. This tragic event forced an acceleration of the selection process. The bylaws, fortunately, provided for an orderly process of succession in the event of an emergency. The plan called for the vice president to automatically become acting president until the next board meeting.

On April 1, 1986, the board voted to elect Louis P. Meyer as president pro tempore. He had been a member of the staff for thirty years, and served for the previous twelve years as the vice president of the board. He was asked to serve until a new president was selected and ratified by the General Assembly.

The required executive leadership characteristics were agreed upon. A top priority was that the chief executive officer must have a demonstrated ability to improve the basic financial health of the board. A letter, along with the list of leadership characteristics, was sent to over three thousand leaders of the church. The letter requested prayer for the board and staff at this crucial time, and asked pastors and lay leaders to send names of persons they felt met the criteria. Names of over one hundred persons were received.

After months of study, work, dialogue, and prayer, the search committee nominated J. Perry Grubbs to be the chief executive officer of the board. Every director agreed with the selection, and Grubbs's name was recommended to the general board. He was elected unanimously in a secret ballot vote by the board in April, 1987, and was ratified by a ninety-five percent vote of the General Assembly in June, 1987.

Subsidiary Corporations

In this decade, persons who wished to make contributions to the board increasingly did so through gifts of property and real estate. A couple in Indiana gave a one-hundred-acre farm. Another individual gave an apartment building. Then, in 1986, the largest contribution the board had ever received came by way of several commercial properties from Allen and Rose Spencer, in Ohio. As this trend increased, it became evident that the board's organizational structure was not adequate to handle this property, and that too much staff time and effort was being devoted to property management. A plan needed to be developed to encourage these types of gifts and to formulate a way to manage real estate and gift properties.

The management team and directors reviewed the situation. Their overall concern for the decade was to improve and increase the board's services to the church, while developing ways to expand its economic base.

From 1986 to 1990, a strategy evolved. In this time period, the BCEHM was the recipient of four separate incorporated businesses/organizations of ministry. The business complexes were Spencer Steel, Inc., and Spencer Enterprises,

Inc., both of Ohio. The ministry corporations were Triple L Youth Ranch, Inc. of Colorado, which had been given to the board by the Colorado Conference of the Church of God late in 1989, and the Breiel Boulevard Care Center, Inc., of Middletown, Ohio, given by its board of directors in August, 1989. The center's primary asset is a one-hundred-bed skilled care nursing home.

A Christian retirement center in Lake Wales, Florida, Genesis Pointe, came under the board's administration in 1988. Twenty condominiums were completed, and plans called for an additional twenty-eight. In addition, the BCEHM had received the Hope Hill Children's Home, Inc., in 1974.

Some of these corporations were not-for-profit, and others were for profit. Each of the two types of businesses was governed by its own set of rules and regulations. In 1987, a subsidiary called Resource Development Properties, Inc., was created by BCEHM directors to manage the business and real estate properties.

The president's report to the board in 1987 gives this insight:

> 1987 has been another year filled with major decisions. In 1986, a major policy decision made by the General Board was that in order to continue an effective ministry of services to the church . . . ways must be found to broaden the Board's financial base, refine our budgeting process, and get the growing general fund deficit under control. . . . As a way to start broadening the financial base, another major decision in 1987 was the formation of the Resource Development Properties, Inc. (AR 1987, 7).

United Management Services, Inc. was set up by the board to coordinate and give overall guidance to the subordinate corporations. Then Providence Companies, Inc. was established as a think tank of lay persons. They were to help generate income to support the ministries of the board. The subsidiaries were owned by and responsible to the Board of Church Extension and Home Missions. Any annual profits realized would be used for the board's program ministries. It was felt that the subsidiaries would build flexibility into the board's organizational structure for the 1990s and beyond. It was recognized that there was a wealth of human resources in the Church of God which was not being used. The strategy was to ask lay leaders with unique business and management skills and expertise to serve as members and officers of the subsidiary boards.

By 1990 three subsidiary companies, including the original Resource Development Properties, Inc., Spencer Steel, Inc., and Spencer Enterprises, Inc., collectively owned and managed approximately ten million dollars of commercial business properties in Indiana and Ohio.

Year of Canadian and United States Partnership

From its beginning, the Board of Church Extension and Home Missions has shared its services with the Church of God in Canada. Over the years, many service requests were received from the neighbor to the north.

In the 1980s, Canada's population was approaching thirty million people of many socioethnic cultures. The time was right for a more coordinated approach to church growth in Canada.

The leaders of the Church of God in Canada requested help from the BCEHM and there were several meetings between the board staff and select leaders from both western and eastern Canada. These efforts resulted in the forming of a Cooperative Canadian Home Missions Task Force of nine members—three members each from the Western Canadian Assembly and the Eastern Canadian Assembly, two board staff persons, and the elected Canadian member on the BCEHM.

After a couple of years of study, the task force drafted a

resolution which was unanimously approved by the General Assembly of the Church of God in 1988. Entitled, Year of Canadian-United States Partnership in Ministry, it called for Canadian assemblies and the Church of God in the United States to set 1990 as a year to highlight the opportunities to evangelize and plant churches in Canada. The resolution also encouraged the general agencies, state and area assemblies, and congregations in the United States to build supporting relationships with the Canadian churches (AR 1988, 21-22, 35-36).

During 1990 this resolution sparked a variety of events and activities. Some took place at the 1990 June International Convention in Anderson to highlight better Canadian and United States understanding. Several congregations from both countries yoked together in fellowship, witness, and mutual support during that year. The Commission on Christian Unity met with the Cooperative Canadian Home Missions Task Force in Toronto. One lay couple from Canada volunteered their summers for 1989 and 1990 to assist in home missions work in the United States.

Church Building Services Over the Decades

A study of the board's seventy-year lending ministry gives some interesting insights. From 1921 through 1990, the board approved 2,944 loans. It was in 1965 that the first million dollars was loaned in a twelve-month period. The year when the largest sum of loan funds was advanced was 1978, when $4,319,177.25 was loaned to seventy-four congregations.

The financial marketplace always dictates the rate of interest the board charges for church loans. The more interest the BCEHM pays its investors, the higher the interest it has to charge congregations. In 1969, the board charged 7.5 percent. By 1979, the interest rate was eleven percent. During the 1980s, the rate fluctuated from eleven to sixteen percent. At the beginning of the 1990s, a first mortgage loan rate was 12.8 percent.

A total of $23,763,280 in loan funds was advanced in the 1970s, and $25,576,450 advanced in the 1980s. This means that 77.4 percent of all funds loaned by the board were loaned in the last two decades of its seventy-year history. These figures portray the growth of demand for church building facilities. They also indicate the pressure on the board to get adequate funds to meet this demand. In 1990, the vice president for Church Building, Investment and Loan Services reported:

> The Board's lending function is increasingly difficult to maintain as a self-sustaining service due to the costs of competing in the financial marketplace. Investors are now far more knowledgeable and have greater expectations of returns. . . . Individuals want the highest earning rate and churches want the lowest cost rate. The two needs are rarely compatible (AR 1990).

The high cost of land and building helped to keep the board's Church Building and Capital Fund Campaigns in heavy demand. 1990 was the thirty-fifth year the BCEHM had provided this service. It has been used by an average of thirty-three congregations per year. During this time it has helped 1,177 congregations to raise a surprising $105,305,307 in pledges. This practical program has been one of the most popular and successful ministries of the board.

Interchurch Cooperation Reaffirmed

Periodically throughout the board's seventy-year history, groups and individuals have became overly concerned about the national agencies' relationships with various church councils and bodies. When questions arose, the BCEHM always answered forthrightly. In 1951 it issued a statement in response to objections about cooperative relationships with the National Council of Churches of Christ. The statement reaffirmed the position that the board had always had a practice and attitude of cooperation with interdenominational agencies in common fields of interest and service. (For details see Chapter Five.)

Several ministers began to raise this same issue in 1984, objecting to national agencies having any relationships with the major ecumenical bodies. The board responded with a Resolution of Affirmation in its annual meeting held April 10-11, 1985, stating that the Church of God, from its beginning, has proclaimed unity and cooperation between Christians, and that in its history the BCEHM:

> . . . has been blessed and enriched by the mutual sharing of information, ideas, plans and programs with other church organizations. . . . Therefore, be it resolved, that the Board of Church Extension and Home Missions reaffirms its commitment to the principles of cooperation and openness and supports the staff in their activities involving cooperation with other church groups and boards involved in ministries similar to the assignment of the Board from the General Assembly.

The resolution received a unanimous vote by the board. A copy was sent to the Executive Council and to the Business Committee of the General Assembly of the Church of God.

The New CEO's View of the Future

In his annual report of April 18, 1990, the new president, J. Perry Grubbs, shared his dream and vision with the BCEHM:

> During the 1980s there was an explosion of knowledge. We can hardly keep up with our own area of expertise, much less with information in other areas;

however, knowledge will double in the 1990s. We must relate knowledge to the way we do business. Openness is mandatory. Diversity is a must. Perception is the key. We have a new perspective of the globe. This year we are beginning a new decade, and in ten years a new century.

As we look at the 1990s, the Board will need to examine its structure, use the expertise of Board members, tap leaders throughout the United States and Canada, articulate our vision of higher purpose, and stress goals and objectives for personnel.

We are committed to be an efficient and innovative enterprise that is sensitive to the ministry to which we have been called. We can see the ministry of Christ as enabling change both in, and on behalf of, others. . . . An element in looking to the future is hope. Hope is the desire to change things in accordance with what we see as God's intention for the future. . . .

The Board has a rich heritage. People have sacrificed over the years to make it the vibrant ministry it is today. The possibilities are unlimited. The Board has integrity. It is dynamic. Never in history has there been a greater opportunity to help people find Christ. . . . In the life of every organization there is a special time when it responds with vigor and relevance to the needs of its day. . . . This is such a time for the Board of Church Extension and Home Missions, a time when dreams, vision, and enthusiasm result in courage and commitment, a quest to fulfill a destiny. It culminates years of expectation, potential and promise. It is a venture of faith. It is a challenge worth pursuing.

Our ministry, which includes equipping the saints, helping the homeless to find shelter, children to find hope and direction, the elderly to find comfort and love, the poor to have food and clothing, is a global ministry and mind set, based upon helping people find Christ. As we look at the next few years, the next decade, and beyond, we see a myriad of opportunities calling for leadership and assistance. . . .

We are so fortunate to have been entrusted with the responsibility to minister to the Church in the areas of church growth, home missions, and facility implementation. The Board does not belong to us; the ministry belongs to God. The Lord has chosen to place His mantle of approval on our ministry. We consider contributions of time, energy, expertise, and finances from loving people as gifts from God. We are constantly seeking divine guidance as well as input from individuals who are deeply committed to ministry (GB 18 April 1990, A).

Early in his administration, Grubbs shared one of his dreams and goals for the board. He feels there are many committed lay persons in the church who have unusual gifts and skills. They have their own dreams and aspirations for the church. However, they have not always been given the opportunity to use their skills and to work on their dreams in kingdom work. He aspires to have the board be that nurturing agency which seeks, hears, and enables such persons to pursue their dreams. This is a vast untouched wealth, not adequately realized by the church.

Program Items in Brief

State Fund Campaigns. As the Church of God state organizations continued to develop campgrounds, camping facilities, retreat centers, and other real estate, their need for capital funds rapidly increased. The board was asked by state leaders to tailor a program to help them raise capital funds for expansion. In 1983 the state of Kansas requested assistance to help it raise $240,000 to resolve campground indebtedness and fund new programs. This pilot project was a successful venture, with three-year pledges totaling $321,520. Over the next five years, State

Capital Campaigns were directed for Alabama, West Virginia, and Northern Indiana. Such fund-raising efforts proved to be very labor intensive, and created a serious problem of staff overload. Thus additional campaigns were not encouraged by the board.

Energy Efficiency Workshops. After the Middle East oil embargo in the 1970s, the cost of fuel and electricity rose dramatically across the nation. This had a negative affect on most congregations, and many local programs were curtailed. In response to this need, the board held Energy Efficiency Workshops, and led conferences at the annual International Convention on the subject. An Energy Savings Swap Shop column was set up in *FOCUS*. Here congregations shared how they were cutting back on energy consumption. The staff also visited congregations to help them become more knowledgeable concerning alternative energy sources for existing and projected buildings.

Computer Applications for the Church. Between 1986 and 1988 the board joined with fifteen other national church groups to sponsor three annual conferences to acquaint local churches with computers and show how they could help expand ministries. Two hundred and thirty persons attended the first Computers-for-Churches conference in Los Angeles in 1986. Over five hundred church leaders attended the next two conferences in Atlanta, Georgia, and Detroit, Michigan.

Internal Matters

From the 1970s on, at least once or twice a decade, the board realigned its management structure in order to get a variety of viewpoints at the management level, to face the ever-increasing complexities of the board's operations, and to improve the delivery system of services to the church. At the beginning of the 1980s, the corporation officers—vice president, treasurer, and secretary—were named to join the president as members of a management team. They met weekly to discuss and review the management issues and administration of the board's work and ministry. Later, in 1988, the structure was again adjusted to include the president, executive vice president, and the three program department vice presidents. This new leadership team was an attempt to include all program aspects of the board in the decision-making process. It also served as a resource advisory group to give direction and focus to the office of the president.

In this decade the board had its first experience, in almost seventy years of operations, of foreclosing on a congregation for not paying its loan obligations. A three-year period of time was covered as the staff worked with the very troubled and difficult situation, which was basically a pastoral leadership problem. After going the second and third mile and beyond in trying to bring healing to the situation, the board was forced to foreclose. It was able to recover the money loaned through the sale of the facilities. There were some feelings of failure, because this was the first such situation, but one foreclosure in 2,944 loans is an enviable record for any lending institution.

Among the many measures taken to cut the cost of operations, the board set up its own self-funded health insurance plan for employees in 1981. The benefits were identical to the commercially funded plan the board had provided in previous years. Thousands of dollars a year were saved through this action.

New program staff members of the decade included: David Fortune (1980) accounting services; Leroy Falling (1983) director of Indian Ministries; Dale Whalen (1984) and Rodney Bargerstock (1986) Church Building Campaigns; Sethard Beverly (1984) Urban Ministries; J. Perry Grubbs (1986) advancement, and president in 1987; James Martin (1989) advancement and marketing; Marlyne Bruce (1983) accounting; Mary Lee Huff (1984) administrative assistant to the president; James Goossen (1984) accounting; Faith Phile (1985) personnel. As administrative assistants: Kay Scott (1983) Church Building Department, Victoria Rice (1988) Home Missions, Karen Helsel (1988) church growth, Paula Snyder (1986) employee health insurance, and Marilyn Guidry (1987) accounting; John Baird (1987) data processing; Gilbert Davila (1988) director of Hispanic Ministries; and Oral Withrow (1989) vice president of Church Growth and Renewal.

Staff retirements for this decade included D. Raymond Troutman (1980), Hattie Morris (1981), W. L. Whitehead (1983), Dorothy Miller (1984), Tom Smith (1986), Forest Carlson and Katherine Williamson (1987), Louis P. Meyer (1988), Isham (Joe) Crane (1989), and June Rohrback (1990).

Because of severe cash flow problems in operational income in 1990, the directors instructed management to eliminate some of the part-time and most expendable positions.

Staff resignations for the decade included: J. L. Hatchel (1983) physical injury; Joann Howard (1983) marriage; Richard Goode (1983), Nilah Meier-Youngman (1987), and James Martin (1991) other employment.

This was a traumatic decade for the board and staff due to the deaths which occurred. In January, 1980, all of the board's presidents from 1921-1986 were alive; by the end of December, 1988, all four had died. Death occurred for Russell Byrum in 1980, W. E. Reed in 1985, Marvin J. Hartman in 1986, and E. F. Adcock in 1988. Added to this trauma were the unexpected deaths of R. Dale Whalen in 1985, after less than two years on the staff, and former staff member Elmer Case in 1987.

In its April, 1987 annual meeting, the board voted to formally recognize and honor the contribution M. J. Hartman had made to the board and the church. A portrait was hung in the foyer of the office building. Friends from across the church sent memorial gifts to the permanent funds of the board. In addition, during the June, 1987,

International Convention, a tree was planted on the office lawn and dedicated to his memory.

Summary of the Decade

Beyond question, the board's paramount priority for this decade was the quest for establishing a broader economic base. The objective was not more money for the sake of money; the goal was a firmer financial structure to guarantee adequate budget for program services to the church. This was a most difficult goal. Various plans were made to achieve it. At this writing, it appears that some of the right moves were made, but it will take more time before success is assured.

The board's characteristic willingness to listen and respond, developed over its seventy-year history, was much in evidence in the 1980s. By listening to the church at all levels of its organizational life, the board heard of several special needs. It responded by forming various coalitions to achieve the desired results. There emerged a more fully developed coalition style of leadership. Board staff and state leadership developed the Ten Year Church Growth Emphasis with the General Assembly and World Service becoming partners. The BCEHM and the Spanish American Concilio of the Church of God developed Year of Hispanics in 1986; the board and a group of urban pastors developed Urban Ministries Mission—1989; and the board, with Canadian leaders, designed 1990: A Year of Canadian-United States Partnership in Ministry.

Decidedly, there was a noticeable shift in the delivery of board program services. From the board's beginning, its primary delivery system was direct—from staff to individual congregations. This strategy was enlarged to include services to metropolitan areas, districts, states, and regions. The focus became more on training the trainers, whether in church growth, evangelism, church extension, or missions education.

There was a noticeable increase in ethnic ministering. This was, for the Church of God, the decade of ethnic mission possibilities, and afforded the board a unique opportunity to exercise its prophetic role. Through identification of areas and regions where ethnic groups were concentrated, the board was in the position to challenge and encourage congregations, districts, and states to become involved with the ethnic people of their areas.

In this ten-year block of the board's history, the task of providing its chartered services to the church became more complex. Not only did the costs of providing the services to the church escalate, but also the risk factors. Inflation, the growing complexity and cost of getting adequate funds for church loans, increasing external controls, and the rising costs of mission station expense are but a few examples of the difficulties and risks of managing a multimillion dollar operation.

The issue of the balance between the board as a business, namely making loans to churches, and the board as a mission enterprise was discussed by the board in the early 1950s and again in this decade. Is the board viewed primarily as a national Church of God bank, or is it fundamentally a mission and evangelism agency? To address this question, the management team developed a position paper in October, 1986. The statement, in part, says that the board's primary role is to serve the church from a posture of servanthood, with mission being the priority in all areas of work, in all areas where services are delivered, and in all methods used to allocate resources. The statement went on to affirm that a commitment to mission is also a call to stewardship. Good stewardship principles have been applied to the utilization of resources provided by the Church of God for mission: "To assure the effective maximum use of these resources, staff will employ solid and sound business principles to serve better the needs of the Church today (DIR 16 October 1986)."

In this decade as in the previous ones, the board's program and business records reveal that its greatest asset was people. First, the gifted members of the staff: a group of persons with high commitment to serve the church and to deliver the board's service ministries; persons with special skills, assigned to positions where those gifts and skills were maximized; individuals of expertise and courage, who found a way to get maximum mileage from each dollar during every lean year and through every general fund deficit.

Coupled with the staff was the host of Church of God people who believed in the board, its work and ministry—individuals and families who insisted that they were partners in ministry with the Board of Church Extension and Home Missions. They responded year after year to call after call for their investment funds to help build Church of God facilities. In addition, many others were committed to the board's work in home missions, church extension, evangelism, and church growth. From these partners, hundreds of thousands of dollars were given each year. Sometime the gift was the widow's mite, and at other times in the hundreds of thousands of dollars.

The investment files of the board reveal many interesting and insightful stories of individual investors and their belief in and commitment to its work and ministry. One such person was Margaret Douglas, of the little farm community of Clear Lake, South Dakota. She made her first investment with the board in 1924. Beginning in 1929, and for over fifty years she, with her modest income, made periodic investments in life-loan notes. She knew that if she ever had a need she could withdraw the funds. If not, she knew that after her death her investments would help to continue the church's missions and evangelism work. Even after she was ninety years of age, she still hooked rugs and sold them to "help out the cause." Asked why she chose to continue investing with the BCEHM, she answered simply, "Well, there I know my money will work for the Lord, and it has provided a reliable income for me down through the years."

Human assets are intangible assets. They are hard to put in a financial statement or to program on a computer spreadsheet. In reality, they are the true assets which, under God, will be responsible for the life, work, ministry, and final destiny of the Board of Church Extension and Home Missions of the Church of God, Incorporated, for the 1990s and beyond.

Chapter 9

The First Four CEO's

(1921-1986)

Many factors and dynamics are at work in the shaping and forming of any organization. After the organization has been brought into existence, it continues to be shaped by persons and events.

Church organizations are also influenced and shaped by church traditions and the theology and background of the church body they serve. The strong anti-organizational stance of the Church of God during its first fifty years of existence was a key factor in the shape and purpose of each organization it brought into being. The institutional nature of its organizations was played down. The Board of Church Extension and Home Missions was well aware of the church's discomfort with the organizing of church life as it structured itself for ministry.

The congregational polity of the Church of God shaped the way the board saw its mission and ministry. From the beginning its services were almost exclusively directed toward the local congregation. In the 1940s, when the board tried to encourage the development of Church of God state organizations and their sponsorship of new congregations, there was strong resistance. The opposition interpreted this as the spreading of institutionalism.

The purpose of an organization also plays a key role in shaping its life and structure. The first board members of BCEHM used its charter as a blueprint as they drafted the bylaws to carry out its mandates. In the seven decades of the board's existence it frequently went back to the charter, and periodically made organizational adjustments to allow for more effective delivery of services to the church.

A service organization's primary reason for existence is to meet the needs of its constituents. As those needs change, the organization has to change. Since the BCEHM's chartered assignment included the starting and developing of congregations in new areas of the country, and challenging the church to meet the needs of the ethnic groups of the nation, it was natural that through the years the board developed organizational flexibility.

Perhaps the most important component in the life and work of any organization is the human factor. This was certainly true in the history of the board. The first fifteen board members adopted policies that have lasted, in principle, for the entire life of the board, and succeeding board members kept the BCEHM and its program within the charter. They established broad policies and guidelines for the program, services, and business of the corporation. They knew that the board's only reason for existence was to serve the church. That they were elected by and responsible to the General Assembly of the church was vividly etched in the corporate mind of this institution.

This human factor is most visible in its chief executive officer (CEO). This person, more than any other, interprets the charter and board policies and sees to it that they are translated into service to the church. The CEO has a primary role in the selection of the program staff, who give personality and tangible identification to the organization. There is a reciprocal reality, a give and take, at work at all times between a board or organization, its staff, and its CEO.

The BCEHM is fortunate to have been guided by talented and resourceful leaders as chief executive officers. From 1921 to 1986, four executives skillfully led this organization through its first sixty-five years of ministry. This chapter is not biographical sketches of the four leaders. The material covered here seeks to point out the times, circumstances, and the leadership contribution each CEO made to the church through BCEHM.

Russell R. Byrum (CEO: 1921—1927)

Russell R. Byrum's name appears early in the written records of the founding of the Board of Church Extension and Home Missions. As was pointed out in chapters one and two, Byrum was a prominent member of all committees appointed in shaping and bringing the BCEHM into existence. He was elected secretary-treasurer (the chief administrative officer) of the board in its first meeting.

Prior to 1920, Byrum had served briefly as a pastor in the East. He also had worked briefly in the banking industry. At the time of his election to the BCEHM, he was teaching at Anderson Bible Training School and was the managing editor of the Gospel Trumpet Company. He continued both of these assignments while secretary-treasurer of the BCEHM.

Because of his background, Byrum was acquainted with local church needs and problems. He understood the dynamics of the banking and financial world. In addition to his experience at Gospel Trumpet Company, in 1917 he served as vice president of the first executive committee of the Anderson Bible Training School. These experiences made him one of the most qualified leaders in the church to take on the responsibilities of forming and shaping a new board which was to make loans to build church buildings and provide help and practical program services to pastors and congregations. He was thirty-two years old.

In addition to his vocational experience, he was endowed with a keen intellect, a perceptive and probing mind, and an extra measure of self-discipline. All of these served him well as he successfully guided the establishment of the Board of Church Extension and Home Missions.

Byrum's organizational skills enabled the BCEHM to begin with a sound charter and well-written bylaws. If there was any area where he lacked knowledge, he was resourceful enough to know where to go to find the answers needed.

He helped set the scope of the board's ministry. From the beginning he stressed the larger picture. The new board was to be concerned with all of the United States and Canada. For Byrum, it was not only permissible to seek organizational guidance and help from other church bodies, it was advisable to do so. His broader view was also evident in his view of missions. He believed strongly in missions in foreign lands, but he felt just as strongly that without a concentrated effort of missions in the homeland, the Church of God could fail both at home and overseas. He labored hard in his speaking and writing to propose an even-handed rationale—that missions is not divided. The church must be on mission throughout the world and at home.

He helped set a standard of excellence for all the board's work and ministry. He often said and wrote that whether the effort were the starting of a new congregation or the setting up of a new mission ministry, the goal was "results which would be permanent."

Sound fiscal policies and conservative money management were also part of the Byrum legacy. In a taped interview with Marvin Hartman in 1971, Byrum said that he was always on the conservative side when it came to money matters. He had a great respect for money. "If you handle lots of money, it is best to be on the safe side," he said (Byrum 1971).

Another solid foundation stone laid by Byrum was a progressive view, with straightforward honesty. His vision of what was needed for mission in the homeland set expectations for the board to be on the frontier. This is expressed in a little booklet, *America's Missions for Christ* (BCEHM 1922). In his chapter, "The Strangers Within Our Gates," he lifts up the needs of over seventeen million ethnic minority persons of the nation. He paints a picture of home missions needs among the native Americans, the challenges in New England as well as the western frontier, the evangelization of southern mountaineers, and ministries to the unconverted across the nation (Byrum 1922).

The Church of God at that time was largely focused on small town and rural areas. Byrum saw that if the church were to make its major impact on the nation, it must also focus on the cities. He was one of the first Church of God leaders to lift up the urban areas as a fertile mission field.

His progressive views are exhibited in another small book written in 1927: *Problems of the Local Church*. He was well aware of the church's anti-organization bias. He felt strongly, however, that if local congregations were to survive and be effective outposts for evangelism and ministry, they should be better organized. He wrote this book as a practical guide for setting up committees, conducting business meetings, electing officers, writing bylaws, setting budgets, promoting giving through pledging, and the use of offering envelopes (Byrum 1927).

Russell Byrum was the BCEHM's chief organizational architect. He set it on its course of successful service to God and the church. He was the George Washington of BCEHM.

Elver F. Adcock (CEO: 1927-1953)

Elver F. Adcock, more than any other chief executive officer or employee of the BCEHM, was thought of as "Mr. Church Extension." In many ways he personified the board. This was largely true because he served most of his adult life on the board's staff. He was its first and only employee, as Byrum's assistant, soon after the board was founded in 1921. In 1927, at the age of twenty-nine, he was elected its executive secretary-treasurer. He was the CEO from 1927 until 1953, and served as treasurer from 1927 until he retired in 1963 at the age of sixty-five. His forty-two years of continuous service establishes the board employee record for longevity.

Byrum said of Adcock, the young man from Iowa, "He was not fast, but he had good judgment (Byrum 1971)." This characteristic of not rushing to make snap decisions, plus being blessed with sound judgment, was just what was needed by this new agency, still in its process of formation. On numerous occasions Adcock's deliberateness in decision making and reasoned response to issues saved the board from difficult times. His good judgment was a premium quality in the process of setting up the board's church building loan program.

Adcock literally learned on the job. There were no experienced Church of God leaders who had organized and operated an agency for church extension, home missions, and church building. Before being elected CEO, he had been on staff for six years and had handled all the mailings, publicity, and date-to-day operations. He was the logical choice to build on the solid organizational foundation Byrum had established.

With only two years at the helm, the greatest test for the young executive and the new agency had to be faced. How do you keep a fledgling national agency solvent and on a steady course during the nation's worst depression? Facing this frightening experience tested Adcock's mental and business skills, and his spiritual maturity. Through commitment, agility, and innovation, under Adcock's leadership, the board survived and kept solvent in the 1930s while hundreds of banks went bankrupt. Although the board had only modest funds to lend to congregations, it was successful in helping almost one-fourth of the congregations from being foreclosed on, due to inability to pay off their indebtedness to local banks.

A second big test for Adcock and the board came with the hardships and restrictions of World War II. During the war no materials could be sold for the building of church facilities. By this time the board had accumulated hundreds of thousands of dollars of loan funds, but could not lend them. Adcock helped the board find creative ways to solve this dilemma. (See Chapter 4.)

The war caused a great dispersion of people across the United States. Some areas had a great influx of new people. Other areas suffered from the out-migration of people. Again, innovation, ingenuity, and determination paid off, and ways were found to help the church adapt to a mobile society. Adaptability and persistence were the traits exhibited by Adcock whenever the board faced extreme or unusual circumstances in the 1930s and 1940s.

Throughout his ministry with the board, he was never one to brag about its achievements. Repeatedly, in his writings he noted that what needed to be done was so large and overwhelming a task that it dwarfed the small victories of the present. He best expressed this in his booklet, *Our American Missions*, written in 1934:

> By comparison with what needs to be done, we have only made a start. So, turning from the small amount that has been done, we face the vast undone that challenges those who will sacrifice and dare to herald the truth (Adcock 1934).

In a personal interview with Louis P. Meyer, June 24, 1986, he was asked to state where he felt BCEHM had made a difference in the life of the church. He responded that there were many areas, but highlighted one. He said, "Because of this board, the Church of God has built better church buildings." Over his entire ministry with the board, he carried a deep concern and commitment to see that each congregation had an adequate and respectable place for worship and training. He studied and applied himself to be able to give wise counsel on the area of church facilities. He became known as one who possessed skills unique in this important area. He served for two years as chair of the Department of Church Building and Architecture of the National Council of Churches.

The Adcock years with the board were punctuated with a pioneering spirit. He relished frontier experiences. This was true whether the frontier was establishing new congregations in Alaska or ministering to minorities across the nation. His compassion for people motivated him to become a friend of minorities. In the same 1986 interview he said, "All minorities needed help in those days, as they do today. Our job as a board and a church was to find out how to provide the help needed." Many of the board's major home missions stations were opened while he was CEO. He often championed the cause of those outside the social and economic mainstream. Part of his endowment to the church was a keen social conscience.

His commitment to the larger picture was also part of the Adcock legacy. The church was needing to move from working as isolated congregations to a cooperative approach to missions and church extension. He helped the church to see the proper roles of the national agencies and state organizations in its common mission. Throughout his four decades with the board, Adcock constantly taught that the mission of the church is best served through wise and sound financial planning, whether by pastors, congregations, or state organizations.

The Adcock years of service helped to plant a standard for church and agency work. This standard insisted that, in spite of overwhelming odds, God expects our best efforts. Regardless of circumstances, we are to be faithful to his vision and mission for the Church of God—to reach out to all people on this exciting continent of North America.

William E. Reed (CEO: 1953-1970)

W. E. Reed left a twenty-year legacy of service to the board. He joined the staff in 1950 as secretary of evangelism. He was elected chief executive officer in 1953 and served for seventeen years in this capacity.

When Reed was in his early teens, his father died. As one of the eldest children, he had to help provide for his mother and family. He worked in a grocery store and at a variety of other jobs in the depression of the 1930s to help his family survive. These experiences taught him early in life that each person is responsible for himself and others, and that each person will be held accountable for his or her responses to life's events.

Reed was not afforded the opportunity for college training in his early ministry. However, he was self-educated, availing himself of other training opportunities. Throughout his ministry, whatever the situation or assignment, he gave himself totally to it. His innate knowledge, wisdom, and unusual analytical skills, plus his ability to see the larger picture, greatly enabled his effectiveness as the third CEO of the board.

Perhaps one of W. E. Reed's greatest achievements was the diplomatic leadership he gave in moving the board from its thirty-two years of single executive leadership to a multi-departmental organization. This feat was even more remarkable when you take into account that the former CEO of twenty-six years was still on the staff. To be sure, there were tensions and times of disagreement, but that it was accomplished is a credit to both men.

Another major legacy of the Reed years was the influence of his personal integrity. Several staff members and agency executives were asked to name a key characteristic of Reed's leadership. Most often named was integrity. One might differ with him on an issue or action, but never doubted for a moment his integrity. It was this personal trait which first attracted the BCEHM to invite him to become chief executive officer in 1953. Some members raised a question about his age (he was thirty-eight years old at the time) and his experience. But his personal integrity won out over both these reservations. In his twenty years with the board he become one of the most respected national leaders of the church.

Early in his administration, Reed began to see the need for strong Church of God state organizations. He felt that they were needed to help develop healthy, growing congregations, and to minister to the growing ethnic minorities of the nation. Throughout his tenure with the BCEHM he was an advocate of church work at the state level.

Before being elected CEO, Reed had served the board as its secretary of the Department of Evangelism. He carried a deep burden for helping the Church of God become more effective in its evangelistic outreach. As CEO, he also served concurrently for a few years as secretary of the Department of Home Missions. This exposure to two of the board's three departments gave him an in-depth knowledge of both the stresses and the opportunities in the program ministries of the board. His leadership was one of even-handedness, showing genuine concern and working hard for each department. For him each department was important, no one more sacred or eminent than another. There was but one mission for the board—to carry out its charter.

There is another legacy of the Reed administration: he reinforced the board's desire to make its service ministries available to *all* congregations of the Church of God. To him, the small congregation and its pastor in rural or isolated areas deserved as much attention and service as did the better-known pastors and larger congregations.

Reed was a diplomatic leader with a high commitment to cooperative ministry. His counsel was sought often by pastors and national colleagues as well. He was a strong team person who felt that each national agency was important, and that much more could be accomplished together than by a competitive approach.

Reed's life and ministry with the board was a model of dedicated leadership. He served with fairness, conviction, and openness. Because of his sterling qualities of leadership, he was invited, and accepted the invitation, to become the executive secretary of the Executive Council of the Church of God in 1970.

Marvin J. Hartman (CEO: 1970-1986)

Marvin J. Hartman came to the chief executive office of the board in 1970 from a successful pastorate of twelve years in St. Joseph, Michigan. He was a third-generation Church of God leader. His grandfather, William Hartman, was a pastor of a congregation in Kalamazoo, Michigan, for fifty-three years.

In some ways Hartman was the best-prepared CEO in board history. In the 1950s, he had served for three years in the World Service office as staff secretary. During his pastoral days he had served for five years as an elected member of the Division of World Service and for ten years as a member of the Executive Council of the Church of God. Five of the ten years on the council he served as its chair. For another five years he chaired the National Budget Committee. This background gave him a broad grasp of the national structure and work of Church of God agencies.

Hartman also came to his post equipped with a clear understanding of the role of elected board members as the key policy makers. He saw the CEO and administrative staff as the ones to carry out the policies and manage the programs, services, and business affairs of the agency. Early in his administration, an annual two-day training event was set up to orient and train newly elected board members as to their role and function.

A major contribution of the Hartman years was his focus on team building. He worked hard and carefully at putting together a strong team of staff members to carry out the board's program services. He also worked hard all of his years as CEO to help the general board, board of directors, executive committee, administrative committee, and program staff to develop a sense of teamship. He frequently stressed that all members were a community of colleagues, and that oneness was best expressed through the concept of teamship.

A review of his years of leadership reveals that his basic

approach to board members, staff, and church leaders was pastoral. Whether the occasion were the confronting of tough, conflicting ideas, a mistake a staff member had made, or illness in the family, Hartman assumed a pastoral stance. This quality of leadership expressed itself in many ways. During his tenure, provision was made for each program staff member to have a private review every three years with the board of directors regarding his or her work assignment. A program staff sabbatical policy was established under his leadership.

He held up a standard of adequate preparation and commitment to excellence. Whatever was to be done must be done with good taste. There is no room for shoddiness in working for God and the Kingdom. Under Hartman, a well-defined plan was established for staff to set annual job and performance goals. These goals were reviewed every six months.

As with his two immediate predecessors, Hartman worked hard at encouraging Church of God development at the state level. He frequently met with the state executive leaders in their annual meetings. At their request, he named a member of BCEHM staff as liaison to work with them in matters of planning and development.

On the personal level, Hartman could handle criticism very well—a key quality for agency leadership. This was partly due to his own sense of humor and his awareness of his own humanity. He enjoyed telling a joke on himself, adding embellishments with each telling. This common touch added greatly to the effectiveness of his leadership.

In the sixteen years of the Hartman administration, he faced his share of difficult decisions. A major one was to have to begin registering the board with the state security office in each state where it did business. This added a layer of controls which the board had never had to face before. But the very difficulty of this and similar events forced Hartman to realize the price of leadership and the need for facing up to the challenge. On the occasion of the annual board meeting in 1972, he wrote in his annual report:

> We, the staff, are your servants, as well as the servants of God and the Church. We find joy when we are able to serve effectively. We are disappointed when our service is ineffective or when we fail. General Board members, as well as staff, who identify themselves with the Board of Church Extension and Home Missions, have always been leaders. Leaders are always out in front; sometimes understood and other times misunderstood. I believe that all of us want to, with a sense of humility, fulfill the stewardship involved in our election as leaders. It is a new day and certainly the Board does not seek to maintain the status quo or to reminisce unduly about the past (GB 25 April 1972, C).

Another Hartman legacy was his innovative style of leadership. He brought to the staff and board a spirit of creativity. He was open to change. He had an appreciation for the diversity of the church and genuine gratitude for its rich history, but for him the past, however glorious, should not dominate the future. He felt the best was yet to be. This progressive, open spirit permeated his sixteen years as CEO.

Some Common Characteristics

By reading the seventy sets of annual minutes of the board and the annual reports of each chief executive officer, one notes leadership characteristics which they had in common. Each spent his life within the Church of God. Each possessed an unquestioned faithfulness and high commitment to the church. Each felt the church could and would make a great difference in the lives of people on the North American continent.

Each executive was guided by the broader picture. None of the four was a single issue leader. None placed a higher priority or emphasis on one phase of the board's assignment over the rest. A balanced program of board services was the burden of each.

In varying degrees, each was a progressive leader who found the future more attractive than the past. Each met the unique challenges of his tenure with a noticeable quality or air of innovation. In varying ways, each was attracted by new fields of service on the American frontier. All four felt that the BCEHM was born to the role of pioneer.

Each of the executives came to his leadership role with the board at a relatively early age: Byrum at the age of thirty-two, Adcock at twenty-nine, Reed at thirty-eight, and Hartman at forty-seven. Becoming a chief executive at an early age might be one reason they all were willing to take risks and were so attracted by the future.

Ecumenical church work and cooperation was a strong factor in each administration. Whether it was going to other church groups to find answers on how to organize a church building and loan program or how to set up a home mission project, or serving on interchurch committees, each executive worked effectively with other church leaders. They knew that the board and the Church of God had much to learn from other church groups. They also felt the Church of God had much to share and contribute to the ecumenical life of America.

In the beginning of the board's ministry there was very little organized Church of God state or district work. Byrum, with a view to the future, saw the possibility and need for such development. Then Adcock, Reed, and Hartman each did much to encourage and assist the development and strengthening of state organizations. Each in his own unique way contributed to the establishment of a partnership in ministry with state executives and assemblies. This resulted in the development of national/state revolving loan funds, joint sponsorship of new congregations, jointly produced programs and films on church growth, and a variety of other cooperative ministries.

Each executive brought his best to the task of serving the church through the board. Each was deeply affected by his years of service with the board, and each made a lasting contribution to its life and work. Their combined sixty-five years of executive leadership illustrate the apostle Paul's writing to the Corinthians:

> There are varieties of gifts, but the same Spirit; and there are varieties of service, but the same Lord; and there are varieties of working, but it is the same God who inspires them in everyone. In each of us the Spirit is manifested in one particular way (I Corinthians 12:4-6; vs. 7 (NEB)).

These four outstanding leaders kept the BCEHM focused on its charter, reminded of its relationship to the church as an institution of service, and aware at all times of its direct responsibility to the General Assembly of the Church of God.

Chapter 10

Looking Ahead

This is an account of highlights in the life and history of one national agency, the Board of Church Extension and Home Missions of the Church of God, as it celebrates seventy years of service and ministry. These pages have recorded many ways that the church, through this board, has carried out its mission here in the homeland. These years have been filled with excitement, challenges, hardships, defeats and victories. The board has a rich and empowering history.

The tasks assigned by the General Assembly to this agency in its original charter were clear, and in many ways timeless. Seventy years later, congregations still need assistance with building needs; new congregations still need to be developed; people still need to be confronted with the claims of the gospel and invited to claim their inheritance in Christ; and the church still needs to be challenged to reach out to hurting, overlooked, and forgotten people in the United States and Canada.

This is an agency seasoned in living on the frontier. It has served the church well on many social, ethnic, programmatic, and mission frontiers. This rich heritage should serve it well as it continues to help the church be effective in the twenty-first century, where new frontiers will abound and proliferate. With a clear sense of its assignment, with commitment and resolve, the uncharted waters ahead should be welcomed as a gift from God.

I have been asked to conclude this writing with a suggestion of some possible trends and frontiers I see facing the church and all its agencies in this, the last decade of this century, and in the coming century. What I have listed below is not a full treatment or development of any trend or coming event. It is simply a hint of what might be ahead, an arrow pointing in the direction of a possible future.

To serve effectively in the century ahead, the church must become far more proactive and less reactive. The Christian belief that God is the God of the future as well as of the past, brings liberation. The desire to return to the past fades, while faith and confidence increase and enable believers to join with God, who is still creating and making all persons and all things new.

The Global Frontier. In June, 1989, the world watched as a Chinese university student, alone, stood before an army tank in Tiananmen Square, challenging its repressive mission. Because of instant satellite coverage, it was as riveting as though one were viewing the event in his or her own neighborhood. Indeed, it was in our neighborhood, our global neighborhood.

A key shortcoming in much thinking today is in the way the world is perceived. Many have not acquired the global neighborhood perspective. This is a challenging frontier for all individuals, institutions, religions, nations, and governments. Whether the world's critical need is environmental restoration, ecological balance, food production and distribution, peace and reconciliation, or meeting human spiritual needs, solutions based on a global perspective will bring more lasting and satisfying solutions.

To be effective in the twenty-first century, the Church of God also needs this specific, enlarged perception of reality—the global community perspective. Proposals, plans, and strategies based exclusively on parochial or national boundaries will not suffice. This frontier will exact the creative energies and skills of all agencies of the church. Perceiving our mission as to a global community will position the church for a positive and effective ministry in the decades ahead.

The Multicultural Frontier. Diversity is God's plan. This is evident in the changing seasons, the mountains and valleys, and in the people of the globe. Yet, human beings have not fully appreciated or come to terms with God's pluralistic creation.

Based on the 1990 census and other demographic studies, if current trends continue, by the decade 2040 European Americans will comprise less than half of the United States population. This country will be a nation of ethnic minorities with no single group as a majority. Such a frontier will challenge the church and all institutions of society. Those who begin now to access the information, assimilate it, and accept the multicultural realities as within God's plan will be far more effective in the twenty-first century.

Anything done to promote and encourage cross-cultural understanding will help lay the foundation for a peaceful, reconciling world. The board, with its seven decades of experience on the ethnic frontiers of America, should feel at home on this multicultural frontier.

The Religious Frontier. It was observed in Chapter Seven that there can be no true understanding of the causes of the world's wars, nor of finding paths to peace without taking into account the religious factor. Peace between the world's peoples will never be realized unless there is better understanding and peace between the religions of the world. Far too often, religion makes people fanatical, angular, and exclusive, rather than cooperative, understanding, and reconciling.

This will be an even more critical frontier in the next century. As the world's population increases, as nationalism continues to rise in many countries, as the United States and other nations become even more multicultural, the religious bodies and their leaders must play a greater role in developing the conditions for peace and justice. To do the work required of the church universal in the twenty-first century, all religions must endeavor, not to form a syncretistic faith, but to understand one another and discover how to work together. New roads must be built for joint ministries to alleviate some of the world's pain, suffering, and misunderstanding.

The Church of God, with its enduring one-hundred-ten-year belief in Christian unity, could carve out an exciting niche for its work and mission on this frontier. The BCEHM and the other national agencies, with their years of commitment to cooperative interchurch work and collaborative ministry, could assist the church to find new applications for this strongly held doctrine of unity.

These three frontiers are but examples of what appear to be exhilarating and challenging decades ahead. The Board of Church Extension and Home Missions has had enough experience in vanguard and frontier life to be of help to the Church of God as it pioneers this intriguing future.

Appendix A
List of Board Members

BOARD OF CHURCH EXTENSION AND HOME MISSIONS
Board Membership 1921-1991

List of charter members and under each charter member the line of membership, with last person named being member now serving. (Note: The * designates deceased members; the ** is explained at end of appendix.)

Committee of nine appointed in 1920:

*J. T. Wilson
*W. D. McCraw
*R. R. Byrum
*A. C. Harrison
*L. W. Guilford
*A. F. Gray
*A. T. Rowe
*Earl L. Martin
*C. E. Brown

Charter members elected in 1921:

*A. T. Rowe
*J. D. Smoot
*S. P. Dunn
*W. A. Sutherland
*J. T. Wilson
*R. R. Byrum
*H. A. Sherwood
*W. P. Long
*C. H. Tubbs
*C. E. Byers
*C. S. Sisler
*L. H. Morgan
*C. C. Mansfield
*W. T. Seaton
*J. L. Williams

These and their successors are listed below.

Elected Board Members

*A. T. Rowe	1921-1934	(13)
L. T. Flynt	1934-1940	(6)
*O. F. Linn	1940-1946	(6)
*J. Edgar Smith	1946-1949	(3)
*H. C. Heffren	1949-1973	(24)

Leroy Bottorff	1983-1976	(3)
One year vacant here due to Leroy Bottorff's resignation		
Morris Vincent	1977-1988	(11)
Leroy Nicholls	1988-	
*J. D. Smoot	1921-1922	(1)
G. T. Neal	1922-1937	(15)
*A. P. Gregory	1937-1949	(12)
*Paul Robinson	1949-1957	(8)
Isham Crane	1957-1962	(5)
Hollie Sharpe	1962-1972	(10)
Robert Atkinson	1972-1977	(5)
Wayne King	1977-1987	(10)
Ralph Allen	1987-	
*S. P. Dunn	1921-1944	(23)
Gabriel Dixon	1944-1972	(28)
Carl Flewellen	1972-1982	(10)
Robert Leeper	1982-1987	(5)
Lawrence Wyatt	1987-	
*W. A. Sutherland	1921-1922	(1)
*W. D. McCraw	1922-1925	(3)
*Earl Martin	1925-1953	(28)
A. E. Brown	1953-1963	(10)
Paul Jenkins	1963-1968	(5)
*John Henry Johnson	1968-1971	(3)
Lawrence P. Wyatt	1971-1983	(12)
Sandy L. Johnson	1983-	
*R. R. Byrum	1921-1929	(8)
*J. Lee Collins	1929-1944	(15)
Charles Weber	1944-1947	(3)
*Naomi Randall	1947-1962	(15)
Nellie Snowden	1962-1970	(8)
Mary L. Brumback	1970-1973	(3)
Jewel L. Carte	1973-1975	(2)
Dorothy Blevins	1975-1985	(10)
Kay Hargett Trick	1985-	
*H. A. Sherwood	1921-1932	(11)
Steele C. Smith	1932-1950	(18)
Wilbur Schield	1950-1956	(6)
C. Ralph Fox	1956-1965	(9)

Guy Kinney	1965-1970	(5)
Robert Reitz	1970-1980	(10)
D. Raymond Troutman	1980-1990	(10)
S. Louis Jackson	1990-	
*C. H. Tubbs	1921-1926	(5)
*W. E. Monk	1926-1950	(24)
*L. R. Wingham	1950-1954	(4)
*W. E. Reed	1954-1962	(8)
Joe G. Davis	1962-1964	(2)
*George Blough	1964-1974	(10)
Charles Hart	1974-1984	(10)
A. Ken Lewis	1984-	
*C. E. Byers	1921-1929	(8)
*Bruce Corey	1929-1932	(3)
*John H. Kane	1932-1935	(3)
*John L. Williams	1935-1941	(6)
*John H. Kane	1941-1954	(13)
Eustace Johnson	1954-1959	(5)
*A. O. Jenkins	1959-1974	(15)
Willard Wilcox	1974-1984	(10)
Gary Hausman	1984-1989	(5)
Felix Colon	1989-	
*J. T. Wilson	1921-1944	(23)
*A. A. Kinion	1944-1967	(23)
*R. Dale Whalen	1967-1977	(10)
Fred Davey	1977-1987	(10)
Earl Pruitt	1987-	
*C. S. Sisler	1921-1929	(8)
*W. T. Wallace	1929-1944	(15)
*C. A. McGillen	1944-1955	(11)
J. L. Hatchel	1955-1965	(10)
J. David Grubbs	1965-1975	(10)
Joseph Blair	1975-1985	(10)
Claude Robold	1985-1990	(5)
Willard Wilcox	1990-	
*L. H. Morgan	1921-1923	(2)
*Marshall Mercer	1923-1924	(1)
*A. L. Byers	1924-1933	(9)
*M. M. Caldwell	1933-1954	(21)
*John Lackey	1954-1959	(5)

E. B. Whalen	1959-1974	(15)
Walter Kufeldt	1974-1984	(10)
Truman Harris	1984-1989	(5)
Leslie Ratzlaff	1989-	
*C. C. Mansfield	1921-1924	(3)
*E. G. Masters	1924-1930	(6)
*U. G. Clark	1930-1933	(3)
*D. W. Patterson	1933-1936	(3)
*Bruce Corey	1936-1939	(3)
*W. B. Crowell	1939-1946	(7)
Eustace Johnson	1946-1953	(7)
W. A. Donaldson	1953-1963	(10)
Francis Jolliff	1963-1973	(10)
Jack Duff	1973-1983	(10)
Gale Hency	1983-	
*J. L. Williams	1921-1924	(3)
*E. F. Adcock	1924-1961	(37)
*Paul Robinson	1961-1966	(5)
Clifford Tierney	1966-1976	(10)
Robert Christensen	1976-1981	(5)
Oral Withrow	1981-1986	(5)
David Shrout	1986-	
*W. T. Seaton	1921-1933	(12)
*E. E. Perry	1933-1939	(6)
*Ross Minkler	1939-1961	(22)
One year vacant here due to Ross Minkler's resignation		
Charles Richardson	1962-1966	(4)
Richard Harp	1966-1971	(5)
G. D. Blackwell, Jr.	1971-1975	(4)
Jewel Carte	1975-1976	(1)
Margaret LaFont	1976-1986	(10)
Dorothy Jackson	1986-	
*W. P. Long	1921-1924	(3)
*J. W. Lykins	1924-1939	(15)
*W. H. Hunt	1939-1956	(17)
*O. C. Lewis	1956-1966	(10)
Calvin Hamilton	1966-1969	(3)
Benjamin F. Reid	1969-1981	(12)
Alex Shumate	1981-1986	(5)
One year vacancy due to Alex Shumate's resignation		
Mike Curry	1987-	

In 1967 membership of board increased to twenty-one members; these served in the new offices:

Donald A. Noffsinger	1967-1971	(4)
Edward Bowser	1971-1980	(9)
Robert Atkinson	1980-1990	(10)
Paul VanNorman	1990-	
Carroll Dale	1967-1971	(4)
Ted Boggess	1971-1973	(2)
Hollie Sharpe	1973-1983	(10)
Karon Shultz	1983-1988	(5)
Paula Stone Quinn	1988-	
Verle Fridley	1967-1977	(10)
Paul Matas	1977-1982	(5)
Jerry Blevins	1982-	
Gene W. Newberry	1967-1972	(5)
Felix Flores	1972-1982	(10)
Joe Salinas	1982-	
*Wilma McManus	1967-1969	(2)
N. Grace Donohew	1969-1979	(10)
Joyce Hall	1979-1984	(5)
Elaine Todd	1984-	
Harold Minkler	1967-1976	(9)
Thomas Pelt	1976-1981	(5)
Don Dennison	1981-	

Persons Who Served on the Board of Directors or Executive Committee Who Were Not Members of the General Board

1920 — *H. A. Sherwood
**1921-1932
1927 — *W. S. Haldeman
1928 — *H. M. Riggle
*W. S. Haldeman
1929 — *W. S. Haldeman
1930 — *D. W. Patterson
**1933-1936
1931 — *A. F. Gray
*D. W. Patterson

1932 — *A. F. Gray
*D. W. Patterson
1934 — *W. B. McCreary
*Oscar J. Flynt
1935 — *Carl Kardatzke
*William Bowser
*Oscar J. Flynt
1936 — *Carl Kardatzke
*William Bowser
*Oscar J. Flynt
1937 — *Carl Kardatzke
*William Bowser
*Oscar J. Flynt
1938 — *William Bowser
*Oscar J. Flynt
1939 — *William Bowser
*Oscar J. Flynt
1940 — *William Bowser
*Oscar J. FLynt
1941 — *William Bowser
*Oscar J. Flynt
1942 — *William Bowser
*Oscar J. Flynt
1943 — *William Bowser
*Oscar J. Flynt
1944 — *William Bowser
*Oscar J. Flynt
1945 — *William Bowser
*Oscar J. Flynt
1946 — *William Bowser
*Oscar J. Flynt
1947 — *William Bowser
*Oscar J. Flynt
1948 — *William Bowser
*Oscar J. Flynt
1949 — *W. E. Reed
**1954-1962
*William Bowser
*Oscar J. Flynt
1950 — *W. E. Reed
*William Bowser
*Oscar J. Flynt
1951 — *W. E. Reed
*William Bowser
*Oscar J. Flynt
1952 — *W. E. Reed
*William Bowser
*Oscar J. Flynt
1953 — John S. Kane
*W. E. Reed
1954 — *John H. Kane
1932-33, 1941-54
John S. Kane
1955 — *John H. Kane
John S. Kane
Nora Angus
1956 — Gene W. Newberry
**1967-1972
*John H. Kane
Nora Angus
John S. Kane
1957 — Gene W. Newberry
*Roy Creamer
Nora Angus
John S. Kane (Rep. Arch. Dept.)
Louis P. Meyer (Rep. Evang. Dept.)
1958 — Gene W. Newberry
*Roy Creamer
Nora Angus
John S. Kane (Rep. Arch. Dept.)
Louis P. Meyer (Rep. Evang. Dept.)
1959 — Gene W. Newberry
*Roy Creamer
Nora Angus
1960 — Gene W. Newberry
*Roy Creamer
Nora Angus
1961 — Gene W. Newberry
*Roy Creamer
*E. F. Adcock
Nora Angus
1962 — Gene W. Newberry
*Roy Creamer
*W. E. Reed
*E. F. Adcock
**1924-1961

Donald A. Noffsinger
**1967-1971
Harold Smith
Loyd E. Hargett
1963 — Gene W. Newberry
*Roy Creamer
*W. E. Reed
Donald A. Noffsinger
Harold E. Smith
Loyd E. Hargett
Kenneth Ritchhart
1964 — Gene W. Newberry
*Roy Creamer
*W. E. Reed
Donald A. Noffsinger
Harold E. Smith
Loyd E. Hargett
Robert Reitz
**1970-1980
1965 Gene W. Newberry
*Roy Creamer
*W. E. Reed
Donald A. Noffsinger
Harold E. Smith
Loyd E. Hargett
Robert Reitz
1966 — Gene W. Newberry
*Roy Creamer
*W. E. Reed
Donald A. Noffsinger
Harold E. Smith
Robert Reitz
Loyd E. Hargett
1967 — *Roy Creamer
Loyd E. Hargett
Robert Reitz
Harold E. Smith
*W. E. Reed
1968 — *Roy Creamer
*W. E. Reed
1969 — *W. E. Reed
1970 — *Marvin J. Hartman

*Deceased
**Elected to General Board for dates indicated, but was not an elected member at the time of serving on Board of Directors or Executive Committee.

Appendix B
List of Home Missionaries

BOARD OF CHURCH EXTENSION AND HOME MISSIONS
Home Missionaries 1921-1991

Name:	Field:
Abold, Henry	Native American (Sioux)
Anderson, Evelyn	Spanish Literature
Arnakin, Simeon & Barbara	Alaska Native Ministry
Austin, James & Alice	Alaska, Field Director
Armey, Willard & Glenna	Pine Crest, Kentucky
Bailey, Earl & Esther	Native American (Sioux)
Bailey, Mr. & Mrs. Maxwell J.	Alaska Children's Home
Baker, Lee & Belledene	Native American (Crow Agency)
Barberena, Mrs. Doris Davis	Hispanic & Migrant
Bennett, Elmer	Hispanic, Baja California
Bentley, Albert & Irene	Hispanic Work & Saltillo, Mexico
Bentley, Paul & Kathryn	Native American (Sioux)
Beyer, Herman and Mazie	Alaska (Juneau)
Black Calf, Mark, Jr.	Native American (Sioux)
Blanchard, Max & Cleo	Native American (Crow Agency)
Braten, Walter & Lyliss	Native American (Toppenish, WA)
Brooke, Robert & LaVitra	Native American (Sioux)
Brown, Calvin & Wanda	Alaska (Palmer)
Brown, Dale	Native American (Sioux)
Butler, Eloise	Japanese Relocation; Migrant
Butler, Loyd & Reba	Mexico Field Director
Caldwell, Maurice & Dondeena	Hispanic; Satillio & Mexico City, Mexico
Cantley, Chester & Esther	Alaska Children's Home
Cardoza, Oscar & Rosa	Hispanic (California)
Castaneda, Gregorio & Josefina	Hispanic (Texas, New Mexico)
Chappell, Paul & Virginia	Hispanic, (Somerset, TX)
Choi, Chong Mook	Korean (California)
Choi, Nak Sin	Korean (Georgia)
Chou, Lien Fu	Hawaii (Honolulu)

Chung, D. K.	Korean (Pennsylvania)
Colunga, Samuel	Hispanic, (New Mexico, California)
Compton, Al & Edith	Alaska (Kodiak)
Conner, Mr. & Mrs. Boyd	Tennessee Mountains
Cotto, David & Tina	Hispanic (Washington, D. C.)
Crockett, Isom & Ola	Mississippi (African-American)
Cultice, Ervin & Gayle	Alaska (Anchorage)
Davila, Gilberto & Melba	Hispanic (Texas)
Davis, Mr. & Mrs. Sanford	Alaska Children's Home
Depue, John & Jane	Native American (Sioux)
Downer, Hattie	Brooklyn, NY Mission
Downer, Ivory	Brooklyn, NY Mission
Drake, Forest & Margaret	Kentucky Mountains
Dyer, Russell & Isabel	Native American (Crow Agency)
Eikamp, Arthur	Migrant Ministry; Alaska
Falling, Leroy & Lucille	Native American
Fillmore, Dale & Connie	Alaska (Juneau)
Francis, Mrs. Lee	Kentucky Mountains (Yellow Rock)
Frazee, Jarrell & Hazel	Alaska (Anchorage & Juneau)
Geiwitz, George & Marie	Alaska; Hispanic; Baja Mexico
Geiwitz, Lewis & Hazel	Alaska; Hispanic (New Mexico)
Germany, Horace & Jeanetta	Mississippi (African-American)
Gonzales, Luz & Carol	Monterrey & Saltillo, Mexico
Gonzalez, Hector & Susan	Hispanic (Arizona)
Grosvenor, John & Nancy	Native American (Lapwai)
Hall, Wiley & LaVaughn	Native American (Park Hill, OK)
Hamilton, James & Doris	Saltillo, Mexico
Hammond, George & Ann	Native American (Crow Agency)
Harriman, Ms. Dorothy	Japanese Relocation/Defense Area
Harriman, Leland & Evelyn	Native American (Tulalip, WA)
Hastings, Raymond & Elna Mae	Saltillo, Mexico
Helsel, Marvin & Pauline	Native American (Crow Agency)
Hossler, Elmer & Jean	Native American (Toppenish, WA)
Hause, Norman & Annabelle	Native American (Sioux)
Hunter, Paul & Elva	Hispanic (California)
Janes, L. Y. & Mrs.	Spanish Literature
Jeffcoat, Ethel (Masters)	Native American (Sioux)
Jenkins, Mrs. William	Defense Area Work (Indiana)
Johnson, Mr. & Mrs. Ballard	Kentucky Mountains
Johnson, Mae (Robinson)	Japanese Relocation Center
Joiner, Ronald & Eunice	Migrant
Kakish, Jacob & Mary Ann	Arabic (Michigan)
Kendall, Paul & Mary Ruth	Alaska (Anchorage)
Kinion, Warren & Devie	Native American (Toppenish); Hispanic

Koglin, LaWanda	Migrant
Kole, Boyd & Beulah	Native American (Crow & Sioux)
Kole, James & Grace	Native American (Lapwai, ID)
Lacy, Garland & Sue	Kentucky Mountains (Pine Crest)
Lancaster, Wesley & Jean	Alaska (Palmer & Anchorage)
Lane, Mrs. S. J.	Defense Area/Japanese Relocation
Lansberry, Orville & Emma	Native American (Sioux)
Lapp, Joe	Saltillo, Mexico
Lautaret, Larry & Maxine	Alaska (Kodiak & Anchorage)
Lavelle, Mr. & Mrs. Noble	Native American (Toppenish, WA)
Lawrence, Jack & Linda	Alaska (Kodiak)
Lawrenz, Richard & Sharon	Alaska (Juneau)
Lobdell, William	Native American (Lapwai)
Lopez, Ernie & Jolene	Hispanic (Texas)
Lopez, Hector & Virginia	Hispanic (Texas)
Lujan, Daniel	Hispanic (Texas)
Maceno, Matthieu	Haitian (New York)
Maciel, A. T. & Ruby	Hispanic (TX, CA, Mexico)
Majors, George & Marie	Alaska (Fairbanks)
Mahuron, James & Susi	Native American (Lapwai)
Mamaloff, Fred & Evelyn	Native American (Crow Agency, Alaska)
Mansfield, Richard & Cindy	Hispanic (New Mexico)
Marble, Stan	Native American (Lapwai & Wounded Knee)
Marshall, Mrs. Helen	Hispanic (Texas)
Marshall, John & Blanche	Alaska (Kodiak & Sutton)
Martin, Earl & Blanch	Alaska (Summer Supply)
Masters, Judson & Ethel (Jeffcoats)	Alaska; Native American (Crow Agency)
Matthews, Marvin & Rosemary	Native American (Sioux)
Matzekiet, Phyllis	Migrant
McAlpine, Mae	Defense Area Work (Ohio)
McDanold, Malcolm	Kentucky Mountains
McKinney, Mrs. Lois (Earl)	Kentucky Mtns./Native American (Oregon)
Miller, John & Edna	Native American (Toppenish, WA)
Miller, William & Ursula	Alaska (Palmer)
Mink, Donald & Patricia	Native American (Sioux)
Mitschelen, Ms. Thelma	Native American (Toppenish, WA)
Mitten, Louis & Gladys	Native American (Toppenish, WA)
Mondragon, Lorenzo & Margaretha	Hispanic (California)
Morton, Gene and Ruth	Kentucky (Pine Crest)
Nez, Bill and Terry	Native American (Navajo, New Mexico)

Nisbet, Carl & Sara	Alaska (Juneau)
Oddman, Ms. Jean	Brooklyn, NY Mission
Ortiz, Frank & Irene	Hispanic (California)
Palmer, Elsworth	Hispanic (Texas); Mexico
Parsells, Ed	Native American (Oklahoma)
Patterson, D. W. & Mae	Alaska; Hispanic (CA & Baja)
Pesquerea, Adolfo & Phyllis	Hispanic (Texas); Saltillo, Mexico
Petterson, Mr. & Mrs. Herbert	Native American (Sioux)
Pickard, Vern	Native American (Park Hill, OK)
Pistole, Hollis & Elizabeth	Kentucky Mountains
Pitts, Calvin & Myrlene	Saltillo, Mexico
Plank, Keith & Gloria	Hispanic (Texas); Native American (Sioux)
Poor Bear, William	Native American (Sioux)
Powell, Mr. & Mrs. T.S.	Native American (Oklahoma)
Ramos, Lorenzo	Hispanic Work (Texas)
Randall, Naomi	Kentucky Mountains
Ratzlaff, Ms. V.	Hispanic Children's Home (CA)
Reeder, Wilma	Migrant
Richard, Edward & Lois	Alaska (Kodiak)
Richardson, Doug	Native American (Sioux)
Robinson, Simon & Mae	Kentucky (Pine Crest)
Rodriguez, George & Lupe	Hispanic (Texas & Florida)
Rodriguez, Juan & Diana	Hispanic (Texas)
Rogers, Jesse & Lyvon	Kentucky (Pine Crest)
Rowe, Howard & Wilma	Kentucky (Pine Crest)
Sailers, Mr. & Mrs. Millard	Tennessee Appalachian Project
Salinas, Joseph & Maria	Hispanic (New Mexico & East Chicago)
Salisbury, Ivyl & Florence	Native American (Sioux)
Sawyer, J. B.	Migrant
Schemmer, Marsha	Native American (Toppenish, WA)
Shaw, J. Frank & Susan	Native American (Tulalip & Toppenish, WA)
Shotton, Ronald and Ruth	Saltillo, Mexico
Shrout, Rick & Toni	Native American (Crow Agency)
Skinner, Arley & Clara	Alaska (Palmer & Anchorage)
Smith, Ms. Eva Joy	Defense Area/Japanese Relocation
Smith, John & Margaret	Defense Area (Washington)
Sommer, Jolene (Mrs. E. Lopez)	Saltillo, Mexico
Sperow, Robert & Alma	Kentucky Mountains (Pine Crest)
Stage, Ms. Virginia	Spanish Children's Home (California)
Tafolla, Mr. & Mrs. M. K.	Founder Hispanic Work in Texas
Telfer, David & Karla	Hawaii (Honolulu)

Thorsen, Mr. & Mrs. Paul	Native American (Sioux)
Torris, Priscilliano & Victoria	Hispanic (Baja California)
Tussey, Ms. Leona	Kentucky Mountains
Tyler, Dennis & Patricia	Native American (Sioux)
Underhill, Charles	Native American (Sioux)
Valdez, Ms. Amelia	Mexico
Van Gundy, Ms. Grace	Hispanic Work (Los Angeles)
Velasco, Saulo & Sylvia	Hispanic (Texas)
Velez, A. E.	Mexico
Wattleton, Ozie, C.	Mississippi (African-American)
Westlake, William & Evangeline	Hispanic (New Mexico)
Williams, Adam & Marjory	Native American (Tulalip, WA)
Williams, Emery	Co-op-Evangelism (African-American)
Williams, Mrs. Julia	Texas (African-American)
Wilson, Russell	Alaska (Fairbanks)
Winland, Jack	Native American (Sioux)
Woodman, Bahe & Mabel	Native American (Navajo)
Woodman, Ron & Efie	Native American (Navajo)
Woodward, James	Native American (Oklahoma)
Woosley, W. D.	Kentucky Mountains
Wright, Harold & Laurena	Native American (Crow Agency)
Yates, Marciano & Carolyn	Hispanic (Texas)
Young, Ms. Lucille	Migrant
Zamorano, Fidel & Sally	Hispanic (California)

(An attempt has been made to list the names of all persons who served in some capacity in home missions work related to the ministries of the Board of Church Extension and Home Missions from 1921 to 1991. It is possible some names may have been missed due to insufficient records. If so, we apologize.)

Appendix C

List of Employees

BOARD OF CHURCH EXTENSION AND HOME MISSIONS
Employees 1921-1991

Name Employee	Date of Employment	Date of Termination	Job Assignment
Acheson, Esther	7/62	12/67	Secretary
Adams, Wilma Cromer	5/59	5/66	Accounting
Adcock, E. F.	9/21	9/63	President/Treasurer
Alexander, Jean	6/56	6/60	Accounting
Alexander, Larry	8/78	6/80	Building Maintenance
Anderson, Rowena Dodge	9/53	3/56	Secretary
Angus, Nora	5/38	5/63	Assistant Treasurer
Austin, James	12/57	10/69	Director of Fund Campaigns
Bair, Glen	8/61	11/65	Accounting
Baird, John	7/87	*	Systems Programmer
Baird, Norma Jean	8/44	8/45	Secretary
Baker, Beckie	1/86	7/87	Accounting
Ball, Mark	5/79	9/80	Building Maintenance
Bargerstock, Rodney	1/86	*	Fund Campaigns
Barnes, Jean	2/49	6/52	Secretary
Barnett, Edgar	6/37	5/62	Accounting
Bates, A. Barrett	4/62	6/63	Maintenance
Baugh, Carol	12/83	10/85	Secretary
Baxter, Helen Jo	8/43	7/44	Accounting
	10/48	8/51	
Beach, David	8/53	11/54	Architecture
Beaty, Esther Mae	8/52	8/55	Secretary
Benson, Roy	5/59	11/60	Accounting
Beverly, Sethard	7/84	*	Director Urban Ministries
Blackwell, George	8/75	2/91	Loan Officer
Blackwell, Klue	6/77	11/90	Receptionist
Blevins, Virginia	5/81	12/87	Mail Room
Bosworth, Merle	8/63	5/69	Loan Officer
Bowman, Edward	10/62	10/63	Building Maintenance
Brandon, Norma	7/76	7/83	Secretary
Bretland, Racheal	11/58	9/60	Secretary

Brewbaker, Ruth Mary	7/86	*	Resource Development Property Manager
Brown, Catherine	11/64	7/66	Accounting
Brown, Cecil J.	8/56	6/61	Dir. Fund Campaigns
Brown, J. Lloyd	1/61	4/71	Fund Campaigns
Brown, Kathleen	8/81	*	Loan Bookkeeper
Brown, Naomi	2/61	1/69	Secretary
	1/84	4/88	
Bruce, Marlyne	8/83	*	Assist. Treasurer/Controller
Bruzzese, Barbara	2/71	2/84	Secretary
Buckle, Claudia	9/75	6/78	Secretary
Bugg, Andrew J.	8/79	*	Vice Pres. Church Building, Investmsnts, and Loans
Bullard, Sandra	7/72	9/73	Accounting
Burford, Barbara	8/57	7/59	Secretary
Burgin, Eleanor	10/61	6/63	Secretary
Burnett, Carol	9/65	4/70	Accounting
Burns, Carolyn	3/88	*	Stock Room
Bush, Judy	2/89	*	Administrative Assistant
Caldwell, Maurice	9/62	10/69	Home Missions Secretary
Carlson, Forest	1/74	12/87	Investments
Carman, Pam	6/88	7/89	Secretary
Carver, Judi	6/87	6/88	Accounting/Secretary
Case, Elmer	10/72	8/76	Fund Campaigns
Casey, Kenneth	10/63	11/64	Building Maintenance
Cassidy, Opal	9/46	8/47	Secretary
Claflin, Lucyanne	11/59	6/61	Secretary
Clingenpeel, Lisa Fowler	11/89	8/91	Secretary
Coffey, John	8/60	6/61	Architecture Dept.
Crane, Isham (Joe)	8/60	6/89	Vice Pres. Church Growth
Critser, Wanda Kay	6/78	7/79	Computer Operator
Crose, Kathy	2/79	*	Printing Department
Culp, Jeanne	9/45	6/46	Accounting
Cultice, Ervin	8/67	5/71	Building Maintenance
Davidson, Tomme	4/88	12/90	General Ledger Bookkeeper
Davila, Gilbert	9/88	*	Director Hispanic Ministries
Davis, Hulbert	6/56	7/57	Building Maintenance
Davis, Margaret	5/66	5/78	Receptionist
Davis, Trina	5/79	11/83	Accounting
Dawson, I. K.	5/44	7/48	Department of Evangelism
Dawson, Sandra	5/62	7/63	Secretary
DeYoung, Joyce	8/58	8/61	Accounting
Dodge, Ginger Johnson	11/87	8/89	Secretary

Downs, Lois Esper	2/54	7/65	Secretary/Accounting
	12/67	7/83	
Eckhardt, Judith	5/64	6/66	Secretary
Edwards, Denise	5/81	6/82	Accounting
Egly, Dolly	9/55	6/56	Receptionist
Elston, Janice Bradley	10/46	6/47	Receptionist
Erion, Judith	7/74	7/75	Accounting
Ervin, Wilazell	6/68	8/69	Mail Room
Fairchild, Delores	1/61	6/62	Accounting
Falling, Leroy	9/83	8/91	Director Native American Ministries
Ferguson, Debbie Yerden	1/85	10/86	Secretary
	11/89	7/90	
Fluck, Stanley	6/52	10/54	Bookkeeper
Foggs, Edward	1/70	7/75	Director Urban Ministries
Fortune, David	8/80	*	Corporation Secretary
Fox, Patricia	10/65	8/67	Secretary
Gallamore, Evelyn	1/44	11/44	Secretary
Gebhardt, Marsha	5/79	4/81	Secretary
Geiwitz, Hazel	6/65	6/67	Accounting
Germany, Philip	9/57	8/59	Building Maintenance
Goode, Richard	7/75	8/83	Director Urban Ministries
Goossen, Jim	1/84	*	Internal Auditor Computer System Analyst
Gordon, Billy	1/87	12/89	RDP Properties Manager
Graham, Regina	8/72	6/85	Secretary
Gramlich, Ann	2/87	6/88	Accounting
Grant, Kay Scott	5/83	*	Director of Investments
Gritzmacher, Victor	3/58	12/72	Secretary of Church Building
Grubbs, J. Perry	7/86	*	President
Grubbs, Marilyn Adams	1/63	6/64	Secretary
Guidry, Gary	6/84	6/85	Building Maintenance
Guidry, Marilyn	6/79	3/82	Accounting
	3/83	3/84	
	3/87	*	
Hackney, Craig	10/68	4/69	Drafting
Hames, Karen	8/63	6/65	Secretary
Harger, Cedric	1/51	6/52	Radio (CBH)
Harris, Phil	7/78	5/79	Stock Room
Harrison, Sally	11/61	4/63	Mail Room
Hartman, Marvin J.	9/70	3/86	President
Hastins, Lucille	8/62	6/63	Bookkeeper
Hatchel, J. L.	6/71	12/83	Director Fund Campaigns
Hausman, Ruthie	4/81	12/83	Secretary

Helsel, Karen	12/88	*	Administrative Assistant
Helton, Kathy	4/89	8/90	Secretary
Higgins, Vickie	6/65	7/66	Accounting
Hill, Alice	6/68	11/71	Secretary
Hinkle, Katherine	5/53	8/57	Mail Room
Hoffman, Edison	2/49	5/50	Building Maintenance
Hogue, Barbara	1/61	8/62	Mail Room
Holden, Zerinda	2/88	*	Administrative Assistant
Holder, Barbara	7/62	6/66	Mail Room
Holsinger, Adrienne	1/65	1/67	Printing
Huber, Ruth	5/85	3/86	Accounting
Huff, Mary Lee	2/84	*	Administrative Assistant
Hunt, Kathleen	9/49	9/53	Secretary
Hunt, W. H.	2/48	3/56	President of General Board
Hutchinson, Elmer	5/55	12/73	Architecture Department
Jackson, Florence	10/40	8/44	Secretary/Receptionist
Jarvis, Penny	6/90	*	Secretary
Johnson, Agnes	11/87	11/88	Mail Room
Johnson, Doris	6/47	12/48	Accounting
Johnson, Jean	4/81	10/87	Secretary
Johnson, A. Wayne	8/59	6/68	Men's Work
Justice, Shirley	4/59	6/60	Secretary
Kane, John S.	9/53	12/71	Architect
Karamitros, Olympia	6/50	11/52	Secretary
Kelley, Amy	9/89	*	Investment Bookkeeper
Klotz, John	6/88	12/90	Building Maintenance
Kurtz, T. D.	12/60	7/63	Accounting
Lammers, Marjorie	5/46	5/49	Secretary
Lantz, Stephanie	7/88	9/90	Bookkeeper
Lawrenz, Sharon	3/65	6/67	Secretary
Leedom, Madonna	5/43	8/46	Secretary
Lemons, Walter	1/84	9/85	Stockroom
Lewellen, Gail	10/90	*	Administrative Assistant
Lewis, Robert	8/83	8/84	Stockroom
Long, Jean	5/51	7/52	Accounting
Loudenslager, Nancy	6/61	7/62	Secretary
Lucas, Betty	7/51	11/55	Secretary
Luttrell, Kathleen	3/77	12/78	Secretary
Macholtz, Dorothy	3/62	6/64	Secretary
Manther, Gladys	7/40	9/42	Accounting
Martin, Dan	10/38	9/39	Accounting
Martin, Earl	6/27	6/47	President of General Board
Martin, James	8/89	1/91	Exec. Director of Advancement
Mauch, Arlene	2/45	6/47	Secretary

May, Marion	9/35	2/38	Secretary
McCaw, Maxine Grubbs	3/62	6/63	Secretary
McCracken, Mary Lou	4/63	5/65	Secretary
McGee, Beverly	5/74	10/79	Secretary (CBC)
Meischke, Richard	8/46	6/52	Director of Radio (CBH)
Metz, Evelyn	9/64	6/68	Secretary
Meyer, Louis	6/56	5/88	Vice Pres. Program, Research & Development/Interim Pres.
Meyer, Marie Esper	10/42	6/45	Secretary
Miller, Dorothy	1/67	7/84	Accounting
Miller, Nancy	6/77	7/78	Secretary
Miller, Sharon	9/56	8/57	Secretary
Miller, T. Franklin	5/43	7/45	Home Missions Secretary
Mix, Kenneth	9/53	12/54	Architechture Dept.
Monk, W. E.	6/32	12/48	Gifts and Investments
Morris, Hattie	5/71	6/81	Mail Room
Morton, Jacquelin	10/53	6/59	Secretary
Nabb, Susan	12/84	3/87	Accounting
Nicholson, Gary	9/89	2/91	Accounting
Oesch, Norma	4/50	10/53	Secretary
Olhausen, Elena	9/85	11/87	Stock Room
Parker, David	7/50	8/51	Maintenance
Pegg, Ella	7/32	3/36	Secretary
Phile, Faith	10/85	*	Director of Human Resources
Phile, Ralph	9/57	7/72	Investments
Phillips, Brian	9/76	6/78	Stock Room
Piatt, Phyllis	6/70	6/71	Secretary
Popp, Warren	9/53	8/54	Architecture Department
Price, Billy	5/71	5/74	Building Maintenance
Randall, Naomi	8/44	10/69	Home Missions Secretary
Rector, Corrine	3/84	7/89	Printing, Mailing
Rector, Daniel	1/85	3/87	Building Maintenance
Reed, William E.	6/53	12/70	President/Treasurer
Rehbein, Esther	6/86	1/89	Secretary
Reitz, Robert	2/87	*	President of Resource Development Properties
Rice, Vickie	8/83	*	Administrative Assistant
Richards, Lois	2/58	12/58	Secretary
Riley, Paula	9/89	*	Computer Operator
Ritchhart, Kenneth	8/54	6/57	Architectural Dept.
Rohrback, June	7/65	6/90	Administrative Assistant
Sanders, Paul	6/74	6/91	Executive Director Hope Hill Children's Home

Schattner, Delight	9/89	12/90	Secretary/Receptionist
Scheller, I. C.	6/49	12/60	Accounting
Seal, Susan	6/89	8/90	Administrative Assistant
Shoot, Risé Wood	5/73	5/76	Secretary
Shotwell, Florence	7/50	6/51	Secretary
Shumate, Charles	5/75	*	Minister for Renewal
Smith, Greg	9/84	6/87	Data Processing
Smith, Joann Howard	2/61	9/83	Corporation Secretary
Smith, Mike	5/75	5/76	Stock Room
Smith, Paul J.	7/70	*	Executive Vice President/ Treasurer
Smith, Steele	7/35	8/38	Church Loans
Smith, Tom	6/67	3/86	Homes Missions Secretary
Snyder, Jean	8/51	6/52	Secretary
Snyder, Paula	11/86	3/91	Administrative Assistant
Spiers, Forrest	6/54	8/58	Architecture Department
Stohler, Sharon	6/65	5/66	Mail Room
Strunk, Nancy	2/80	6/81	Accounting
Stummer, Darcy	2/78	5/79	Accounting
Tarr, Charles	4/71	6/75	Evangelism
Taylor, Bonnie	5/87	7/90	Mail Clerk
Taylor, Mary	10/42	3/44	Secretary
Telfer, David	1/69	9/91	Vice Pres. for Home Missions
Terrill, Brad	5/81	5/82	Building Maintenance
Terrill, Nelson	2/66	9/91	Properties Manager
Terrill, Twyla	1/72	*	Data Processing
Terry, Herman	2/53	9/62	Building Maintenance
Thompson, Jay C.	2/49	9/62	Investments
Tinsley, Janice	8/62	1/67	Secretary
Townsend, Donald	6/85	8/88	Building Maintenance
Troutman, Raymond	12/65	12/80	Office Manager/Accounting
Upshaw, Joy	9/89	*	Accounting
Van Gundy, Grace	8/46	7/47	Accounting
Warren, Roxie	6/75	8/79	Secretary
Watson, Cecil	9/75	*	Director of Planned Giving
Welton, Ruth	4/46	7/50	Secretary
Whalen, Kathy Reminder	4/79	8/89	Accounting
Whalen, R. Dale	1/84	6/85	Fund Campaigns
White, Betty	6/59	3/61	Secretary
Whitehead, W. L. (Wink)	6/74	2/83	Building Maintenance
Whitesel, Patty	12/78	8/80	Secretary
Williams, Roxann	5/90	*	Mail Clerk
Williamson, Katherine	3/74	6/87	Accounting

Willis, Verna	4/67	7/77	Printing
Withrow, Oral	10/89	*	Vice President Church Growth Ministries
Wolfe, Connie	9/56	8/63	Secretary
Wolford, Elmer	10/68	1/70	Fund Campaigns
Wood, Rich	5/75	7/76	Computer Programmer
Workman, Norma	8/55	9/56	Secretary
Wright, Flora	6/61	7/70	Printing
Youngman, Nilah Meier	7/75	9/87	Director Hispanic Ministries

*Denotes a current employee as of 2/1/90

Appendix D
Picture Captions

Group 1 (page 119)
Photo 1 Open Air Service, Anderson Camp Meeting, with BCEHM in charge, 1951.
2 Russell R. Byrum, first CEO of BCEHM from 1921-27.
3 W. E. Monk, Board member, 1926-50; staff: 1932-47.
4 Celebration of BCEHM's 50th anniversary at the G.A. 1927. Left to right: Russell R. Byrum, 1921-27; Elver F. Adcock, 1927-53; W. E. Reed, 1953-70; and Marvin J. Hartman, 1970-86.
5 BCEHM office in the Gospel Trumpet building, 1934. Left to right: Elsie (Manthie) Gaulke, Glenda Sayre, Elver F. Adcock, and Elda (Parker) Pegg.

Group 2 (page 120)
Photo 1 Earl L. Martin, Board member, 1925-53; president, 1927-47.
2 The Sunday school of the Omaha, Nebraska Church of God Tabernacle, one of eight new congregations the BCEHM helped plant during its first three years of operation.
3 Russell R. Byrum in 1971; he had been the BCEHM's first CEO when he was only 32 years of age.
4 The Executive Committee of the BCEHM in 1939. Left to right: William Bowser, Steele C. Smith, Oscar Flint, Elver F. Adcock, and Earl L. Martin.
5 General Board members at Anderson Camp Meeting, June 1939. Left to right (front): Earl L. Martin, John L. Williams, J. Lee Collins, J. W. Lykins, Steele C. Smith, and S. P. Dunn; (back): W. T. Wallace, W. E. Monk, E. E. Perry, L. T. Flynt, J. W. Wilson, M. M. Caldwell, A. P. Gregory, and Elver F. Adcock

Group 3 (page 121)
Photo 1 The Executive Committee, 1964. Left to right: Loyd Hargett, Gene W. Newberry, Roy Creamer, W. E. Reed, Esther Acheson (secretary), Robert Reitz, Harold E. Smith and Donald A. Noffsinger.
2 Board and staff, 1971. Left to right (seated): Charles Tarr, Robert Reitz, George Blough, Harold Minkler, Mary Brumback, Grace Donohew, Emmitt Whalen, Hollie Sharpe, Marvin J. Hartman, and Gene W. Newberry; (standing): D. R. Troutman, Verle Fridley, Francis Jolliff, L. P. Meyer, Dale Whalen, Tom A. Smith, Richard Harp, Donald

A. Noffsinger, W. E. Reed, Benjamin F. Reid, Clifford Tierney, Isham (Joe) Crane, David Telfer, Edward Foggs, V. J. Gritzmacher, Ralph Phile, and Paul J. Smith.

3 Annual Meeting, BCEHM, 1980, Board members and staff. Left to right (seated): Robert Reitz, Paul J. Smith, Nilah Meier/Youngman, Felix Flores, Joyce Hall, Carl Flewellen, Edward Bowser, and J. L. Hatchel; (standing): Charles Shumate, L. P. Meyer, Lawrence Wyatt, Richard A. Goode, Isham (Joe) Crane, Joseph Blair, Paul Sanders, Andrew J. Bugg, Dorothy Blevins, Tom A. Smith, M. J. Hartman, Walter Kufeldt, Forest F. Carlson, Fred J. Davey, Hollie Sharpe, D. R. Troutman, Charles Hart, Paul Matas, Margaret LaFont, Robert G. Christensen, Jack Duff, Morris R. Vincent, Wayne King, George Blackwell, Jr., and Cecil Watson.

4 General Board and staff, 1990: Left to right (front row): Sandy Johnson, Leroy Nicholls, J. Perry Grubbs, Elaine Todd, Paul J. Smith, Gilbert Davila, Leroy Falling, Faith Phile, Marlyne Bruce, and Michael Curry; (back row): Robert Reitz, Leslie Ratzlaff, Cecil Watson, George Blackwell, Jr., Earl Pruitt, D. R. Troutman, Ralph Allen, James Martin, Gale Hency, Rodney Bargerstock, Jerry Blevins, Don Dennison, Robert Atkinson, Kay Scott Grant, Ken Lewis, David Telfer, Charles Shumate, Joe Salinas, Felix Colon, Lawrence Wyatt, David Fortune, Oral Withrow, David Shrout, Andrew J. Bugg, and Sethard Beverly. Board members not in picture: Paula Stone Quinn, Dorothy Jackson, Willard Wilcox, and Paul VanNorman.

Group 4 (page 122)
Photo 1 Dedication of new office building at the corner of Nursery Road and Third Street in Anderson, 1966. W. E. Reed is giving special recognition to C. C. and Ina Mansfield for their gift annuity of $250,000 that made the building of the new facility possible.

2 Another view of the new office building in 1966.

3 The BCEHM office building on the International Convention grounds, 1946; this building was constructed in 1946-47 and served as home of the BCEHM for 18 years.

4 Part of the crowd at the 1966 dedication.

5 Office worship time, 1954. Left to right: Wilma Cromer, Elver F. Adcock, Nora Angus, (unidentified), W. H. Hunt, Irwin Scheller, Kenneth Ritchhart, Naomi Randall, (unidentified), Forrest Spiers, John S. Kane, Barbara Marshall, (unidentified), Lois Downs, Evelyn Clear, and W. E. Reed (leader).

6 Staff meeting, 1955. Left to right: Elver F. Adcock (treasurer), Naomi Randall (associate secretary of home missions), W. H. Hunt (president), W. E. Reed (general secretary), and John S. Kane (secretary of Department of Architecture).

Group 5 (page 123)

Photo 1 Richard Lee Meischke, the first director of the new Church of God radio program, The Christian Brotherhood Hour. (1946)

2 Nora Angus: staff member, 1938-63; assistant treasurer and office manager (1940).

3 Edward L. Foggs, first director of Urban Ministries. (1970)

4 John S. Kane and Elmer L. Hutchinson in the Department of Architecture, formed in 1953. (1956)

5 Nilah Meier/Youngman, first director of Hispanic Ministries. (1975)

6 Leroy Falling, first director of Native American Ministries. (1983)

7 J. Perry Grubbs, incumbent president, BCEHM, elected 1987. (1988)

8 W. E. Reed, outgoing CEO, works with incoming Executive Secretary, M. J. Hartman. (1970)

9 Program staff; left to right (seated): David Telfer, Isham (Joe) Crane, Charles Shumate, M. J. Hartman, Nilah Meier/Youngman, and Forest F. Carlson; (standing): Cecil Watson, Elmer Case, Tom A. Smith, J. L. Hatchel, George Blackwell, Jr., Paul J. Smith, L. P. Meyer, Richard A. Goode, and D. R. Troutman.

Group 6 (page 124)

Photo 1 The Palmer, Alaska Church of God, 1949.

2 Mae and D. W. Patterson, pioneer workers for the BCEHM in Alaska. (1947)

3 Alaskan Church of God pastors, 1954. Left to right: Tom Moyer, retired; Jerry Frazee, Juneau; Ervin Cultice, Potter Community; Wesley Lancaster, Palmer; James Austin, Anchorage; Russell Wilson, Fairbanks; Judson Masters, Kodiak.

4 Wendell and Mignonne Byrd, pastors at Palmer, Alaska, 1937.

5 J. Frank Shaw, an early worker with Indians, seen here in an open air service at Anderson Camp Meeting, 1952.

6 Leaders at the Klagetoh, Arizona Navajo mission, 1976. Left to right: Samuel and Ellen Walker, pastor Bahe and Mabel Woodman, Charlie Redhouse (back center), Ron Woodman, and Betty and Francis Key.

7 James and Alice Austin receive a new carry-all for their work in Anchorage.

8 The forming of a Church of God Indian Council at Klagetoh, Arizona, 1974. Left to right: Tom A. Smith, Leroy Falling, Bahe Woodman, David Telfer, Fred Mamaloff and Adam Williams.

9 The meeting of the American Indian Council, held in Anderson, 1981.

Group 7 (page 125)
Photo 1 The chapel at Toccoa, Georgia, built with BCEHM loan #12, 1924.

2 The Warsaw, Indiana Church of God building was completed with help from the BCEHM, loan #401, 1937.

3 Pastors John Clarke and Roscoe Snowden see their applications for loans for church buildings on the *approved* list.

4 Leaders of The Disciples of Christ's Board of Church Extension invest $1,000,000 with the BCEHM of the Church of God; the money will be used to help build Church of God church buildings. Left to right: Harold Watkins, Disciples executive; Emmitt Whalen of BCEHM; Rolland Sheaffer, Disciples executive; and M. J. Hartman of the BCEHM.

5 A Spanish leaders' consultation, Corpus Christi, Texas, 1975. Left to right: Elsworth Palmer, Rafeal Campos, Antonio Grizzell, Samuel de la Cruz, Joe Salinas, Arthur Cuellar, Roberto Oliva, Gilbert Davila, Evelyn Anderson, L. P. Meyer, Warren Kinion, Nilah Meier, George Melendez, and Mel Martinez.

6 M. F. Tafolla, home missions leader, celebrates his 74th birthday with his wife and children (and their spouses), and grandchildren; San Antonio, 1947.

7 David Cotto, chair of the Spanish Council, 1989.

8 First Church of God Hispanic Youth Convention, Anderson, November, 1978.

Group 8 (page 126)
Photo 1 Church of God Korean pastors in the U.S., 1984. BCEHM staff member, David Telfer, in background; left to right: Pastor Kim Gap Soo and his family from Wichita, Kansas; D. K. Chung and Chong Mook Choi.

2 Leaders of the Haitian Church of God congregation of New York City visit with leaders of a similar congregation in Washington, D.C., 1983.

3 Pastor Hashem Sweis, minister of the Arab congregation of the Church of God in Yonkers, N.Y., with his daughter, Amel, son, Ghasson, and wife, Siham.

4 The church building of the Aina Haina Church of God, Honolulu, Hawaii, 1974.

5 Children of the Atlanta Korean Church of God; Chong Mook Choi, pastor. (1983)

6 Mother Ivory Downer, co-founder (with daughter, Hattie) of the Williamsburg Mission in Brooklyn, N.Y. (1970)

7 Hattie Downer (co-founder) Williamsburg Mission, Brooklyn; Hattie was director of the mission from 1950 to 1987. (1960)

8 The church building at Pinecrest, Kentucky, 1979.

Group 9 (page 127)

Photo 1 Children and staff of Hope Hill Children's Home, Hope, Kentucky, 1978.

2 Willard Wilcox and trustees of Hope Hill Children's Home explain to the General Assembly of the Church of God in Anderson, Indiana, 1975, why they have voted to deed the home to the BCEHM.

3 Pastors attending the Town and Country Church In-Service Training School at the University of Tennessee, 1957. Left to right: James I. Turner, Richard Turner, L. P. Meyer, Harry Redmond, and Silas Turnbow.

4 The Church and Community Committee of the BCEHM meeting in Chicago, 1962. Left to right: Wayne Johnson, L. P. Meyer, Verle Fridley, James Massey, Leroy Fulton, Tom Pyeatt, Frank Couversier, Donald Collins and John Conley.

5 Paul and Lana Sanders, directors of the Hope Hill Children's Home, 1975-90.

6 The national men's committee, 1965. Left to right (seated): Wayne Johnson, Don Ritchey, and Virgil Robold; (standing): Cal Hamilton, Henry Johnson, Roger Lewis and Neal Rafford.

7 Leaders attending the "Pastoring in the City" conference, Kansas City, Kansas, 1975.

8 Church of God state coordinators at Deer Valley Ranch, Colorado, 1971; BCEHM staff also in photo. Left to right: Raymond Miller, Elmer Case, Carl Peterson, Riley Phillippe, A. D. Semrau, Jesse Barber, Forest Carlson, Fred Pinyoun, George Blackwell, Jr., Elver F. Adcock, Elmer Rich, and Gale Hetrick.

Works Cited

(Note: The following abbreviations were used throughout the book to identify various groups and documents.)

AR	Annual Report of the Board of Church Extension and Home Missions, Church of God Archives, Anderson, Indiana
BCEHM	Board of Church Extension and Home Missions of the Church of God
COG	Church of God, Anderson, Indiana
DIR	Board of Directors of the Board of Church Extension and Home Missions of the Church of God; minutes
EX	Executive committee of the Board of Church Extension and Home Missions of the Church of God; minutes
EX Council	Executive Council of the Church of God
GA	General Assembly (formerly General Ministerial Assembly) of the Church of God; minutes
GB	General (full) board of the Board of Church Extension and Home Missions of the Church of God
GMA	General Ministerial Assembly (now General Assembly) of the Church of God; minutes
GTC	Gospel Trumpet Company (now Warner Press), publishing house of the Church of God
MB	Missionary Board of the Church of God; minutes
NBC	National Budget Committee of the General Assembly of the Church of God; minutes
NEW Persons	New Persons and Drop Out Study
UTC	Urban Training Center
VC	*Vital Christianity*, journal of the Church of God (formerly the Gospel Trumpet)
WP	Warner Press (formerly the Gospel Trumpet Company), publishing house of the Church of God
YB	Yearbook of the Church of God

Adcock, E. F. 1934. *Our American Missions.* Anderson, Ind.:BCEHM.

——. 1986. Some Recollections of The Board of Church Extension and Home Missions. COG Archives, Anderson, Ind. Manuscript.

BCEHM. N.d. A Proposed Urban Training Center for Christian Mission in Chicago. Prospectus. BCEHM Archives, Anderson,

——. N.d. The Church of God Mission to People. Summary of New Persons and Drop Out Study. BCEHM files, Anderson, Ind.
——. 1974. *FOCUS* Summer:1.
——. 1975. *FOCUS* Fall:4.
——. 1980. A Ten Year Perspective. *FOCUS* Spring:1.
——. 1989. Review of Home Missions Department Current Program. Study document. 20 October. BCEHM.
Byrum, R. R. 1922. *American's Millions for Christ.* Anderson, Ind.: BCEHM.
——. 1927. *Problems of the Local Church.* Anderson, Ind.:GTC
——. 1971. Interview by M. J. Hartman, 1 September. COG Archives, Anderson, Ind. Cassette tape recording.
——. 1976. Interview by M. J. Hartman, 5 January. BCEHM Archives, Anderson, Ind.
Crose, L. A. 1981. *Passport for a Reformation.* Anderson, Ind.:WP.
EX Council. 1970. Consultation of the Church of God Workbook. Anderson, Ind.
NBC. 1976. A Million for Missions, proposed special project. 13 February. Minutes.
Phillips, H. L. 1979. *Miracle of Survival.* Anderson, Ind.:WP.
Riggle, H. M. 1924. Pioneer Evangelism. *Gospel Trumpet.*
Smith, J. W. V. 1980. *The Quest for Holiness and Unity.* Anderson, Ind.:WP.
Stokesbury, J. L. 1981. *Short History of World War I.* New York:WM Morrow & Co.
Telfer, D. R. 1981. *Red & Yellow, Black & White, and Brown.* Anderson, Ind.:WP.
WP. 1962. *Vital Christianity* 16 December. Vol. 82, p. 14. News note.